Futurecast

Also Available from BarnaBooks:

EXTENSIVE NEW RESEARCH on how our behaviors, attitudes, and beliefs are shaping our future—and what we can do about it now

FUTURECAST

what **TODAY'S TRENDS** *mean for* **TOMORROW'S WORLD**

GEORGE
BARNA

BARNA
AN IMPRINT OF
TYNDALE HOUSE PUBLISHERS, INC.

Visit Tyndale's website at www.tyndale.com.

TYNDALE is a registered trademark of Tyndale House Publishers, Inc.

Barna and the Barna logo are trademarks of George Barna.

BarnaBooks is an imprint of Tyndale House Publishers, Inc.

Futurecast: What Today's Trends Mean for Tomorrow's World

Designed by Jon McGrath

Published in association with the literary agency of Fedd and Company, Inc., 606 Flamingo Blvd., Austin, TX 78734

Library of Congress Cataloging-in-Publication Data

Barna, George.
  Futurecast : what today's trends mean for tomorrow's world / George Barna.
    p. cm.
  Includes bibliographical references.
  ISBN 978-1-4143-2406-7 (hc)
  1. Christianity—United States—Forecasting. I. Title.
  BR526.B363 2011
  277.3'083—dc22   2011008124

Printed in the United States of America

17   16   15   14   13   12   11
7   6   5   4   3   2   1

Table of Contents

WHY FUTURECASTING MATTERS

Making Sense Out of Information Overload

As RED AUERBACH, the great Boston Celtics basketball coach, used to say, let me tell you a story . . .

When I initially became immersed in conducting national research studies, it was to better understand our society and figure out how to influence it in positive ways. Gathering and analyzing the data, trying to discover how all the pieces fit together, developing compelling strategies to address needs and challenges—I was like a kid in a candy store with my dad's wallet in hand.

For a number of years, I was captivated by the adventure, the chase, the process of trying to make sense of reality and do something significant about it. As a committed follower of Jesus Christ, I believed that studying and reporting on the intersection of faith and culture was the best way I could contribute to the advance of God's Kingdom on earth. That pursuit kept my energy flowing for years.

And then I hit the wall.

I had worked with a number of organizations (churches, denominations, and parachurch entities) and devout individuals who were just as excited as I was about making a difference in the world, and together we had played our respective roles in the ongoing cultural and spiritual battles with passion and intensity.

But nothing had changed—or at least that's how it seemed.

In fact, as the keeper of the numbers, I had to admit that things were actually getting worse in many ways, both in the areas of life and ministry that my comrades and I were doing our best to positively influence and in areas in which we had no direct involvement.

I couldn't figure out what the underlying obstacles were that kept us from seeing tangible, positive results.

It wasn't for lack of marketplace intelligence.

It wasn't for lack of funds.

It wasn't for lack of passion.

It wasn't for lack of plans and tactics.

Honestly, it went beyond discouraging to downright depressing. Some days it all seemed hopeless. I was overwhelmed by the magnitude of the shift in people's lives away from the things of God and toward the things of self. I was dismayed by the lack of leadership for growing true disciples. I was aghast at the lack of focus and energy among parents for raising their children with one central goal in mind: becoming spiritual champions. In my weaker moments, my assessment of the church in America was that it couldn't have found the path to victory if Jesus Himself had been holding a neon road sign pointing the way.

When you get to the point of depression over your life's work, you either give up or find a new way to attack the problem. Thanks to God, I was led to a new way of thinking about the issues at hand. It wasn't a groundbreaking perspective or something no one else had ever thought of before; it was simply a new way for me to think. Others had been there long before I arrived. As is often the case when something isn't working, the best solution turned out to be the simplest.

For me, the breakthrough came when I realized that the key to spiritual health in America (if not the world), and a general about-face in our culture, did not hinge on our facilitating some kind of grand, nationwide revolution that would hit with fury and force all at once. Instead, it was bound up in a return to the way Jesus did things—that is, changing one life at a time.

Maybe that doesn't sound revolutionary to you, but it was for me. Still, even though I understood the concept, I didn't immediately see how it applied to a massive and complicated nation like the United States—more than 310 million people dispersed over nearly 3.8 million square miles. But I came to realize that a nation, a culture, or even a local community isn't changed all at once. If we're alert and prepared, we may get the privilege of participating in the reconstruction of one other life. If that works, then perhaps another life, and then another. In the end, those humble efforts may add up to a revolution or they may not; but when we're realistic about what can happen through our efforts, the big trends are no longer overwhelming and depressing. They are simply new opportunities to be mastered so that we can change the world for Christ, one life at a time.

When we adjust our perspective to a more realistic point of view, it changes everything. The day's headlines no longer bring us down. The absurd statements of leaders do not crush our hopes and dreams. Church splits and electoral defeats are no longer game changers. Anything is possible with God, and He can use anyone to do the impossible when we are willing to take it one life at a time.

So why do I tell you this story? Because we're about to review the character of some national trends, and it's a rather jarring picture when we put it all together. But if we keep our focus on changing one life at a time—starting with our own—it need not throw us into paralysis or depression.

America is undergoing significant changes, and the nature of those changes is both complex and chaotic. The historical foundations on which our society was developed are facing some severe challenges. It's not easy to be the kind of Christian that Jesus longs to have as His ambassadors in this place, at this time.

It's not easy, but it's not impossible.

Getting Good Information

You are responsible for your own choices—not the president, not society, not your spouse, not your friends, not your mama. Every day, you make thousands of choices. Meanwhile, everyone else is making thousands of choices too. If you step back and look at the terrain, you'll realize that some people make consistently better choices than others. In some cases, it's because they have superior instincts. In other cases, it's because they have superior intellect. Sometimes the difference is the availability of superior information.

I cannot do much to hone your instincts or raise your native intelligence, but I *can* serve you by providing useful information. That's one of the objectives of this book.

No one has to tell you how much our world has changed—even in just the past few years. Thanks to the Internet, the expansion of numerous other media channels, and the explosion in social-networking sites, the world is overwhelmed with information. The challenge has shifted from collecting and disseminating facts to winnowing through the multiple storehouses of available information to pluck out the useful morsels, place them in a viable context, and provide a reasonable interpretation of their meaning and application.

The reason we bother to track trends is different from what

many people might think. The purpose is not to *predict* the future, for such proclamations are often terribly off the mark and create hardships for those who put their trust in the projections. The true value of trend watching is to see the *possibilities* for the future and discern how to shape that future. Predictions can be fun and interesting, but if you want to make a difference with your life—and a large majority of Americans would say they do—then you need the right tools.

One indispensable tool is information that can be converted into awareness, which leads to the ability to anticipate options, which in turn provides a chance to exhibit influential behavior—which, of course, is one of the primary functions of leadership. Leadership is based on the ability to see future possibilities and shape the environment to facilitate desired outcomes. So, if you want to lead effectively, you must be well informed and ready to act on the possibilities that emerge.

Years ago, when I was a young researcher learning the ropes, I served in three diverse industries and saw how the process of information gathering and analysis works at its best. In the political realm, working both in election campaigns and in state government, I discovered the power of understanding what people think and feel and of correlating those insights with government policies that would address the public will. In the business realm, working with Disney and other corporations, I learned the importance of having a solid grasp on consumer preferences and experiences in order to provide products and services that would meet felt needs. And in my early work with a handful of forward-thinking churches and parachurch organizations, I realized the value of connecting people's beliefs and lifestyles with biblical principles to effect a better integration of scriptural values and practices in their lives.

Upon reflecting on those divergent experiences, a philosophy of trend watching and information application became clear. Here are the central components:

- Information is critical for decision making.
- Information for its own sake is worthless; valuable information is that which can be converted into action.
- Not all information is created equal: Some is accurate and adds value; some is unreliable and potentially harmful.
- We cannot make good decisions if we have bad information.
- More information is not the same as useful information.
- The earlier in the decision-making process we have good information, the wider our range of options for productive action.
- Good information improperly or inaccurately interpreted leaves us worse off than if we had no information.
- Information without context is usually misleading.
- Great strategy is built on current and accurate information, placed in a proper context, interpreted within that context, and resulting in specific and targeted behavior.

These insights taught me to respect good data and interpretation as treasured resources. Anyone can obtain information, but it takes time, effort, and a bit of skill (or guidance) to gather the right information and to explain it in a proper and meaningful fashion. Without data, you're just another person with an opinion. Without good interpretation of the data, you're just another source of noise. Bad interpretation—that is, drawing conclusions that do not logically or reasonably flow from a sufficiently broad and reliable base of data—is not only misleading but also a potentially harmful distortion of reality.

The purpose of this book is to help you wade through the flood of available information to find that which is helpful, accurate, and useful and to consider ways of connecting disparate facts and ideas into a coherent picture of today and the future. The ultimate goal is not simply to inform you, but to equip you to make strategic decisions about how to make the world a better place to live. This is your God-given challenge and privilege. Trend tracking is a tool you can use to help fulfill that calling.

As you read these pages, you will notice they contain a limited number of predictions and forecasts. That's because predictions that look more than five years down the line are tenuous speculations at best. Many researchers who follow cultural trajectories contend that present-day cultures in developed nations are now reinventing themselves every five years or so. Projecting beyond a half decade is risky business and often proves foolish. It's one thing to forecast demographics five or more years out, but you're swinging at a moving target in such areas as technology and lifestyle, or even core values and attitudes. Yes, there are books in the marketplace that predict what life will be like fifty years from now (or even about life in the year 3000), but this is not one of those books. My objective is not to offer amusing, wild speculations that none of us will live to verify, but to give you practical ideas about becoming a person of positive influence right now.

This book is also not a comprehensive road map of current and future trends. The life dimensions we'll explore will touch on the following critical areas:

- Lifestyles
- Hopes, dreams, and aspirations
- Family life
- Relationships
- Attitudes and values
- Media and entertainment
- Technology

- Religious beliefs
- Religious behavior
- Churches and parachurch organizations
- Demographics

For regularly updated information and commentary on these and other trend areas, you can check my website (www.georgebarna.com) as well as that of The Barna Group (www.barna.org).

CHAPTER 1

HOW WE LIVE AND HOW WE WANT TO LIVE

Our Lifestyles and Aspirations

As RECENTLY AS twenty years ago, people around the world longed for the American way of life. The global fantasy was that Americans had it all figured out, and anyone living in the United States had it made. But times have changed. Not only has the standard of living risen in many countries around the world, but the lifestyle of the average American has suffered some serious setbacks over the past quarter century—especially during the recession of 2007–2010. The United States is still a wonderful and desirable place to live—as evidenced by the millions of immigrants who still attempt to gain entry each year and cross-national surveys showing comparatively high satisfaction levels among American residents—but conditions and expectations have dropped a few notches.

What's Happening with Our Standard of Living

Americans are generally comfortable with their standard of living. Almost two-thirds say they have a higher standard of living than their parents did at the same age, even though median household income levels have fallen in the past ten years. Because median household income has risen by 40 percent since 1970, people fifty and older have less angst about the recent economic collapse than do younger Americans.[1] Almost six out of ten adults (57 percent) believe that as time goes on, it will be increasingly difficult to achieve the American Dream.[2]

Thanks to the recession, Americans have received an overdue wake-up call that has altered their economic thinking and behavior. Personal savings were in the 7 to 8 percent range during the 1960s and 1970s—until the onset of the 1973–1975 recession. At that point, savings ballooned to 14.6 percent in 1975 before declining to prerecession rates once the economy returned to health. During the economic insanity of the 1990s, though, the savings rate declined again, this time due to excessive personal spending and risky investing. By 2000, the savings rate had plummeted to just 3.5 percent, and it dropped to a mere 1.3 percent in 2008.

Americans have received an overdue wake-up call that has altered their economic thinking and behavior.

While savings dropped, debt rose to unprecedented levels: Household debt rose from 60 percent of household income in 1982 to 130 percent of income in 2007. Saving money became a thing of the past. Federal Reserve Bank statistics show that between 2005 and 2008, many people had blown through their savings and were literally spending more than they were making.

Public hysteria about the economic crash began a reversal of people's unrestrained spending, such that by April 2008, the savings rate had "rebounded" to zero. Since then, scared by high unemployment rates and declining salaries, people have begun to save again, and the savings rate has climbed back to the 4 to

5 percent range—not enough for many families to recover from previously incurred debt, but a move in the right direction. Whether it is too little too late, given the federal government's $13 trillion debt load, remains to be seen.[3]

Equity declined substantially as people borrowed against the value of their homes, relying on the prospect of better times in the years to come. But those hopes were destroyed with the crash of housing prices and stock market values. Home values, which had quadrupled from 1982 to 2007, declined by more than 25 percent during the slump, producing record numbers of foreclosures. Families whose net worth was tied up substantially in their home equity took a particularly hard hit.

Families whose net worth was tied up substantially in their home equity took a particularly hard hit.

Further, over the preceding twenty-five years, the stock market had soared as well, creating sizable gains for many investors. The Dow Jones Industrial Average, one popular indicator, increased by a factor of fifteen during that period. But when the market crashed, it took with it many people's dreams of a secure future. Money invested for retirement plummeted so much that by 2010 the number of people who believed they would be able to draw anything from their savings or home equity was in decline, and growing numbers of citizens were counting on a potentially bankrupt Social Security system to keep them afloat once they left the labor pool.

At one point, Federal Reserve Board statistics estimated that the economic freefall had cost Americans about $15 trillion in net worth. Mincing no words, a recent Nobel Prize winner in economics, Columbia University professor Edmund Phelps, warned that it could take up to fifteen years for people to restore the money they lost in the recession.[4] Indeed, the nationwide financial blow is largely responsible for about half of all small-business owners

(47 percent) eliminating retirement from their future plans. Many (41 percent) expect to reduce their workload at some stage in the distant future, but a greater share are concerned that the magnitude of their recent losses—in savings, personal income, and business revenue—precludes the possibility of retirement altogether. In their minds, retirement would be forced on them only by poor health.[5]

Millions of Americans justifiably lost confidence in the system as they watched news of record layoffs.

Millions of Americans justifiably lost confidence in the system as they watched news of record layoffs—and dreaded the possibility that they, too, could lose their jobs and benefits; saw numerous small businesses go under; and realized that they could be stuck in their current jobs for years to come without a meaningful raise in salary. They were angered by the unimaginable greed and dishonesty of a parade of busted financial managers (starting with Bernie Madoff and Goldman Sachs) who squandered people's investments and by mismanaged corporations (including AIG, Bank of America, and General Motors, among others) that received federal bailout money. The result is an era characterized by widespread fear, discouragement, confusion, anxiety, and doubt.[6]

The Boston Consulting Group estimates that roughly 100,000 households in the United States have a net worth of $20 million or more (including real estate). That's a lot of money, but let's put those numbers in context: Those 100,000 households represent *less than one-tenth of one percent* of all U.S. households, and even that number may be too high. The IRS estimates that only half as many households are actually in the $20 million–plus category. In 2007, according to the Federal Reserve Board, the median household net worth was $120,300, and the mean was $556,300. More recent data, through the end of 2009, suggests that those figures have declined, with the median closer to $100,000 and the mean in the neighborhood of $450,000.[7]

Of course, the recession did not hit everyone with equal force. We still have a "wealth gap"—a situation in which the top one percent of households earns 19 percent of all pretax income (up from 12 percent in 1990). Households making $100,000 or more comprise 17 percent of the population but account for 37 percent of the nation's spending. On the other hand, according to the Congressional Budget Office, the wealthiest one percent paid out 28 percent of all federal tax revenue in 2008, and the wealthiest 10 percent contributed 55 percent of all tax dollars. The effective tax rate for the top one percent of earners is 31 percent, compared to a rate of just 4 percent among the bottom 20 percent of earners.[8]

Despite this disparity in taxes paid, the bottom line is that millions of Americans are now living on the edge. A December 2009 survey by TNS revealed that half of all American consumers fear an unforeseen financial challenge because they no longer have any personal financial reserves or external means of handling a sudden economic crisis. And that doesn't even include major crises such as funding cancer treatments or rebuilding a home destroyed by a natural disaster. In fact, more than 150 million adults believe they couldn't cover even a minor personal crisis, such as the need to replace the transmission in their cars, the need to replace the roof—or even the furnace—in their homes, or the cost of a non-life-threatening illness that required hospitalization. Adults would consider a wide range of options to get through a crisis. Half said they would be willing to drain their savings (but we know that the average American household saved less than $700 in 2008); one-quarter said they were willing to ask relatives for help (but their family members may be close to the edge as well); one-fifth said they would try to get an extra, part-time job (but the competition for those limited opportunities has stiffened considerably); another fifth reluctantly noted that they would run up bills on their credit cards, despite paying horrendous interest rates; and one out of five also agreed that they would be likely to sell some of their possessions to generate quick cash.[9]

In sum, roughly two-thirds of the nation's people are changing their minds—not only about spending and savings patterns, but also about what a "reasonable" lifestyle looks like. The consequences of decisions made before the recession continue to produce both suffering and redefinition, which in turn have altered our national psyche and affected our lifestyles—but not always in ways you might imagine.

People are changing their minds—not only about spending and savings, but also about what a "reasonable" lifestyle looks like.

For example, you might expect to see Americans turn to a lot of creative solutions—but would you expect more couponing? That's right, those little cents-off slips of paper that were so common in the 1960s, '70s, and '80s, but fell out of favor during the following decades of excess, are making a comeback. Inmar, a leading coupon processing firm, says the number of redeemed coupons rose by 27 percent in 2008, from 2.6 billion to 3.3 billion—the largest single-year jump in more than twenty years. Nielsen, which tracks consumer spending patterns, reports that the rise was aided by "extreme couponers"—generally upscale females, 54 and older, who redeemed 104 or more coupons over a six-month period.[10]

In the years ahead, you'll likely hear a lot more about *value* in products and services and see the emergence of a new generation of businesses that cater to discount-minded shoppers. Walmart, of course, already has a leg up on the competition in that market niche, but soon you'll see discount offerings in everything from funerals (increased cremations, cheaper caskets, no-frills ceremonies) to concert tickets (lower prices, greater quantities of cheaper seats, and more artist products available for sale at the show to compensate for revenue lost through lower ticket prices). More companies will introduce loyalty programs that reward consumers for consistent patronage. (One study, by Colloquy, found that one-third of consumers are now drawn by such programs, citing them as a "more important" part of their household's financial model.[11])

If Americans were truly committed to lowering the cost of living, one step they could take would be to reduce the number of lawsuits filed and pursued each year. The aggregate cost of legal action topped $250 billion in 2007, an amount that represents a "litigation tax" of $835 per person, up from $722 in 2001, and compared to just $12 in 1950. Resolving disputes in less costly and less hostile ways—the financial burden of which is often passed along to consumers—could lower our cost of living considerably, while potentially diminishing our stress levels at the same time.[12]

The aggregate cost of legal action topped $250 billion, an amount that represents a "litigation tax" of $835 per person.

What's Happening with Our Perspective on Life

Given the shock to the system that many Americans have received over the past few years, it's not surprising our stress levels have been rising. On any given day, about one-third of adults, and even higher proportions of teenagers and college students, report that they are feeling "stressed out." Dr. Richard Rahe, creator of the widely used Life Changes Stress Test, has also discovered that the nature and intensity of our life stresses have changed since 1967. Certain events—including several that are now common for a growing proportion of Americans—have become relatively more stressful than they were in years past. Those events include the death of a family member, being laid off or fired, pregnancy or the birth of a child, the death of a friend, a child leaving home, and changing one's job field. Interestingly, events that are relatively less stressful than before include the death of a spouse and divorce—indications that our marital relationships may have less emotional impact on us than we'd like to believe.[13]

Beyond the obvious financial challenges that many Americans face, what ignites our emotions and causes stress in our lives?

On the one hand, we are a people who worry. Among the dominant worries we harbor are concerns about the moral condition of the nation (86 percent worry about that). More personal worries include things such as addictions (12 percent) or feelings of loneliness and isolation (9 percent). And though most people believe they are fulfilling their calling in life (71 percent) and are making a positive difference in the world (78 percent), those two goals become burdens as people seek to reach their potential.

We are a people who try to look to the future and who typically believe the best is yet to come.

On the other hand, we are a people who try to look to the future and who typically believe the best is yet to come. Still, the recent downturn and the long-term economic challenges facing the nation have reduced both the number of people who are optimistic and the level of certainty about the good times they hope to encounter. Some everyday things we look forward to include a good night's sleep (71 percent), time with friends (55 percent), and listening to music (54 percent). We also embrace long-term hopes, plans, and dreams that give shape and identity to our lives—such as being in good health (85 percent), living with a high degree of integrity (85 percent), having one marital partner (80 percent), having a clear purpose for life (77 percent), having a close, personal relationship with God (75 percent), having close, personal friendships (74 percent), living a comfortable lifestyle (70 percent), enjoying a satisfying sexual relationship within marriage (66 percent), having children (66 percent), living close to family and relatives (63 percent), and being deeply committed to the Christian faith (59 percent). Whew! That's a lot of pieces to the puzzle for a person to develop and organize, but it gives a good sense of what really matters to us and how we will apply our resources.

Perhaps you've noticed that a few outcomes you might have expected to rank high on the list didn't register—such as achieving fame (7 percent), having the latest and greatest technology and electronics (11 percent), owning a big house (18 percent), or working at a high-paying job (28 percent). Most adults are not opposed to those experiences, but such things are not the life outcomes that motivate most Americans to get out of bed every morning.

By the same token, Americans have adopted some distinct limitations when it comes to decision making. For instance, there is a widespread reluctance to sacrifice downtime just to make money or to become better informed. Likewise, people are generally unwilling to give up public services in order to cut taxes, or to reduce personal pleasures and entertainment to be more connected to other people.

People are generally unwilling to give up public services in order to cut taxes.

What does it take, then, to be happy? One recent study discovered that it takes a healthy annual income, but that money alone doesn't do it. Based on an analysis of surveys among 450,000 adults, Angus Deaton and Daniel Kahneman concluded that the more money people earn, the more contentment they experience in the moment—until income reaches $75,000. After that point, the additional toys and comforts afforded by increased income do nothing to improve their current mood. However, additional income beyond that point does seem to improve people's overall satisfaction with their quality of life and place in the world, if not their level of day-to-day contentment. So, making money is not a magic formula for joy and contentment—but anyone who reads the Bible closely already knew that.[14]

But old dreams die hard, even in the face of empirical evidence to the contrary. For instance, a substantial plurality of adults dream about becoming rich. When offered the option of being richer, thinner, smarter, or younger, 43 percent opted for the money, with fewer desirous of being thinner (21 percent), smarter (14 percent), or younger (12 percent). The remaining 10 percent had no interest in any of those four options. Wealth was of slightly greater interest to men (46 percent) than women (41 percent), whereas being thinner was twice as appealing to women (29 percent) as men (14 percent). Surprisingly, men were twice as likely as women to desire being younger (16 percent versus 8 percent).[15] In a culture in which celebrities are often thought of as glamorous and carefree due to their wealth, it may be natural to pine for more money, but wealth is a lure that rarely fulfills people's expectations.

What's Happening with Our Use of Time

Americans are keenly aware that time is a nonrenewable resource that must be used judiciously to accomplish our goals and dreams. Nevertheless, we make some surprising choices in how we spend our time.

You might imagine, for instance, that skyrocketing gasoline prices and expanding commute times would change where we live, where we choose to work, and how we get there. But they haven't. Our choices of where to live continue to be driven by the size and value of the homes we can afford and by the perceived security of the area and the quality of local schools rather than by proximity to work. The average commute has actually increased by nearly 20 percent to twenty-five minutes each way, while ride sharing has grown by less than one percent during the past three years. Perhaps the pressure of those longer commutes is what has caused nearly four out of ten adults to suggest that road rage is on the upswing, and why two out of every ten drivers admit to reading or sending text messages while on the road.[16]

And given the government's strategy of building more roads rather than creating incentives for commuters to use mass transit, we can expect traffic jams to get worse in the coming years.

Given the government's strategy of building more roads, we can expect traffic jams to get worse in the coming years.

The variety evident in American lifestyles means that surprisingly few activities are common to most people on a daily basis. Some that are common include watching television, driving a car, talking to (or texting) someone on the phone, using a computer, and catching up with the news. Also, did you know that two-thirds of Americans recycle materials on any given day? Other activities common to a majority include drinking at least one cup of coffee or tea, praying to God, and discussing moral issues (or the moral implications of specific situations or choices) with others.

Although specific media choices vary by age and other demographics, the inescapable reality is that we are a nation addicted to media input. Statistics vary, but we know that the typical adult allocates more than fifty hours per week to media absorption. In fact, the only activity that takes more of our time is sleeping. Based on criteria developed by the American Psychiatric Association, our devotion to media content is literally an addiction—perhaps the most widespread and insidious addiction in our society today.[17] (If you think that statement is overblown, try wrestling the cell phone away from a teenager for a couple of days, or tell a college student that he or she is banned from the Internet for a week.) We'll undertake a more complete discussion of media use in chapter 4.

Some activities are not yet mainstream daily behaviors but are moving in that direction. Among those are drinking energy drinks (the super-caffeinated beverages consumed regularly by one-third of young adults); playing video games; using profanity in public (more than one-quarter of adults already do so, including one-third of men); changing the TV channel because of displeasure with the moral content of a program;

We are a nation addicted to media input. In fact, the only activity that takes more of our time is sleeping.

discussing spiritual matters with other people; viewing pornography; and engaging in gossip. Notice the paradox in some of these emerging trends—for instance, growth in spiritual discussions as well as gossip; or switching channels to avoid immoral content, but also increased viewing of pornography. These contradictions reflect dominant patterns in American lifestyles: both the polarization of the population on moral and spiritual matters and the inconsistency between how people see themselves and how they behave.

Some activities might already be more common than you think. Our surveys show that one out of every ten adults had a sexual liaison outside of marriage last week. Also in a typical week: one out of every eight adults (12 percent) took revenge against someone who had wronged them; a similar proportion got drunk (though the numbers are substantially higher among adults under thirty-five); one out of every five (20 percent) bought a lottery ticket or gambled (and twice as many do so in a typical month); and one-fifth (22 percent) chose not to watch a particular movie or television program because they believed it would contain objectionable content. One behavior that is taking the country by storm is napping: 34 percent of adults take a nap each day, a percentage that is likely to grow in the coming years with our aging population.

Increasingly popular activities that are undertaken less frequently include "adventure vacations" (nearly half of all households have taken one in the past five years) and vacationing with family or friends (this number has fluctuated between 35 and 55 percent in recent years). Travel remains a favorite activity for Americans, with roughly three-quarters of all overnight (or longer) trips in 2009 taken for pleasure. These trips averaged four nights in duration; four out of five were by car (air travel is more common for business-related jaunts); and less than half involved a stay in paid lodging.[18]

Other national pastimes may not be as popular as you think. For instance, did you know that half of the adult population (50 percent) did not eat in a restaurant last year? Or that six out of ten adults did not read a single book? Only four out of every ten adults entertained a friend in their homes last year. And even though a majority of Americans live within a hundred miles of the coast, only one out of four adults actually went to the beach in the past twelve months.[19]

Even though a majority of Americans live within 100 miles of the coast, only one out of four adults go to the beach.

Our sporting and exercise preferences are varied as well. The most popular physical and athletic activities among adults include exercise walking (37 percent took at least two walks during the past year), exercising with equipment (22 percent), swimming (16 percent), bowling (14 percent), working out at an exercise club (14 percent), and weight lifting (13 percent). Children ages seven to seventeen have a different set of physical priorities. They were most likely to engage in swimming (37 percent), bicycle riding (30 percent), bowling

(27 percent), basketball (27 percent), exercise walking (20 percent), and soccer (19 percent). Notice that sports requiring significant numbers of participants, such as baseball, football, and volleyball, are now less common than they used to be. But even some sports requiring less human capital, such as tennis, have fallen out of favor.[20]

During the recent recession, as discretionary income became scarce but not the desire to have a good time, millions of people rediscovered the family room as a location for leisure time. The result was a renaissance of home entertainment, relying on new equipment such as large-screen TVs, video game consoles, and computers loaded with free or low-cost programs (now known as *apps*). As Americans recover from the recession, the adoption of these new tools for filling our time may be one of the changes that remain in place. Look for the tech industry to continue to capitalize on this opportunity by providing a tidal wave of additional apps, powerful and accurate voice recognition software, and myriad alternatives available through "cloud computing"—that is, Internet-based applications. The social-networking craze is another recent in-home entertainment trend.

During the recent recession, millions of people rediscovered the family room as a location for leisure time.

Don't overlook the unfolding generational differences. Specifically, it seems that Busters (those born 1965 through 1983) prefer technology and entertainment devices that can be used to meet group needs (e.g., HDTV, DVRs), whereas Mosaics (those born between 1984 and 2002) prefer devices that provide more exclusive personal use and content customization (e.g., MP3 players, mobile phones).[21] These preferences reflect each generation's ideas about relationships and identity.

Naturally, many other endeavors continue to enjoy widespread popularity as well. During the recession, surprisingly few consumers reduced their trips to the movie theater or video retailer (even if it was now a vending machine dispensing their DVD of choice); those options still provided a relatively inexpensive and memorable experience. Music remains hugely popular, though it now comes in a different format (digitized), in different quantities (single-song downloads rather than entire album purchases), and from a different source (online retailers) than before. You may have noticed that independent record shops have all but disappeared over the past twenty years. And the continued digitization of other media has now set video stores and bookstores on a similar path.

And how could we possibly discuss how we spend our time and resources without considering the role of shopping? The trends here may be more significant than you think. One recent study concluded that women spend an average of eight years of their lives shopping. The typical American woman will make 301 shopping trips per year and devote slightly less than 400 hours per year to those excursions. (And this only involves trips for the purpose of buying—it excludes window-shopping experiences, which occur at a rate of almost one per week.) The most common shopping trip was to the grocery store—eighty-four trips per year, consuming ninety-five hours. The most time-consuming trips, though, were those focused on clothing, shoes, and accessories—171 hours per year, distributed across sixty-three shopping trips. Before you criticize such devotion to shopping, remember this: 70 percent of our nation's gross domestic product (GDP) is based on retail sales. Women, it seems, are simply doing what they can to bolster the sagging economy.[22]

Despite the inroads made by online retailers in some industries (such as books and music), for the most part attempts to replace the physical act of shopping with a combination of online ordering and home delivery have been slow to catch on. This is largely because shopping is a multipurpose task: for millions of Americans, it is both a necessity and a source of entertainment or pleasure. Retailers, sensitized to this reality, commonly receive higher marks for the shopping experience they offer consumers than for the customer service they provide.[23]

Attempts to replace the physical act of shopping with online ordering and home delivery have been slow to catch on.

It's also interesting to note that, even with our economic woes, Americans generally choose not to simply buy the cheapest available product or service. And even though the word *value* is no longer in vogue—because people think it has too often been misappropriated and abused—the concept of value shopping is alive and well. Half of all consumers are willing to pay more for a product or service that is of demonstrably higher quality, largely because they believe it will last longer, perform better, and thus save them money in the long run. Only one out of four consumers believes that cheaper products and services are of the same quality as more expensive ones and therefore represent a better option. However, because of the nation's financial squeeze, some consumers have had to purchase cheaper brands, even if they don't want to, simply because they lack the money to stretch their budgets as far as they must go. That will likely change once more people get back on their feet economically, probably around the middle of this second decade of the new millennium.

What's Happening with Our Personal Connections

A persistent knock on Americans by foreigners visiting the United States—and there are some twenty-five to thirty million who flock here every year, not including the half-million foreign students enrolled in American colleges—is that we are rude and unfriendly.

Given the time and effort we devote to interpersonal relationships, though, another interpretation might be that we simply have a different approach to relationships than is practiced by people from other countries. Still, the research confirms that Americans do have some relational issues to address.

When asked to identify the most fulfilling relationship in their lives today, Americans give an unexpectedly diverse set of replies, with no single type of relationship dominating the list. The most frequent response (32 percent) is that family members provide the most fulfilling relationships, followed by spouse (22 percent), God (19 percent), and children (17 percent). Just 2 percent named a non–family member as their most satisfying relationship. When we asked about groups of people with which respondents were associated, we learned that the most significant groups were the people from their church (29 percent), friends from their workplace (18 percent), or aggregations of friends with whom they frequently spend time (14 percent).

Perhaps some people struggle to develop and maintain strong relationships because of their desire for control. A Barna Group study discovered that two-thirds of Americans (66 percent) like to be in control of whatever is happening in their lives and circumstances. (That desire is more common among men than women, by a 70 percent to 61 percent margin.) As anyone knows who has ever had a spouse or a boss who was determined to exert control over the relationship, involvement in such a connection is not pleasant. Yet, in a society where independence is seen as a virtue, the penchant for control is an almost inescapable outgrowth of the self-reliant, me-first, can-do mind-set.

The penchant for control is an almost inescapable outgrowth of the self-reliant, me-first, can-do mind-set.

We also recognized that it has become common to mistake

physical proximity—being in the presence of others—for genuine relationship. Americans are generally well connected with one another, yet a huge number feel disconnected. According to our national studies, as many as 40 percent of adults admit they are trying to find a few good friends. The absence of such friends can be explained in various ways: the mobility of our population, diverse work schedules, family pressures and stresses, poor communication skills, selfishness, financial constraints, and radical independence. But the fact remains: more than ninety million adults are looking for just a few good friends. That need is particularly acute among people in the Mosaic generation. Two-thirds admitted to seeking a few good friends.

There may be fewer limitations on the nature of friendships than ever before. In a dramatic reversal of past trends, Americans have become much more comfortable with people of different backgrounds—not only being in their midst, but becoming their friends. A study by the Pew Research Center, released in December 2008, reported that six out of ten adults say they like the idea of living in a community that is mixed politically (63 percent), racially (65 percent), religiously (59 percent), and economically. That is a startling shift from the conventional wisdom that people prefer a homogeneous neighborhood and friends who reflect their own backgrounds. This shift is a work in progress, however, as demonstrated by research data showing that people vastly prefer living in an area with a limited immigrant population over residing in a community with a large immigrant presence. And despite their progressive attitudes, most people live in an area dominated by others who share their racial or ethnic backgrounds. Most whites live in majority-white neighborhoods, as do about half of all blacks and just less than half of all Hispanics. You find the same racial and ethnic segregation patterns in churches across the country. Fewer than one out of ten Protestant churches has a congregation that is multiethnic or multiracial to any noteworthy degree.

But again, the distinction between proximity and connection is important. Recent studies inform us that despite the plethora of new communication technologies that make interaction easier and more frequent than ever before—texting, cell phones, e-mail, instant messaging, social networks, video calls, tweeting—those means do not supply the depth and satisfaction that a traditional face-to-face relationship provides. In fact, it is possible to have hundreds, if not thousands, of digital friends but to feel lonely, isolated, or abandoned and to lack trusted individuals with whom one can share significant moments and concerns.

Fewer than one out of ten Protestant churches has a multiethnic or multiracial congregation to any noteworthy degree.

Relationships that used to form within neighborhoods are less common today. And though tens of millions of Americans volunteer in community service groups and churches, even those environments have failed to provide the kind of friendships that people used to form through those associations. In fact, insights from the Pew Research Center indicate that the number of meaningful relationships—and the diversity of those friendships—has been in modest but steady decline for the past couple of decades.[24] The Pew findings are supported by a project undertaken by the University of Southern California's Center for the Digital Future, which found that more than one-quarter of adults now spend less time with family members, largely replacing those interactions with time devoted to the Internet and television. The report also noted that for several consecutive years parents have regretted that their children spend too much time with television, Internet, and other technologies to the detriment of their family ties.[25]

Will our untamed appetite for new communications

technologies serve us better in the future, facilitating healthier relationships? Nobody can know for sure, but some recent innovations hold promise. For instance, a few new tools use technology to facilitate face-to-face interaction. Services such as Foursquare, Brightkite, Loopt, and Google Latitude provide people with ways of knowing where friends are at any given moment, fostering in-person gatherings on the spur of the moment without any direct communication required. It's a kind of planned spontaneity. Similar innovations may help to foster more genuine and lasting interactions.[26]

Some people fear that social-networking sites might actually contribute to the ongoing demise of healthy friendships.

The eight-hundred-pound gorilla of online engagement, of course, is the universe of social-networking sites, led by Facebook. Some people fear that social-networking sites might actually contribute to the ongoing demise of healthy friendships. And though the share of the population that uses such sites more than quintupled from 2005 to 2010, there is a growing level of push-back from users who acknowledge that it has somehow cheapened their relationships. When such networks simply become ways of killing time or create boredom through insignificant interactions with others, as some social network users have proclaimed, the relationships involved are devalued. On the other hand, recent studies indicate that, at least among young people, interaction through social-networking sites actually serves as a stimulant for more extensive in-person socializing. Many young users of such technology utilize those tools to facilitate shared, in-the-flesh experiences, with online communications often sparking ideas or alerting friends to the availability of others in their network.[27]

But old-fashioned, face-to-face relationships also continue to evolve. In a recent, helpful study, Geoffrey Greif, a faculty member at the University of Maryland's School of Social Work, evaluated the nature of men's relationships with each other, allowing a comparison to the friendships that women maintain. Women are well known to be physically and emotionally expressive with each other, and the depth of such expressions often indicates the perceived strength of the relationship. With intimacy as their goal, the ability to share feelings and ideas is important. They operate best when they meet in person. Though women may lose touch with friends during their twenties and thirties, they typically reconnect later in life in order to gain trusted perspectives that help them make sense of the ever-changing world of work and family. Those reattachments provide highly desired guidance and emotional support.

Dr. Greif showed that male-to-male relationships can be just as strong but appear less intimate. Men can receive significant support through their friendships with other men, but they are generally not physically or emotionally expressive. In fact, male friendships are most likely to form, provide value, and endure when they are low-maintenance and based on shared experiences that do not require excessive talk or displays of emotion. Simply being in the same place at the same time and experiencing the same event—for instance, playing golf or attending a football game together—is sufficiently satisfying.

Men tend to resist friendships with other men whom they perceive to be too needy.

Men tend to resist friendships with other men whom they perceive to be too needy or who reflect what they see as the negative aspects of female relationships: cattiness, drama, the likelihood of holding grudges, or being overly competitive. Male relational stages unfold differently than women's, often reflecting the same loss of focus on friendships when career and family demands are highest, but followed by a return to the same friends with whom they had lost touch. For men, the Internet is a treasure because it facilitates those reconnections. Guys are less likely to pursue an entirely new pool of friends.[28]

A different form of relationship that bears attention is the sexual engagements that occur so regularly across America. Some people in other countries have suggested that the dominant export of the United States is sex—in movies, music, television, online, bedroom products, and so forth. The truth of the matter is that, whether media content simply reflects the sexual obsessions of the public or the public's obsession was ignited by the sexual emphasis in media content, the focus on sexuality is inescapable in our culture.

Efforts to promote sexual abstinence notwithstanding, sexual intimacy is common in America from the time people hit their teen-age years. Depending on which organization's statistics you trust, the average age of a person's first sexual intercourse is fifteen, sixteen, or seventeen. For more than four out of five people, their first sexual experience occurred prior to marriage. In fact, the most recent data available show that just 24 percent of all men and women ages fifteen to forty-four who have never been married are still virgins.[29] This reflects not only the relaxed moral standards of the nation but also that people are delaying marriage until their mid-to-late twenties in the midst of a sexually charged culture that makes abstinence exceedingly difficult.

Just 24 percent of all men and women ages fifteen to forty-four who have never been married are still virgins.

Few Americans stop at only one sexual partner. The median number for men ages fifteen to forty-four in a lifetime is nearly six (though 23 percent say they've had fifteen or more partners), and women average three partners (with 9 percent citing fifteen or more partners). Along the way, a majority of women under forty-five experience an unintended pregnancy, with more than one-quarter of those terminated by an abortion.

As it turns out, sexual adventures are among the most common forms of personal entertainment in America. A recent survey of college students revealed that 60 percent had been involved in a "friends with benefits" relationship—the term used to describe a no-commitment sexual arrangement. The primary attraction of these relationships, according to the survey, was the absence of commitment or responsibility, providing the participants with what they perceived to be "a relatively safe and convenient environment for recreational sex." The couple involved gained the benefit of trust and comfort without the complications of romantic involvement or a jeopardized friendship. With the growing acceptance of such interactions on campuses across the nation, it is little wonder that the United States has literally millions of unwanted pregnancies, abortions, and births out of wedlock. Since 1980, the number of children born to unwed parents has climbed from 18 percent of all live births to 40 percent today.[30]

It is worth noting that another challenge to traditional sexual values—"gender neutral" dormitories—is also emerging on college campuses. These are dorms where students of the opposite sex are allowed to share rooms. Originally championed at Columbia University, this practice is gaining ground (more than fifty schools now facilitate such arrangements) and is expected to become commonplace in the next decade or so.[31]

Reflections

Our chaotic world sometimes moves us to yearn for life as it used to be. That's usually an exercise in wasted time and energy. In this turbocharged global era, we will find life more fulfilling and fruitful if we commit to doing our best without simultaneously possessing unrealistic expectations and paralyzing anxieties about things we cannot change. Life satisfaction is more closely tied to attitudes and values than to possessions and fame. Rather than lament what we used to have, don't have, or cannot have, we can choose to make the most of our blessings and opportunities. Only then will our lives blossom.

Toward that end, we need to create an updated sense of the American Dream—a Dream 2.0, if you will, or what some have called "the new normal." If the original dream has largely been achieved and surpassed—after all, who would be satisfied these days with a postage-stamp lot, two-car garage, and family of four in the suburbs?—what is the new dream?

Here's a thought to ponder: Can you envision a life that moves beyond a quest to acquire "stuff" and toward a dream that defines how you can contribute more to the lives of others? In practical terms, what would that look like? Most Americans want to make a lasting mark on the world, leaving it a better place than they inherited. Perhaps your new dream can encompass how you can optimally apply your gifts, abilities, and resources toward a better tomorrow. It doesn't have to be a big *program*; simply begin by touching the lives of the people right around you, the people God has already brought into your sphere of influence. Affecting one life at a time, when multiplied exponentially, can truly change the world.

> **Most Americans want to make a lasting mark on the world, leaving it a better place than they inherited.**

En route to developing your new dream, you must learn from the mistakes of the past—both your own and others'. Consider the advantages inherent in debt-free living, adhering to a savings plan, wise investing, living within your means, and pursuing simplicity. What would it be like to seek consistency in your self-image, beliefs, behavior, and understanding of the common good? None of these outcomes is beyond your reach. They become an impossible dream only if you allow them to. Incorporating clear goals, stringent self-examination, determined effort, and accountability will improve your chances of success.

Technology provides useful tools, but we must be careful not to take the lazy way and use technology as a substitute for relationship. Life is about knowing, loving, and serving God and other people. Technology simply provides tools for the journey.

Never lose sight of the nature and purpose of that journey, despite the plentiful distractions and temptations you encounter from moment to moment. Success is not about comfort or survival; it is about transcending the mundane circumstances of daily existence to experience a dynamic partnership with God, one that results in your desire and ability to bless people. Anything less lofty will leave you disappointed and unfulfilled. Of course, in the end, it's your choice.

Chapter 2

FAMILY LIFE

Foundations, Continuity, Disruptions, and Possibilities

From our nation's humble beginnings in the earliest settlements and colonies, the family unit has been the foundation on which the American experiment is anchored. Given the nature of our humanity, family-related stress has always been part of the equation. But over the past half century, in particular, the traditional family unit and its customary practices and assumptions have been under increasing pressure.

One thing that hasn't changed is the widespread perception of the family's importance in our nation's stability. Surveys show that more than four out of five Americans continue to believe that for the United States to remain a strong and secure nation, its families must be strong and secure as well. When we ask people to identify their single highest priority in life, half of all adults list elements related to their family lives. Yet, regardless of the goodwill felt toward the family unit, this is not an easy era for families to navigate.

What's Happening with Marriage

As with most things in our contemporary culture, change is apparent, even in relation to such foundational institutions as marriage. Though one might expect marriage to be on the way out, the data show just the opposite: Marriage, perhaps the oldest interpersonal practice of all, is demonstrating a fierce resilience in the face of constant and ever-morphing challenges to its future.

Believe it or not, roughly nine out of every ten Americans get married at some point in their lives. With divorce now a common practice, though, only 56 percent of adults are currently married—a statistic that hasn't changed in twenty years. In 1970, 71 percent of the adult population was married; and even though the proportion declined continually over the next two decades, it has remained virtually unchanged since then.[1]

Nine out of every ten Americans get married at some point in their lives.

The how and when of marriage have also been shifting, of course. The average age when a person first marries has risen from twenty among women and twenty-three among men in 1960 to twenty-six among women and twenty-eight among men in 2010. Postponing marriage has had some discernible benefits for the longevity of marriages. For instance, when people wait to tie the knot, they tend to have greater financial and career stability, are more thoughtful about the mate they choose, have a heightened likelihood of sharing responsibilities (such as earning money, taking on household chores, and parenting), and are more realistic about the challenges of marriage and the hardships of divorce. As a result, according to recent research, later marriages produce longer-lasting unions.

But putting off marriage has had another significant effect: dropping the marriage rate. When combined with the high number of divorces, this decrease in the rate of marriage has left us with a stable number of homes (and thus a lower percentage) containing two married heterosexual parents with children. In 1970, the nation's population reached two hundred million, and there were twenty-five million such homes. In 2009, when the population reached three hundred million, there were still twenty-five million two-parent households.[2]

In the intervening years, social scientists have devoted much time and money to studying marriage and family dynamics. A lot has been learned about what makes marriages last these days. Critical characteristics of couples with lasting marriages include the following:

- There is a limited age gap between husband and wife.
- The couple waited to get married until after age twenty-five.
- The couple did not have children until married (and, in the best of all worlds, they did not have children from prior relationships).
- The spouses have a similar intensity of desire to have children.
- Both partners come from homes in which their own parents had not been divorced.
- Neither partner was previously married.
- The couple is not on the edge financially.
- Either both partners or neither partner smokes.[3]

Depending on how we ask the survey questions, we find that anywhere from 60 to 90 percent of married adults are satisfied with their marital relationships—it really depends on how satisfaction is measured. Asked why they remain married, 71 percent do so out of love, yet 73 percent identified companionship as a key factor. Only half described their union as "loving and joyful," and nearly one-third simply labeled it "a peaceful coexistence." Three out of ten admitted that they remain married solely because of financial need or that leaving the marriage would be "too much trouble."[4]

To gain a broader perspective of what goes into people's thinking about their marriages, consider the following: Nearly half of married women and one-third of married men at least occasionally think about leaving their spouses. The temptation to do so isn't usually driven by a desire to take up with someone else; more often, it's about relational tensions, financial pressures, parenting stress, or health challenges. In fact, only one out of ten married adults claim they would cheat on their spouse if they were guaranteed that their spouse would never find out (although most adults admit that they would never confess their indiscretion to their spouse).[5]

Marriages are less likely to dissolve because of sexual infidelity than for other reasons.

Unexpectedly, researchers have discovered that marriages are less likely to dissolve because of sexual infidelity than for other reasons. Approximately one out of five married men admits to having cheated on his wife, usually engaging in affairs with at least two other women. About half as many married women have cheated on their husbands. Yet more than two-thirds of those marriages continue, albeit with very different dynamics. That's not to say that sex isn't a big tension point in marriages; it is, in several ways.[6]

One common tension is the lack of sex in a marriage. A majority of married adults (55 percent) complain they do not have sex often enough (a more common gripe, not surprisingly, among men). Currently, nearly one-third of married adults (31 percent) coexist in what sociologists have termed "sexless marriages"—those in which the married adults have sex fewer than ten times during the year. That may be one reason why nearly all married adults admit to having sexual fantasies about someone other than their spouses—and the likelihood grows as the person gets older. More than eight out of ten adults don't engage in sexual affairs, but they do ponder the possibilities. Some researchers have reported that what is most likely to restrain most married people from affairs is the lack of opportunity. It is interesting to note, as well, that the dominant reason for sexless marriages varies. Among men, their reasons for abstaining revolve around health issues or boredom with their sexual partner. Women's primary reasons relate to control issues (withholding sex as a punishment or to exert authority), anger toward the husband, or disinterest in sex itself.[7]

One of the latest trends affecting marriage is unions between people of different races or ethnicities. In 1960, only slightly more than 2 percent of marriages were multiracial or multiethnic. That grew to 7 percent by 1980 and constitutes 15 percent of new marriages today. Such marriages are more likely among Asians (31 percent of all new marriages) and Hispanics (26 percent) than among blacks (16 percent) or whites (9 percent). And the probability of entering a mixed marriage within groups varies by gender: black men are more than twice as likely as black women to intermarry, whereas Asian women are twice as likely as Asian men to do so. Things have changed dramatically from forty-five years ago, when it took a 1967 Supreme Court decision to force a number of states to drop their laws against interracial marriages. Today, 80 percent of adults believe it is acceptable for one of their family members to marry outside their own race or ethnicity.[8]

Men don't fear marriage, but some fear a failed marriage, so they avoid it altogether.

Marriage is not for everyone. Presently, one out of four adults in the United States has never been married—though half of those will eventually enter into a marriage covenant. One of the primary reasons why men tarry at "popping the question"—and why millions never do—is fear of having a bad marriage. Recent studies have indicated that men don't fear marriage, but some fear a failed marriage, so they avoid it altogether. In 1980, just 6 percent of men in their forties or older had never been married, but that number has almost tripled to 17 percent today.[9]

If an unmarried man or woman is searching for a virgin to marry, that task is getting more challenging all the time. Among the never-been-married, non-cohabiting adults in America today, only one out of every four (24 percent) has abstained from sexual intercourse. Among the 76 percent of never-married, non-cohabiting adults who have had sex, men have averaged four sexual partners; women have averaged three.[10]

Traditional marriage—the legal union between one man and one woman, who become husband and wife—will continue to face opposition in the coming decade. The most obvious form of opposition is from supporters of same-sex marriage. At the time of this writing, five of the country's fifty states—Massachusetts, New Hampshire, Vermont, Connecticut, and Iowa—legally permit same-sex marriages, and three others—New York, Rhode Island, and Maryland—legally recognize unions performed in those states.

> *Proponents of same-sex marriage have been most effective working through the political system rather than in the public square.*

Proponents of same-sex marriage have been most effective working through the political system rather than in the public square. All five states that permit "gay marriage" have paved the way through legislative or court action, whereas proposed changes to state constitutional laws by referendum have been defeated by voters in all thirty-one states in which such efforts have been made. Currently, thirty-six states have passed legislation defining marriage as the legal relationship between two adults of the opposite gender. Changing those laws will be difficult in many states, given the public's general discomfort with homosexuality and the notion of gay marriage. With an increasing number of gay marriages now becoming gay divorces, public advocacy for gay marriage is not likely to shift until later in the decade, when younger adults (who generally support same-sex marriage) represent a larger share of the voting public.[11]

The nation's attitudes toward gay marriage have continued to soften over time, faster than many social analysts expected. In 2003, 54 percent of survey respondents considered two homosexual men living together with a child to be a family; by 2010, the figure had escalated to 68 percent.[12] Part of this accelerated rate of acceptance toward gay families is due to extensive media coverage of celebrities and public figures discussing their homosexual lifestyle or their support for such, which has served to both educate the public about nontraditional families and to wear down the resistance of people whose opposition was not deeply held. If conservative groups continue to express reasonable opposition, however, there is a real possibility that public acceptance of gay families may waver over the next decade, just as people's position on other volatile moral issues (such as abortion) have seesawed over the years.

Another quietly emerging alternative family form is the triad, or "polyamory," in which three adults are married and become spouses to each other. While such unions are relatively rare—at least in the public's view—they are also likely to expand in the future. The main support for such relationships comes from the notion that if marriage is to be defined by the participants—the underpinning of same-sex marriages—then if all three (or more) parties have genuine feelings for each other and are willing to make a public commitment to their joint relationship, then polyamory is no less valid a form of marriage than traditional or same-sex unions.[13]

What's Happening with Divorce

Divorce has become a natural part of the American lifestyle. Every year, more than one million divorces are finalized in the United States—a rate of one divorce for every two new marriages. In 1960, the ratio was vastly different: one divorce for every four new marriages, a ratio that dropped to 1:3 by 1970, and reached the 1:2 level in the mid-seventies.

The good news about divorce is that the divorce rate has dropped in recent years, from a high of 5.3 per thousand people in 1981 to 3.6 in 2007. That's the lowest rate since 1970. The bad news relates to the reasons why the rate has dropped. More and more people are substituting cohabitation or homosexual relationships for marriage, producing fewer marriages (and consequently fewer opportunities for divorce). For instance, in 1970 there were 10.6 marriages per thousand people; today that number has plummeted to 7.3, a decline of 31 percent.[14]

The United States continues to lead the world in number of broken marriages. After the initial five years of marriage, nearly one in four Americans (23 percent) have split through separation or divorce. That is double the rate in Canada, Finland, Austria, Germany, and Sweden; triple the rate in England and France; and about five times the rate in Italy, Belgium, and Spain. Part of the reason for this difference is the brief waiting period for a divorce to be finalized in the United States. Other nations require a cool-down period of three to five years, during which many marriages are reconciled. But in the United States, thirty-three states have no waiting period at all, despite that, in about four out of five cases, one of the spouses does not want to get divorced.[15]

Among Americans who have been married, one-third have also been divorced.

Our studies show that among Americans who have been married, one-third (33 percent) have also been divorced. The stigma that used to go along with divorce has largely dissolved in our society. With no-fault divorce laws and people's awareness of the hard work that must go into making a marriage work in a chaotic, distracted, selfish, fast-paced society, many people almost expect marriages (though not necessarily their own) to wind up in divorce court. Our research has also discovered that, particularly among the younger generations of adults, doubts about the durability of marriage sometimes become a self-fulfilling prophecy: Afraid to fail, they never fully devote themselves to do what it takes to build and maintain a strong marriage, putting that union at risk right from the start.

Our most recent exploration of marriage and divorce revealed that religious faith may not have much to do with the solidarity of a couple's marriage. In 2008, evaluating only adults who had ever been married, 32 percent of born-again Christians had been divorced, compared to 33 percent of people who were not born again. In roughly one out of ten cases, the born-again individuals had divorced prior to becoming Christians, altering the statistics slightly in terms of how faith in Jesus Christ had affected their marriage vows. The study also showed that Protestants were more likely than Catholics to ever get a divorce (34 percent vs. 28 percent). Evangelical Christians were the least likely faith group to get divorced (26 percent), while people aligned with non-Christian faiths were the most likely (38 percent). Atheists and agnostics were in the middle (30 percent). In terms of racial and ethnic background, Asians were the least likely to dissolve a marriage (20 percent) and blacks were the most likely (36 percent). Ideologically, conservatives were less likely to get divorced (28 percent) than were those who were mostly moderate in their political views (33 percent) or mostly liberal (37 percent).[16]

Nobody enters a marriage expecting to get divorced. Instead, couples are overtaken by extreme pressures and tensions that build until the marriage is perceived as no longer sustainable. Those difficulties most often include financial hardships, sexual differences, parenting pressures, and health challenges. Recognizing these realities, the nation has done a dramatic about-face in its attitudes: 69 percent now contend that divorce is morally acceptable, an increase in the past decade of ten points and an increase over the past quarter century of more than twenty points. Once again, Americans have become comfortable maintaining a belief in opposites: the importance of marriage and the acceptability of divorce.[17]

Americans have become comfortable maintaining a belief in opposites: the importance of marriage and the acceptability of divorce.

The median duration of marriages in the United States is eighteen years (and declining). Medical researchers have learned that the physical stress of a broken marriage continues long after a divorce. People in their fifties and sixties who have endured a divorce are 20 percent more likely than those who have not been divorced to experience chronic health problems. Many others also struggle with emotional or mental problems. Contrary to popular belief, however, the existing pattern shows that people sixty-five or older are three times as likely to experience involuntary singlehood through the death of a spouse (30 percent) than through divorce (9 percent). But, of course, as time goes on, that pattern will change significantly as Busters and Mosaics feel the effects of their broken marriages. It was not until the 1980s that America had more divorced than widowed adults, but since that turning point, the gap has continued to grow between those two conditions.[18]

One of the reasons for both the decline in the number of marriages and the continued frequency of divorce is the nation's recent and growing infatuation with cohabitation. In 1960, fewer than a half million couples were cohabiting, but today the number exceeds 6.4 million—about a fifteenfold increase in the past fifty years. Amazingly, in any given year, America has three to four times more couples living together than getting married during the year (between 6 million and 8 million cohabiting couples versus 2.2 million newlyweds).[19]

There is a wide variety of perspectives on the impact of cohabiting. Research conducted years ago showed that cohabitants who marry have a greater chance of divorcing than do non-cohabiting couples—a 61 percent greater likelihood. But many people either never knew about or never bought into that argument. A recent Gallup study on cohabitation showed that the younger a person is, the more likely he or she is to believe that living together before marrying is an insurance policy against divorce. That same study showed that cohabitants are not likely to get conflicting perspectives from other adults: half the public (49 percent) believe that cohabitants are less likely to divorce than are non-cohabitants, and 20 percent say it makes no difference or they have no idea.[20]

The latest studies show that living together no longer automatically dooms a relationship.

The latest research on cohabitation shows that things have changed dramatically in the past three decades—not surprising in a society where our core values, common behaviors, and attitudes about relationships have also changed significantly. The latest studies, using massive samples of both cohabiting and non-cohabiting couples, show that living together no longer automatically dooms a relationship. Though it remains true that most cohabiting couples break up within three years of moving in together, those who remain together are no worse off than those who never lived together—as long as the couple either gets engaged or has solid plans to get married prior to moving in together. Those couples who share a household but do not have such plans are significantly more likely to get divorced than are non-cohabiting couples. With the numerous changes in society's views of relationships, marriage, family, and sexuality, a couple's intentions prior to moving in make a big difference in the fate of their union.[21]

But the research also points out that most cohabiting couples move in with each other as a way of spending more time together rather than as a precursor to a committed, long-term relationship. In fact, only about one-third of all cohabiting couples planned their move-in and had serious discussions about their intentions and about long-term plans and the potential impact of their decision. Further, it seems that neither religious beliefs nor traditional moral considerations play much part in the decision to live together. Less than half of all cohabitants say that their religious beliefs indicate that living together outside of marriage is wrong. The typical moral convictions of most of today's young adults suggest that sexual activity while unmarried is acceptable as long as the two people love each other. Similarly, living together is often thought of as a more moral choice than refusing to cohabit because cohabiting either propels the couple toward and prepares them for a strong marriage or protects them from a doomed one. The new behavioral map seems to start with dating, followed by cohabitation, bearing a child, and perhaps marriage.[22]

One of the most serious consequences of cohabitation is that 41 percent of cohabiting couples have at least one child together, reflecting a tenfold jump in the number of cohabitants giving birth to a child outside of marriage (from 196,000 in 1970 to 1.95 million in 2005). Generally speaking, life does not go well for those children. Studies have shown that they are three times more likely to be expelled from school, three times more likely to have a child of their own outside of wedlock, and six times more likely to commit suicide.

They are not likely to get much community support, because fewer than two out of five adults believe that cohabitation has a negative effect on the lives of the children those relationships produce.[23]

Much has been written about single-parent families. There are more than fifteen million such households in our nation, and though cohabitation contributes a growing share of those households, most are the result of divorce. In six of seven single-parent homes broken by divorce, the family is maintained primarily by the mother. That ratio varies across racial and ethnic groups, however: Mothers are the primary caregiver by a 3:1 ratio in non-Hispanic white households; 4:1 in Asian families; 8:1 in Hispanic families; and 10:1 in black single-parent households. Sustaining a viable lifestyle for the children involved is a continual strain for single mothers; their median annual income drops by more than 50 percent after their divorce, from an intact-family average of more than $70,000 to barely $30,000.[24]

Analysts suggest that divorce is a very costly event for society, draining an estimated $122 billion annually from the economy through the cost of antipoverty

Divorce is a very costly event for society, draining an estimated $122 billion annually from the economy.

programs, criminal justice expenses, additional educational costs, and lost tax revenue—not including the value of human and social capital lost as a result of family fragmentation. Others point out that the absence of one parent from the home—especially the father—has debilitating effects on children. Department of Justice data indicate that more than 60 percent of the people in prison grew up in a home without their father, and nearly 70 percent of the juveniles in state-operated institutions were from homes where the father was absent.[25]

Adults who divorce do not want to mess up the lives of others, and there are situations in which divorce may be the only safe and sane solution to a violent or otherwise toxic home environment. But the hardships that result from most divorces are undeniable and significant, especially for the children involved—although some couples are most desirous of sparing their children the pain of ugly legal battles or the sorrow of knowing that their parents will no longer be together. It is not unusual for such couples to occasionally attend events together, depending on the nature of their relationship. As one man explained, "I appreciate and care for my wife; I just can't stand living with her." Among well-known individuals who have had such relationships are investment guru Warren Buffett, artist Willem de Kooning, and publisher Jann Wenner. In light of recent economic woes, it would not be unexpected to witness growth in the number of marriages that dissolve into endless separation.[26]

What's Happening with Parenting

All the research I've conducted or seen regarding parenting agrees that Americans recognize how difficult it is to raise children these days and that parenting has become tougher over the last quarter century. About three-quarters of adults, whether they have young children in their homes or not, concur that parenting is a challenge, to say the least.

It isn't just the culture in which children are being raised that has shifted so dramatically in the past couple of decades; so have the characteristics of parents themselves. As usual, it's a rather complex mixture of behaviors and attitudes that intermingle to form new patterns.

We can start with the most obvious factors regarding parenting, such as the fact that Americans are still having a lot of children—something that cannot be said for the populations in many of the other developed nations of the world. Every year since 2000,

Americans have produced more than four million live births—a threshold that equals the birthrate from 1954 to 1964 (and exceeds the birthrate from 1946 to 1953) during what came to be known as the Baby Boom. When the number of live births dropped below four million per year, from 1965 to 1988, the name coined for that generation was the Baby Bust. Since the beginning of the new millennium, however, the numbers have returned to more robust levels (including 4.2 million births in 2009). And keep in mind that these numbers refer to live births; they do not include the 1.2 million abortions that have been performed annually in recent years.[27]

The huge number of new lives entering the United States masks some subtle changes related to our newest citizens and their situations. For instance, the number of births to unwed mothers has skyrocketed. In 2008, a new record was set: Slightly less than 41 percent of all births were to single women. In 1963, the year before President Johnson initiated the "war on poverty," just 7 percent of births happened apart from marriage.[28]

Pregnancies among unmarried teens now represent only about 8 percent of all births out of wedlock.

Similarly, we have undergone changes in the number of unwed teens who get pregnant. That was one of the circumstances that ignited the abortion battles and led to the Supreme Court's *Roe v. Wade* decision in 1973. Pregnancies among unmarried teens have leveled off in recent years and now represent only about 8 percent of all births out of wedlock. Notably, a *majority* of all births to women in their twenties were to unmarried women. And shockingly, three out of four births among African Americans occurred to single women.[29]

The demographic profile of mothers has changed as well. These days, mothers are older, better educated, wealthier, and more likely to be working. Not only has the average age of a woman's first childbearing experience risen, but the number of births to women thirty-five and older has jumped by 64 percent in the past twenty years. A majority of all first-time mothers this year will have some level of college education—an idea that seemed an unrealistic fantasy a quarter century ago. Thanks in part to that education and to advances in the workplace, women now earn higher salaries and hold more responsible positions, giving them greater freedom (including the freedom to place their children in day care). In fact, a growing proportion of adults believe it doesn't matter if a child's mother is employed outside the home and are decreasingly convinced that a child is better off with a stay-at-home mom than with an employed-outside-the-home mother. In fact, only one out of four married-couple families had a stay-at-home mother in 2007.[30]

Parenting is one of the most stressful experiences for today's families. Researchers have discovered that the presence of children in the home reduces parents' happiness and emotional health—levels that rise once the children have moved away. It's not that parents dislike their children or wish they hadn't given birth to them. It's just a long, hard (and expensive) road to bring children to maturity and their life launch. At the same time, parents report a higher sense of meaning and purpose in their lives than do adults without children. Almost nine out of ten mothers say they feel appreciated. (Fathers somewhat less so.) And even though 87 percent said they wanted to have children simply for the joy of having them, almost half also admitted that when they began bearing children, it was something that "just happened." As one delves more deeply into the experiences and feelings regarding family, the results become even murkier. In short, parenting throws most people into turmoil for a prolonged period, with the pace and pressure of parenting taking the edge off their joy.[31]

One clear outcome of the challenges of parenting is that family size has not changed—neither getting larger during the economic good times nor shrinking during the times of financial struggle. The national fertility rate has remained at 2.1 for more than two decades now. As our population grows during the decades leading up to 2050, the Census Bureau expects that growth to be largely attributable to births among the immigrants who arrived in 2005 and later and to their descendants.

More than one-third of our population born between now and 2050 will be immigrant-related, especially among Hispanic newcomers. Alternative means of growing our families, such

Parents report a higher sense of meaning and purpose in their lives than do adults without children.

as adoption and the use of reproductive technologies (e.g., in vitro fertilization), play only a minor role in our expansion. (There are fewer than one hundred thousand international adoptions each year and only about fifty-five thousand children born via reproductive technologies.)[32]

Raising children is difficult—by one estimate, it costs a middle-class, two-parent family about $286,000 to raise a child from birth to age seventeen—but it is not all hardship and despair.[33] A survey by Pew Research reported that the harsh battles between Boomers and their parents are quite different from the battles that take place today between Boomers and Busters and their children. Only one-quarter of today's parents contend that the fights they have with their children are serious; for the most part, parents these days say that the conflicts are well managed and peacefully resolved. There are substantial gaps between parents and children: 73 percent identified a technology gap (in both use and understanding of the personal value of current tech tools); 69 percent cited a music appreciation gap; 53 percent indicated that they have disparate views of respect; 80 percent listed a chasm in moral perspectives; and 80 percent also noted a big difference in work ethic and related views. But the elements that seem to smooth out such differences are the commitment of parents to establish meaningful dialogue, a genuine desire to understand their children's views, and a commitment to maintain a viable relationship.[34]

Undoubtedly, these calmer and more interactive relationships between parents and their children are related to the recalibration of the roles embraced by mothers and fathers and husbands and wives. Many married women have released some of their control over family decision making to their husbands, who have shown an increased willingness to pitch in and take more family responsibility. These days, it is actually considered cool to be an active dad, one who is involved in and gains satisfaction from participation in family life. Transitions in the marketplace such as the rise of entrepreneurship, advances in technology that allow for telecommuting, and the heightened sensitivity and flexibility of companies regarding their employees' family needs have allowed this to occur.

Mothers still make most of the family-related decisions, but fathers have assumed a growing role in that process. The result seems to be more families in which the mother/father dynamics are being worked out without as much nagging and tension. The significance of that cooperative partnership is underscored by the fact that seven out of ten Americans (71 percent) believe that being a father is one of the most significant roles a man can fill these days, and 64 percent concur that motherhood is one of the most important roles a woman can fill in today's world. A huge majority of Americans (80 percent)—a group comprising both respondents who grew up in dual-parent homes and respondents who grew up in single-parent households—affirm that it is very important for children to be reared in a two-parent home. Almost as many (72 percent) also contend that growing up in a two-parent home

> *Mothers still make most of the family-related decisions, but fathers have assumed a growing role in that process.*

gives a child an advantage over peers who grow up in single-parent households. Expect to see further advances in the sharing of family and household roles in the years to come as parents attempt to do their best to raise emotionally and spiritually healthy children.[35]

What's Happening with Family Life

Not surprisingly, the dynamics *within* the family have changed a lot over the last decade as well. The biggest changes relate to the onslaught of media use (discussed more thoroughly in chapter 4) and the decrease in at-risk behaviors by adolescents and teens.

Family members spend less time with each other than in the past, even though they are slightly more likely to be in close physical proximity than before. The reasons have to do with technology. Parents can now accomplish much of their work and connecting from home using cell phones and computers. Emulating that example, kids these days spend enormous amounts of time glued to their screens as well—a tendency facilitated by the omnipresence of those screens (television sets in every bedroom, cell phones for every family member, computer connectivity in all rooms via various devices). One result is that even when parents and their children are in the house together, they spend less time in eye-to-eye interaction. In fact, some analysts argue that the social needs that used to be met through family engagement have to some extent been replaced by the network of relationships that both parents and children now nurture every day online, in social-networking environments.

While developmental specialists warn parents not to overschedule their youngsters, there is trouble at the other end of that continuum as well, if young people do not have enough commitments to occupy their time. It has been shown that children who are the least busy are more likely to suffer from depression, anxiety, unhappiness, low self-esteem, and lagging academic performance and are more likely to engage in at-risk behaviors. Children whose parents help them stay immersed in one or two major activities each week, consuming up to ten hours per week with such endeavors, tend to

Children who are the least busy are more likely to engage in at-risk behaviors.

be the most well adjusted and happy. That level of engagement is especially important as children reach the teen years, when peer pressure and the lure of questionable behaviors beckons most strongly. For instance, a national study among teenagers found that participation in each of three at-risk behaviors (smoking, alcohol use, and drug use) triples from eighth grade to twelfth grade.[36]

When family members are not glued to their electronic devices, how do they spend their free time? A lot of it comes down to what's considered cool at the moment. The "cool quotient" changes frequently, but at last check-in the things that made the cut were listening to music, watching movies, playing video games, being smart (i.e., doing well in school), owning peer-approved electronics, playing sports (for boys), and being fashionable (among girls). Those attitudes explain the most common playtime experiences. Girls are especially fond of reading (52 percent do so regularly in their leisure hours), shopping (42 percent), listening to music, and hanging out with friends. Boys tend to choose adventurous or athletic activities, as well as reading. Most kids, though, list entertainment derived from video games, television, movies, and online experiences as their preferred way to pass time. But most adolescents and teens (85 percent) also say that family is an important part of their lives, and a huge majority (70 percent) claim that Mom and Dad are among their best friends. While that news might come as a shock to millions of haggard parents, this trend has held steady among children for many decades.[37]

And don't imagine that you're the only one counting the hours until the weekend starts. There is actually research showing that weekends are our happiest times. During those days off, we feel the greatest sense of personal autonomy, competence, and connection with people we like, all of which contribute to our sense of well-being. The things that cause us the most stress—academic or occupational performance, financial struggles, and feelings of emotional estrangement— are least likely to creep up during extended downtime. TGIF indeed![38]

Most adolescents and teens say that family is an important part of their lives.

It would be unfair to finish a chapter on trends related to families without mentioning the effects of influx and outflow. For instance, one widely reported pattern of the past decade, which accelerated during the recent economic misfortunes, is the return home of adult children. Even if your adult children have not moved home after a period of absence (for college, career, or marriage), chances are pretty good that you know someone who has experienced this trend firsthand. Influx is especially common among twentysomethings. The twenties are a time of tremendous turbulence, as seen in the fact that one-third of the people in this group change their residence every year and 40 percent move back to their parents' house at least once. People in their twenties now average seven jobs during that decade; two-thirds cohabit during those years; and about six out of ten will marry before age thirty. Not only is it a decade of stress and anxiety for these young adults, but it becomes a time of unpredictable highs and lows for their parents, as well, as they navigate the changes with their grown children.[39]

The other end of the spectrum relates to the trend of aging parents relying on their grown children, or on social services, to take care of their daily needs. The numbers are massive. Nearly twenty million Baby Boomers now live with their elderly parents, and another thirteen million adults are providing significant health care for their aging parents. Among seniors, nearly eight million receive some type of professional in-home health services, and three million more live in nursing homes or other types of senior housing communities. For the adult children taking care of their parents, the task is taxing. A majority feel appreciated by their parents, but most also admit that the challenge affects their emotional well-being. More than one-third of the adult children providing care admit to feeling frustrated, overwhelmed by the responsibility, and worried about their inability to keep up with the demands. One-third also struggle with the associated costs—not surprising when a year of assisted-living care runs about $40,000 and the average cost of a private room in a nursing home is double that. And here's the kicker: The number of adults sixty and older will double between now and 2030.[40]

One widely reported pattern of the past decade is the return home of adult children.

Reflections

Our nation is in the midst of a seismic reconceptualization of marriage and family. Think about some of the changes in behavior and attitudes we've explored in this chapter. In essence, we're introducing a new era of family life. For better or worse, some of the core components of this new family reality include the following:

- Family is no longer about a husband and wife's emotional and sexual intimacy, solidified by producing children, as much as it's about experimentation, shared experiences, pleasure, and personal fulfillment.
- For women, child rearing is not as directly related to marriage as it is to physical conditions (such as age and optimal fertility), emotional passions, and lifestyle fit.
- Marriage is less about delivering on a commitment to

permanence and reconciliation than about satisfying the felt
needs of the moment.

- Divorce is not desirable, but our society has grown accus-
  tomed to it and comfortable with it, and we understand that
  it is a distinct possibility—and one that we know we can
  survive.
- Marriage no longer signifies the commencement of adult
  life; it is now a middle step in that journey, after one has
  completed his or her education, experimented with multiple
  lovers, relocated to a desirable place, become established in a
  career, and perhaps even had a child or two.
- Critical life decisions—related to health, education, lifestyle,
  faith, childbearing, and career path—are less often made in
  tandem with one's life partner than on one's own, or with the
  assistance of friends and relatives, putting in place realities
  that one's partner will just have to accept.

This new profile of the American family may be the most tangible
evidence available that the culture wars are over. Religious leaders
lament the decline of traditional morals as seen in abortion, cohabitation, divorce, the content of the media we worship, and the lifestyles of the celebrities we idolize. But as time goes on, the changes
in what we truly believe are undeniable. Those values and beliefs
are adopted by our families (whether explicitly or tacitly), absorbed
by our children, and merged into the mainstream of the marketplace. More changes are coming as we adapt to the latest shifts in
family values and behaviors. There is not much chance that the
family perspectives and experiences that defined America in the
twentieth century will make a comeback in the twenty-first.

However, that does not mean we are stuck in a hopeless mess.
Years of research persuasively reveal that the future is largely determined by the outcome of our parenting—that is, who we raise

our children to become. In fact, most of a child's life foundations are firmly in place by the age of thirteen. The data show that the behavioral habits, core values, primary spiritual beliefs, relational strategies, and entertainment preferences that emerge so clearly when we reach adulthood are developed and solidified by the time we reach the age of thirteen as well.

The new profile of the American family may be the most tangible evidence available that the culture wars are over.

In other words, if you want society to change, change the people who will determine the nature of that society: today's children. Yes, it is important for us to continue to interact with adults about the current state of the family and our culture, but the greatest legacy you will leave behind is in the lives of your children and the choices made by the variety of children whose lives you are able to significantly influence.[41]

Focusing on young people is one of the biggest opportunities that Christian churches fail to exploit to its fullest potential—or anywhere close. It is perhaps the one area in which churches and parents could most comfortably work together to produce life-changing outcomes, yet such partnerships are uncommon.[42] Pastors are often frustrated because they see little or no change in the lives of the adults to whom they devote their lives. The reason is that the etchings imprinted on the minds and hearts of the adults they teach and counsel were inscribed so deeply during their formative years that it is incredibly difficult to alter their intellectual and emotional paths. The reality is that human beings change their fundamental perspectives on life very little after they transition from adolescence.[43] The ways in which we express those perspectives may change, but the views and values themselves typically remain stable. The upshot should be obvious: Invest heavily in shaping the minds and hearts of your children and their friends.

Too few parents and families recognize the incredible opportunity they have to change the world by how they raise their children and influence their children's friends. A society is never without hope of positive change as long as families are intentional and diligent in shaping the moral and spiritual character of their offspring.

A society is never without hope as long as families are shaping the moral and spiritual character of their offspring.

Family remains one of the dominant influences in people's lives. There may be nothing you can do as an individual to steer the national conversation about family in a different direction. But you can certainly influence a handful of young lives in your midst and make a lasting mark on the world through that investment. If you are married, a healthy relationship with your spouse can serve as an effective model for friends and young people. If each of us would faithfully and confidently recognize and pursue available opportunities for strengthening the family— and, through it, our entire society—God may allow us to live long enough to see the fruit of our most important labor.

CHAPTER 3

ATTITUDES AND VALUES

The Mind Stuff That Defines Us

EVERYONE HAS TO make choices in life, and we base our choices on our values and attitudes. Actions follow convictions; we do what we believe, and when we don't know what to believe, we typically reserve the right to decide and act once matters become clear. The foundational beliefs that trigger our choices are based on the perspectives we develop after considering a flood of facts, assumptions, experiences, observations, hopes, popular ideas, new concepts, conversations, personal opinions, and expectations. That we make important decisions in a split second is a testimony to the existence of core values: They serve as a shortcut to making sense of reality and directing our responses according to what we believe to be right.

Our brains are constantly absorbing new information in order to recalibrate the trajectory of our lives in accordance with ideals and viewpoints that provide us intellectual, spiritual, and emotional resonance and peace. Each new fact or experience either fortifies our existing perspectives or challenges and perhaps realigns them. The combination of all the attitudes and values we possess is the substance of our worldview, which enables us to live in a manner that makes us comfortable with ourselves.

Our brains are constantly absorbing new information in order to recalibrate the trajectory of our lives.

Perhaps you've been in situations where you felt paralyzed. Faced with a perplexing situation or body of information, you did not know how to respond in a manner that felt right to you, so you froze up, waiting for clarity. In those situations, you have what psychologists call *cognitive dissonance*—an internal conflict caused by the clash of inconsistent perspectives that prevents you from having sufficient peace of mind to respond in a manner that accurately reflects you. Until the tension between the competing factors is resolved and harmony is restored in your mind, you will feel anxious and incapable of acting appropriately. The values and attitudes that you unconsciously rely on to guide you through the day work together as an invisible glue that both defines and supports you.

Societies are constantly in flux concerning the dominant values, attitudes, and opinions that determine the character of the culture. Some of the stress that people feel each day is the result of changing perspectives within their culture, especially if those new norms and mores are moving in an uncomfortable direction. The culture wars of the past quarter century are a tangible expression of the clash of values in our midst.

What's Happening with Our Cultural Values

One of the major dividing lines in American society in recent years has been the escalating tension between the older generations (Builders and Boomers) and the younger segments (Busters and Mosaics). Though it is natural for each successive generation reaching adulthood to shift the culture in ways that reflect its own collection of values and attitudes—creating its own generational brand, if you will—the realignment is always jarring. Boomers, of course, are famous for the radical redefinition of cultural values and attitudes that occurred in the 1960s and '70s. The Busters in turn rejected some of the central Boomer values in order to establish their own presence, as well as to reflect their distaste for the prior generation's standards. The Mosaics have since followed suit by ignoring some of the primary Buster values and attitudes to create their own unique personality and fight for their share of cultural attention and acceptance.

What are the emerging values and attitudes that now define American culture? Here is a peek at how we've changed—and continue to change.

From Excellence to Adequacy

In 1980, extensive research among successful companies produced the best-selling book *In Search of Excellence*. If a similar study were conducted today, the revised title might be *Satisfied with Adequacy*.

In the rush to express our feelings and ideas, we have moved toward becoming a nation in which expertise is less esteemed than passion and participation. Expertise, of course, comes from a commitment to doing the hard work in the trenches, learning the vagaries of the subject in question, and figuring out how to bring viable and lasting solutions to the table. Increasingly, however, Americans (especially young adults) are less interested in collecting and examining empirical evidence or in heeding wisdom born from years of hard work and learning. Instead, we increasingly favor a freewheeling dialogue that allows all people to voice their ideas and to feel good about their contributions, regardless of the quality of that input. In this approach, lots of stories are shared. Some are directly relevant; others not so much. The prevailing belief is that if a person invested some effort, the result is good enough.

This shift in standards has occurred in part because Busters and Mosaics are often more interested in the *process* than the product. One possible advantage of this strategy is that more people can feel a sense of ownership of the outcome and the work it takes to produce it. The downside is that the rush to *finish* prioritizes conversation and inclusion over arriving at the best possible solution. In other words, this new mentality is reshaping our values; now, instead of demanding the highest possible quality of output, we willingly accept lesser quality as long as we have facilitated a greater quantity of input. As with many other modifications of our values, this represents a trade-off—one that makes Boomers bristle with frustration and Busters bubble with excitement.

> *We have moved toward becoming a nation in which expertise is less esteemed than passion and participation.*

What has fostered this letdown in quality? There is no single culprit, but add up a variety of conditions and the picture begins to emerge. Start with what has happened to children in our schools: grade inflation (allowing mediocre work to pass), lengthy vacations (children in other developing nations attend school more hours per day and more days per year), teachers focused on training students to score well on tests rather than teaching life lessons, and colleges keeping their best faculty from teaching undergraduate students (often having graduate students teach classes instead). One-third of college students believe that if they simply show up to class, they deserve at least a B.[1]

It continues with how adults think about and carry out their employment responsibilities. Gone are the days when an employee will stick with a job or a company for years (and develop expertise); now it seems as if workers are on a never-ending search for newer, more exciting opportunities. Employers contribute to this mind-set with an emphasis on bigger, faster, cheaper at the expense of better.[2] It's now rare to find anyone who will stay with a company or organization from college graduation through retirement, a commitment that was once common (and remains so in some other developed nations). There is also now a groundswell of support for a four-day workweek, driven by the desire to have an extra day off.

Additional insight comes from several studies into the value of happiness. Our surveys show that almost everyone wants to be happy, but our perception of our own happiness has been on the decline for years. One reason for this is the high correlation between happiness and the sense of meaning people derive from their work activities. With increasing numbers of people viewing work as a necessary evil—something to be endured— rather than as an opportunity to experience achievement and fulfillment, fewer people even look to their employment to provide them with meaning and joy. They would rather put in their time, collect their paycheck, and get on with the fun stuff of life outside of work. Another reason for the demise of happiness is the rise of choices: When people have a bottomless pit of options from which to choose, they tend to be less satisfied than when they have a restricted menu of options.[3]

> *It's now rare to find anyone who will stay with a company or organization from college graduation through retirement.*

Another attitude that hinders quality output is the notion that success is the result of luck. A study by the National Bureau of Economic Research tracked the attitudes of people who entered adulthood during times of economic distress since 1972. Those individuals are more likely than others to believe that success is random and that hard work is not tied to financial success. The analysts reported that people who adopt luck as the key to success are less likely to work hard, produce less, and fare worse financially.[4]

From Optimism to Pessimism

Americans have a long tradition of believing that the best is yet to come, seeing the future as the messenger of even greater achievements and satisfaction. But that unbridled hope has come to a crashing halt. The recession delivered a much-needed reality check for many Americans, causing us to scale back on out-of-control spending and unrealistic expectations. But long before the economic meltdown, the public had begun to fear that our best days are now behind us. Half of all adults (52 percent) say the nation's best days are history; only one-third (35 percent) argue that the best is yet to come. In like manner, an overwhelming majority (62 percent) say that the country is headed in the wrong direction; less than one-third (31 percent) say things are moving in the right direction. The ultimate statement of such pessimism is that only one out of five adults (21 percent) says that America's children will experience a brighter future than their parents had; 60 percent are convinced otherwise.[5]

An overwhelming majority say that the country is headed in the wrong direction.

Who can blame them? The media, the most powerful coalition of influencers in our society, constantly use every trick in the book to grab our attention and explain why things are bad and getting worse: scandals, misappropriations, crises, mismanagement, dishonesty—you name it. The relentless pounding of negative messages has motivated many people to wonder why it seems the only news is bad news. Of course, some of our daily experience *is* bad news: massive unemployment, terrorist attacks, natural disasters, economic failures, political gridlock, the rising cost of living, and so forth. In our media-saturated society, each new challenge receives 24-7 coverage, eroding people's confidence that the future will bring a better life.

People's confidence in critical institutions and leaders is on the wane as well. Gallup has been tracking the attitudes of Americans toward the nation's major institutions for years. They report that only five of the sixteen institutions they track generate "a great deal" or "quite a lot" of confidence with the public these days. Similarly, the Harris Poll has tracked public perception of the leaders of major institutions for the past forty-five years. Their most recent surveys regarding sixteen major institutions found that faith in our key leaders continues to decline for all leadership groups except one—the military. In fact, the military was the only leadership group out of sixteen in the survey that garnered "a great deal of confidence" among more than half of the public. The leaders of the other fifteen, including educational institutions, organized religion, medicine, the White House, Congress, and the press—failed to inspire the confidence of a majority of the public.[6]

Most people do not believe it is possible to work one's way out of poverty.

People's confidence in their own efforts has become anemic as well. Most people do not believe it is possible to work one's way out of poverty—a significant dip from years past, when the can-do spirit led people to believe that anything was possible with the right attitude and a lot of hard work. That lack of optimism mirrors the finding that only three out of ten Americans now believe that anyone can work hard and get rich in America.[7]

From Common Good to Individual Advantage

One of the unique qualities that enabled the American experiment in democracy to succeed for so many years is the notion that we all give a little to get a lot—that is, we voluntarily surrender some of our individual rights and resources in order to create an environment in which everyone is treated well and our national interests are cared for, so that individual opportunities will abound. But as often happens in societies that become powerful and wealthy, over the course of time the agreement to protect the common good gets lost in the rush to enjoy the freedoms and benefits that such an agreement has produced. Today, constructs such as *citizenship, the common good,* and even *community interest* are foreign to our way of thinking. Instead, it's all about *me.*

To the amazement of many teenagers and college students, citizenship was once a required class in public schools; today, most students have little concept of what it means to be citizens and no firm ideas about the responsibilities or privileges of citizenship. (I suspect that if American-born high school students were asked to pass the citizenship test required of immigrants who apply for naturalization, a large percentage would fail. Many adults in our society would probably not fare much better.)

The concept of the common good is a casualty of war in a society that has become increasingly narcissistic.

The sum-is-greater-than-its-parts, we-can-do-it-together mentality that undergirded many technological innovations and the determination to rally from our national disunity in the 1960s is largely absent today. A good example of this is the discovery that less than one-quarter of adults (23 percent) believe the nation has lived up to John F. Kennedy's challenge to "ask not what your country can do for you—ask what you can do for your country."[8]

The concept of the common good—sacrificing a personal benefit or opportunity to advance the good of the community—is a casualty of war in a society that has become increasingly narcissistic. Psychiatrists have taken note of this bent, reporting that about one out of ten twentysomethings show evidence of narcissistic personality disorder—several times the rate found among other generations. College students have traditionally been a universe unto themselves, disregarding and breaking rules simply because the parameters existed. But the demanding nature of many young Americans today strikes fear into the hearts of academic officials as they observe uncontrolled behavior and unwarranted expectations becoming normative (e.g., unreasonable demands, disregard for the needs of others, disrespect toward those who disagree with them). In one survey among college students, two-thirds proclaimed that their generation has outperformed any other—in terms of narcissism, overconfidence, attention-seeking behavior, and self-promotion.[9]

An obvious outgrowth of the egotism of our society is that we want to shirk the personal responsibilities of citizenship without giving up what we believe to be our rights. Societal rights are privileges we receive as a result of hard work and personal sacrifice; without such trade-offs and compromises, there can be no guarantee of rights.

From Delayed Gratification to Instant Gratification

Patience? That's what they call people in hospitals, right? For growing legions of Americans, that's what comes to mind when they hear the word. (Yes, I'm aware of the difference in spelling.) Lack of patience is endemic in a culture that wants to have all of its needs met *immediately*. Think about the changes we've made to accommodate our desire for instant gratification:

- We've all but eradicated "blue laws" so that businesses can now be open seven days a week.
- We've essentially done away with the notion of "business hours," with many stores now open more than twelve hours a day and a growing share approaching 24-7 operation.

- Speed limits are now taken as a suggestion; adhering to the letter of the law merely eats up valuable time.
- Dial-up Internet connections are on their way out—too slow!—and high-speed connections are growing by leaps and bounds as Americans want more stuff faster. These lightning-fast connections have also facilitated "instant messaging."
- Mobile telephones now give us instant access and accessibility; texting allows us to send and receive messages even when a phone call would be inappropriate.
- Documents that had to get someplace faster than the postal service could deliver them used to be sent by messenger, then fax, then overnight delivery. Now those same documents can be delivered in seconds via e-mail.
- Driving to the video store and shuffling through the aisles takes too long; now we have pay-per-view options that allow us to get virtually any movie we want with a few clicks of the remote and curbside kiosks so that we barely have to get out of the car to get our movies, which we searched and reserved online.
- State lotteries have enhanced the games they offer, with big-money jackpots now available up to five nights a week. And for people who aren't willing to wait a day or two to see if they've won, we have plenty of instant-winner options.
- Fast food—enough said.

The list could go on, and it's actually a fun game to play, but it speaks to a significant shift in our understanding of the value of time and to the need to move through life faster. In many cases, we are willing to pay a premium to get the same resources or experiences more quickly. Time is of the essence.

Look at how this has affected the business world. The average tenure of executives is far shorter than it used to be because shareholders and directors now want short-term results. Business leaders who focus on building long-term health and strength for their companies may not last long enough to enjoy the fruit of their foresight and planning. The irony is that great leaders learn they can maximize their influence only by delaying their own gratification in order to build for the future by incorporating teams of people into the flow of the organization's success. The leaders reap their rewards after others have realized theirs—but often the leader is not kept around long enough to experience those benefits.

I don't have research to back up this next statement, but I imagine we're all guilty of seeking instant gratification even when there is no compelling reason to do so. For some people, it is spending money that could have been saved in order to buy

The average tenure of executives is far shorter than it used to be.

the latest and greatest gizmo; for others, it is taking out loans to purchase something that could have been acquired without debt if we were willing to save up. Some people refuse to work their way up the corporate ladder, choosing instead to hop from job to job. Millions of Americans have abandoned diet and exercise in favor of fat-reduction surgeries. When conflicts arise, we make halfhearted attempts (or maybe none at all) to negotiate our differences before we bring in the lawyers and go to court. Whatever it is, we want our way and we want it now.

From Respect to Incivility

We are losing a national sense of etiquette. Young people routinely watch movies and television shows that glorify rude behavior and profane language. The notion of chivalry is a foreign concept to millions of people; basic behaviors such as politeness, graciousness, and restraint are lost arts. If manners represent an agreed-upon behavioral code that portrays the heart of a society, America is losing its civility.

On the fortieth anniversary of the Woodstock music festival in 2009, a national survey conducted by Rasmussen Research found that fewer than four out of ten adults believed that four hundred thousand people could gather peacefully for such an event today. That is just one indicator that our selfishness has overcome our patience and willingness to sacrifice. If there is any doubt that we have lost our sense of propriety, spend a few hours surfing through the blogosphere and catch the tenor of the interactions. Crude language, name-calling, ridiculing competing ideas, and harsh criticism are de rigueur on numerous pages.

More than two out of every three adults admit that Americans are becoming more rude and less civilized.

This probably comes as no surprise. One recent study revealed that more than two out of every three adults (69 percent) admit that Americans are becoming more rude and less civilized; only one out of seven contend that we are becoming a kinder and gentler nation. Most adults think we are becoming ruder as time goes on, as evidenced by how customers treat salespeople—and vice versa. Part of the issue may be a fading memory or unclear notion of what constitutes rude behavior. For instance, 43 percent consider it rude to talk on a cell phone while sitting next to someone in a public place, yet an equal number say such behavior is not rude.[10]

The very idea of good manners is losing steam. Refined behavior is considered quaint. Giving respect to other people—whether to their ideas, property, family and friends, accomplishments, goals, or themselves as individuals—is increasingly uncommon. Yet, at the same time, we're constantly on alert lest someone disrespect *us*. We seem caught up in the practice of gaining credibility and respect by tearing it away from others. Half of all adults (51 percent) have confronted someone over rude behavior in public, with many more such confrontations likely in the future.[11]

A common sociological pattern is for societies to become more refined as they become wealthier. Desiring increased security and safety, they pass laws and introduce customs that foster heightened civility. We seem to be moving in the opposite direction—perhaps a reflection of the fact that our youngest adults are relatively less well-off, their economic prospects not as rosy, and thus they feel unconstrained. As media gluttons, perhaps their constant exposure to television programs, movies, and music that use profane language and endorse violence and sex has had its influence.[12]

Experts estimate that kids now use eighty to ninety swear words per day.

How bad has it gotten? Experts estimate that kids now use eighty to ninety swear words per day. Not only are they encouraged to do so by imitating their peers and media celebrities, but it creates an edgier image that they covet. A recent survey among a national sample of parents of school-age children found that 70 percent said disrespect in the classroom was a serious problem (including 45 percent who labeled it "very serious"). Reports of rude and disruptive behavior among college students are rampant. A recent study across nine universities— including several Christian schools—noted that 83 percent of professors had experienced disrespectful behavior that disrupted their classes.[13]

From the Christian God to an Amorphous God

Gone are the days when the word *God* referred exclusively to the divine deity described in the Bible. Increasingly, when young Americans talk about "God," they are describing a prototype—an interchangeable "superior being" or concept not tied to a particular religion or profile. This is clearly a generational trend: Six out of ten Mosaics, seven out of ten Busters, and nearly eight out of ten Boomers and Builders possess a traditional, Bible-based idea of God. A growing share of younger adults have adopted the notion that the god of every religion is equally valid and essentially the same.

Part of this perspective is attributable to the belief—again, especially common among younger adults and teens—that all religious faiths are fundamentally the same, although they use different language and stories to communicate their core messages. Young adults increasingly respond with dismay if it is suggested that any one god is the only true deity, any one set of scriptures is the only reliable and accurate representation of spiritual truth, or any one faith is the only way to spiritual fulfillment.

> *Most adults—and a vast majority of teenagers—no longer believe that absolute moral or spiritual truth exists.*

From Truth to Tolerance

Most adults—and a vast majority of teenagers—no longer believe that absolute moral or spiritual truth exists. Relativism is the rule of the day: Your truth is your truth, nobody can dispute it for you, and everyone's truth depends on the circumstances. This is a huge shift from the era in which people believed that unchanging moral and spiritual truths create non-debatable standards of right and wrong. The prevalent view today is that ethical and moral decisions change according to the individuals involved (what's right for me may not be right for you) and the situation (this moral choice is appropriate for this situation, but it might be inappropriate under other conditions).

This shift in morals has a direct bearing on the economic downturn of recent years. Without moral standards and restraint, governments, businesses, and individuals push the boundaries to exercise the maximum level of freedom in order to achieve personal gain. But when we practice unrestrained freedom, our greed and selfishness inevitably affect the well-being of the marketplace and individuals. The only solution to the abuses that occur without such restraint is for government regulation to curtail some degree of our freedom, which in turn makes the markets less efficient. If, instead, people were to make choices based on a biblical worldview, in which truth is founded on God's precepts and principles, fewer external restrictions would be necessary and greater freedom and efficiency would result.

In the absence of an anchored set of standards, we wind up with values that are ever-shifting, somewhat unpredictable, and often self-serving. In practical terms, it means we have growing numbers of people who contend that society is unjust and unfair because standards based on a shifting set of norms will never perfectly coincide with their individual desires and expectations. It also means that people feel free to manipulate the system for their own ends.

Recent research supports these observations. A growing percentage of adults (40 percent) do not believe that America is "fair and decent." Large and increasing numbers of young people are abandoning traditional definitions of integrity to satisfy their momentary needs and desires. For example, teenagers are five times more likely than Boomers to believe that lying and cheating are necessary to succeed (51 percent vs. 10 percent, respectively). Those 51 percent—whom researchers labeled "cynics"—are three times more likely than others to lie to customers or exaggerate expense reimbursement or insurance claims. They're also twice as likely to lie to a spouse or significant other about an important event, keep excessive change received by mistake, cheat on their taxes, and hide or misrepresent information when communicating with a boss.[14]

Things are not much better among teens in general. They are four times more likely than older adults to intentionally deceive their employer (31 percent vs. 8 percent) and three times more likely to keep change that was given to them by mistake

(49 percent vs. 15 percent). Young adults (18–24) are twice as likely as older adults to lie to a spouse or domestic partner (48 percent vs. 22 percent), and they're much more likely to make unauthorized copies of copyrighted music or video content (69 percent vs. 27 percent). Substantial numbers of teens also admit to stealing from a store in the past year (30 percent), lying to a parent about something significant (83 percent), lying to save money (42 percent), cheating on a test (64 percent), and plagiarizing material from the Internet (36 percent).

A growing percentage of adults do not believe that America is "fair and decent."

Is this a sign of trouble? If you don't think so, then consider this: 93 percent of the teens interviewed said they were satisfied with their personal ethics and character. How could they possibly feel so smug about their recital of indiscretions? Three-quarters of these respondents (77 percent) said that "when it comes to doing what's right, I am better than most people I know."[15]

So how do people who make their own truth standards respond to accusations from the old guard that their behavior is inappropriate? A great example is the retort offered by Helene Hegemann, a seventeen-year-old German writer whose first novel, *Axolotl Roadkill*, was hailed as a startling first novel, especially for a teenager. However, after the book made the best-seller lists, a blogger discovered that large blocks of text had been lifted verbatim from novels written by other barely known authors. Confronted by critics, Hegemann apologized for not being more forthcoming about her sources, but she dismissed the criticism by noting that, like many in her generation, she freely integrated portions of other people's work with her own—which she called "mixing"—to produce something she believed to be original and personal. Her crowning argument? "There's no such thing as originality anyway, just authenticity."[16]

How are we to respond to this transition from traditional ideas about ethics and integrity? With tolerance, many would say. That's the new ideal: Let it go, get on with your life, that's just the way it is. Perhaps the soul of this emerging, and newly dominant, worldview is seen best in its ubiquitous catchphrase: *whatever.*

How are we to respond to this transition from traditional ideas about ethics and integrity?

In this environment, however, the cultural intelligentsia fail to make an important distinction between judgment and discernment. They are quick to rail against judgment (which is seen as unwarranted negative criticism), without seeming to understand that discernment (the ability to distinguish between right and wrong or good and evil) is a vital part of what makes us civilized. If the ability to discern is stripped from our grasp, we become defenseless in the face of shallow, unrighteous behavior.

Proponents of the new values contend that where there is no moral standard, there cannot be moral clarity; without moral clarity, one must accept as valid and appropriate whatever moral choices are made. In their minds, it is simply an application of the Golden Rule: Treat others' worldviews with the same respect and acceptance that you want them to give to yours.

From Trust to Skepticism

Perhaps it is not surprising to learn that, in a society in which there is no standard of truth, the ability to trust others is now archaic as well. Americans have adopted an automatic posture of skepticism toward any position or statement that hinges on a truth claim, regardless of its nature.

Earlier it was noted that Gallup and Harris tracking studies have shown a steady decline in our trust of leaders and institutions. But our skepticism has become even more personal. Barely half of all Americans believe that other people can be trusted. One study, by a consumer research firm, concluded that "the intensity of consumer distrust is at the highest level in the past thirty years." (Example: two-thirds believe that businesses intentionally make transactions and agreements more complicated than necessary, simply to hide things from the consumer and protect the business.)

Americans have adopted an automatic posture of skepticism toward any position or statement that hinges on a truth claim.

And even though we are infatuated with media content and spend more time absorbing such information than anything else we do besides sleeping, 85 percent of American voters trust their own judgment more than that of the average reporter when it comes to significant national issues. A majority believe that there is a substantial ideological gap between themselves and reporters, and two-thirds contend that reporters use their platforms to present information that promotes candidates and positions that match the reporters' predispositions.[17] Six out of ten (57 percent) do not trust the media to report news and events fully, accurately, or fairly—and the percentage who lack such trust is growing. Almost half of adults (48 percent) say that the bias contained in the media is liberal, and a whopping two-thirds (63 percent) of adults say there is significant ideological bias of one type or another in the news reporting to which they are exposed.[18] In fact, two-thirds of adults (66 percent) say they are angry at the media for the distorted and inaccurate view of the world presented day after day.[19]

This wariness has had the effect of turning us more inward when it comes to decision making—taking in the ideas of others and the factual information reported in the media, but using a heavy filter on all those sources.

From Heroes to Celebrities

Pop culture has the effect in our nation of cheapening the value of life. With the need to generate an endless volume of content to fill the 24-7 news cycle, we have shifted our attention from the marvelous deeds and firm foundations of true heroes to the vacuous words and absurd lifestyles of celebrities. Worse, we've made these celebrities into role models, further misleading our young people about what is important and valuable in life.

Six out of ten do not trust the media to report news and events fully, accurately, or fairly.

Heroes are ordinary people who rise to the occasion, displaying courage, integrity, and humility in performing acts that leave a positive mark on society. Celebrities are people who perform acts of clever marketing to arrest the public's attention and promote themselves. A society built on its attentiveness to heroes will have heart and hope. A society devoted to celebrities will debase itself through an obsession with fame, frivolity, superficiality, and gossip.

Psychologists and medical experts have identified a disorder they call celebrity worship syndrome, which is affecting more and more people. Staying informed about celebrities can be a harmless diversion for those who are leading full and meaningful lives. The danger arises when people become overly fascinated with the details of celebrities' lives and use it as a cover for the lack of meaning in their own lives. Some experts explain that it is natural for us to pay attention to "alpha males and females"—that it is part of our DNA, an inbred desire to follow the leader. However, when too much attention is paid to those individuals, such dedication can lead to depression, anxiety, and diminished self-esteem among the devoted. The obsession with the lives of strangers hinders this group from making progress in their own lives. It can also introduce some of the celebrities' habits—smoking, drug use, use of specific phrases, physical quirks—into the lives of the fanatics.[20]

Many celebrities are not pleased with the side effects of their fame. (How would you like being followed by paparazzi every day?) But they have come to accept their loss of privacy and the absurd focus on the details of their lives as the price of stardom. Just as important, our society suffers from misplaced attention when it envies fame and the perceived benefits that accompany stardom.

Medical experts have identified a disorder they call celebrity worship syndrome, which is affecting more and more people.

From Knowledge to Experience

Children are sometimes cured of a lust for something by being given an abundance of it. Once they can have all they want of the treasured item, they lose interest in it and turn their attention elsewhere. It seems that this is what has happened to America when it comes to information. Overwhelmed by the tidal wave of facts, figures, sources, and visual stimuli available through the Internet, we have turned our affections away from information and have riveted our hearts to the allure of shared experiences.

Examples of this pattern are diverse. Students attend college but don't finish a degree program, preferring instead to experiment with different entry-level jobs or personal adventures. Rather than study an in-depth review of a movie, people will sample a selection of reviews online in hopes of finding one that suits their desires. Instead of immersing themselves in research from which they can develop an informed opinion and make good choices, people rely on texting and sound-bite conversations to gather a handful of opinions that lead them to their conclusions. When assessing an organization—such as a church—discussions focus on how an experience made the person *feel* rather than what he or she learned and applied from the event. And, of course, we've probably all launched into situations where we followed through on spur-of-the-moment decisions based solely on the emotional appeal of an experience without ample consideration given to their likely consequences or larger implications.

Americans increasingly engage in unexamined behavior—the kind of nonstrategic activity that would have brought Socrates (he of the expression "the unexamined life is not worth living") to tears. Personal growth is most likely when we balance purposeful and intelligent reflection with a related action designed to produce a particular outcome. Instead, Americans increasingly choose to load up on feel-good adventures, prompting some economists to refer to ours as an "experience-based economy."

People rely on texting and sound-bite conversations to gather a handful of opinions that lead them to their conclusions.

One recent management study, for instance, showed that performance can best be improved by combining education and experience. The most productive performance enhancers not only ensured that employees understood the nature of the assigned task, related standards, and the details of how their performance would be measured, but also selected assignments based on how the experience would increase the employees' growth and helped employees see the task as a stepping-stone to greater capacity. Other research has demonstrated that one of the benefits of some video games (e.g., Halo) is their ability to teach people how to interact rather than simply download information. The best outcomes occur when knowledge and experience work together, resulting in understanding and action.[21]

The danger in society today is a newfound zeal for moving straight to experience and bypassing, or becoming impatient with, the need to acquire knowledge. One without the other produces problems. Teaching knowledge and skills alone does not generate excellent performance. Offering wonderful experiences without sufficient insight and understanding hinders growth and diminishes the fullness of the final product. Knowledge facilitates meaningful experience, and experience produces invaluable knowledge. Would you want a surgeon to operate on you who hadn't acquired the requisite knowledge before picking up the scalpel? Likewise, would you want a surgeon with knowledge but no prior experience?

Knowledge facilitates meaningful experience, and experience produces invaluable knowledge.

What's Happening Regarding Morality?

Not surprisingly, our studies indicate that, given the continuing redefinition of our society's dominant values, moral behaviors are shifting too. We discovered that even though four out of five adults say they are very concerned about the moral condition of America—a statistic that has grown by about fifteen percentage points in the past fifteen years—our collective views on morality are in constant flux. A large part of that unsteadiness is that we generally base our moral choices on feelings rather than on intellect or an absolute moral standard. And we continue down that path despite evidence that it is not working.

In a Gallup study of moral conditions in America, 76 percent of adults contended that the nation's moral values are getting worse, and by a ratio of 3:1, adults are more likely to describe the moral values of the United States as "poor" than as "excellent or good" (45 percent vs. 15 percent). Few people see much in the way of positive movement: Less than 5 percent said that people are becoming more honest and responsible, parents are raising more moral children, or young adults are demonstrating good values.

More common responses were that disrespect and a general decline in morality is evident everywhere and that parents are largely responsible by failing to inculcate appropriate values into their children's lives.[22]

Gallup also regularly tracks people's moral convictions. If you haven't been following such matters closely, you may be surprised by some of the prevailing attitudes. For instance, the 2010 study showed the following attitudes:

- 69 percent say divorce is morally acceptable (up from 59 percent in 2001)
- 61 percent describe gambling as morally acceptable
- 59 percent believe that sexual intercourse between an unmarried man and woman is morally acceptable (up from 53 percent in 2001 and 2002)
- 59 percent argue that medical research using stem cells from human embryos is morally acceptable (up from 52 percent in 2002)
- 54 percent claim that having a baby outside of marriage is morally acceptable (up from 45 percent in 2002)
- 52 percent see gay or lesbian relations as morally acceptable (up from 38 percent in 2002).[23]

Our own tracking of these same moral challenges finds that feelings-based morality is just as common among born-again Christians as non-Christians. In addition to the moral issues evaluated by Gallup, we learned that more than half of all born-again adults also believe that cohabitation is morally appropriate; half say that entertaining sexual fantasies about someone other than one's spouse is morally acceptable; and one-third condone the use of profanity in public and the viewing of pornography. Deeper analysis of the data showed that the segments of churched adults who are most at risk were men, people under thirty-five, upscale adults, and people who attend large churches.

Our research also confirmed that because people tend to do what they believe, Christians engage in most of the activities they deem morally acceptable. About three out of ten admitted to using foul language in public during the past week. Likewise, millions had gambled, viewed pornography, enjoyed sexual fantasies, and so forth—pretty much mirroring the kinds of values they espoused.

Because people tend to do what they believe, Christians engage in most of the activities they deem morally acceptable.

Cultural hot buttons, such as abortion, provide another angle on contemporary morality. Though this issue is no longer the lightning rod controversy it was during the past three decades, it continues to spark conflict and passion. When we asked a national sample of adults if they believed abortion should be legal in all cases, legal in most cases, illegal in most cases, or illegal in all cases, the usual split was observed: 49 percent would prefer to keep abortion legal in all or most cases, and 42 percent would opt for making it illegal in all or most cases. But despite the furor over this important matter, most people (two-thirds) do not have strong feelings about abortion one way or the other. Religious faith makes a difference in people's ultimate choice, but perhaps not as much as you'd imagine. Only 55 percent of born-again Christians leaned toward making abortion illegal, compared to 38 percent who would choose to make it legal. People who describe themselves as Christian (but not born again) were the mirror opposite (54 percent preferred to keep abortion legal, compared to 31 percent who prefer it to be illegal). Our research continues to show that these views shift from time to time, indicating that they are not necessarily anchored to an unwavering position about the moral overtones of this issue.

Reflections

Inevitably, as conditions and opportunities change, so do our values. It is the degree to which they change that defines the nature of our society and the direction of our personal lives. The danger in how fast our world moves these days is that we sometimes allow changes in our values to occur without having thought through the implications. Ideally, we would take time to reflect on possible revisions in our values and attitudes and consider the parameters for evaluating those components. Making changes in core values and attitudes without time to reflect, and without a solid and reliable foundation from which to reconstruct our values system, is dangerous. We live in dangerous times.

The current shift in values is not simply a result of the transition of power from one generation to the next.

The current shift in values is not simply a result of the transition of power from one generation to the next. The new set of values, now widely adopted, reflects the essence of the culture wars. Fundamental viewpoints about God, truth, reality, relationships, vocation, meaning, identity, and value are being tested. The good news is that values are pliable; if we venture into an area and find it distasteful, we can always revise our values and embrace something more satisfying. The bad news is that even though we are not locked in to a given set of values, the nature of values is that they produce action, and the consequences of actions motivated by bad values often cannot be undone. That's why it is important to do our best to get it right the first time. We tend to be a fast-paced, superficial society; developing values based on unsophisticated judgments can and will produce harmful outcomes.

The emerging American values set is one that features relaxed standards. To many people, that feels positive—as if we have a greater stake in the development of the minds and hearts of the collective. But a more reasoned analysis of these new values also indicates that they leave us less hopeful, less joyful, and less competitive in a competitive world. It may feel as if the process has been democratized to the benefit of the masses, but research suggests that all we're doing is creating a society with fewer points of positive consistency and more opportunities for fear, doubt, mistrust, and chaos to reign.

The bottom-line question for America is this: What kind of nation do we want to be?

What kind of environment do we wish to live in? Do we want a culture that is refined or coarse? Are we seeking a place where anything goes or where there are agreed-upon limitations to what is acceptable? Until recently, Judeo-Christian principles served as the basis for our cultural parameters—and they served us well. It appears, however, that a growing contingent of the public (most notably the population of young adults) is bent on moving us toward a yet-to-be-defined framework of alternative values in which personal choice is the pivotal value. If that system takes hold for the long run, it will launch the nation in an entirely new direction that is highly individualistic in all phases of life.

If you don't like what's happening, the resistance starts by your living a firm, persuasive, and consistent Christian life.

How do values gain traction in a society? By people deciding that what they believe is right and both defending their values verbally and demonstrating them actively. If you like the direction the country is moving, then by all means support the changes being brought to fruition in opposition to our original Judeo-Christian framework. If you don't like what's happening, the resistance starts by your living a firm, persuasive, and consistent Christian life. You can complain all you want, but if your life's example does not convey a compelling alternative to the current trend, you are simply filling the air with empty words.

CRITICAL SHIFTS IN VALUES AND ATTITUDES	
WHAT WE USED TO EMBRACE	**WHAT WE NOW EMBRACE**
Excellence	Adequacy
Optimism	Pessimism
Common Good	Individual Advantage
Delayed Gratification	Instant Gratification
Respect	Incivility
Christian God	Amorphous God
Truth	Tolerance
Trust	Skepticism
Heroes	Celebrities
Knowledge	Experience

CHAPTER 4

MEDIA, TECHNOLOGY, AND ENTERTAINMENT

The Tools and Conduits That Define Our Lives

FEW AREAS OF life seem to change more frequently and rapidly than those related to media, technology, entertainment, and communications. Every day we encounter breaking news in each of these areas, often in ways that reshape the contours of that dimension of life. Trying to keep up with it, much less get a bead on where these dimensions are headed, is a challenge.

However, if we take a step back and try to get a grip on the big picture related to media, technology, entertainment, and communications, here are some of the central patterns that seem to be evolving:

- *Interactive and participatory.* A growing component of the media world is about allowing people to participate in the conceptualization, communication, and criticism processes. Information these days is most influential when it is interactive; it takes on a bigger role in our culture once people participate in the process and feel as if they have an ownership stake in the information and how it is adopted.

- *Eliminating the lines of demarcation.* We are witnessing a blurring of the distinctions between aspects of life and media that were formerly clear. For instance, it is difficult to distinguish news from entertainment; trivia from significance; truth from marketing; content from intent; value from intrigue; fair use from abuse of content; and reality from hyperbole and fantasy.

- *Rough and ready—and rude.* By extending the platform to give everyone a voice, the result has been the eradication of the rules of civility and an extreme ideological polarization. In what one researcher called "cyberdisinhibition," the anonymity offered to communicators on the Internet seems to give some people license to take on a different, darker personality. The rules of etiquette, in other words, have been altered by the technological landscape.

- *Cut-and-paste, stand and deliver.* With the postmodern worldview embraced by growing numbers of people, we experience content "mixes" and "mash-ups" (unusual combinations of preexisting content into new forms) as well as an emphasis on deconstructionism (providing the reader's interpretation of a creator's content and motivations rather than a faithful rendering of the original content). The result is that everyone is in competition to make his or her own voice louder than those of the critics, interpreters, and deconstructors as the only means of gaining a fair hearing.

- *Faster is better.* No longer content to have an avalanche of information at our disposal, we now seek immediacy in the availability and provision of that information. We expect a refined search process with instantaneous delivery of information.

- *ADD communications.* What used to be deemed a distraction is now often considered added value in a fragmented daily experience. We're more interested in being connected than profound—or even substantive.
- *No fat in our media diets.* To maximize our time, we demand that everything be reduced to its essence: sound bites, video clips, summaries, ratings, reviews, synopses. "Long form" resources are more abbreviated than ever before.
- *Your business is everyone's business.* Increasingly, the very concept of privacy is under assault. Many feel that because all is fair in a consumption-driven marketplace, privacy is no longer a right but a privilege that one must pay and fight for.
- *Learning to juggle.* Media multitasking is a basic survival skill. Absorbing content from just one medium at a time is increasingly viewed as evidence of aging, poverty, fatigue, or disability.

These patterns are not just a lot of shape-shifting; in many cases they signify a real transformation in both thinking and behavior. Little of this is troubling to young adults; they have pretty much grown up with a world in flux and are comfortable with constant cultural twists and turns. For older Americans, though, the constant unpredictability and the ever-present need to learn new tricks just to stay even can be disconcerting. But, as the younger folks observe with typical understated wisdom, it is what it is.

Understanding these alterations is critical because our society is now driven by the points of view provided to us by the media, whether through news reporting, entertainment, or instructional formats. If the media don't report on an event, it might as well not have happened; it will have little if any influence in our society.

Our understanding of morals, values, prevailing attitudes, dominant behaviors, and even facts is now shaped largely by media filters and formats. Notice how much time and energy public officials and business executives devote to shaping a message and shepherding that message through media channels. Like anyone else who seeks to have influence these days, they know they must buy time or persuade media outlets to convey their messages and then rely upon whatever means are at their disposal to craft and control the character and durability of the messages they wish to convey.

If the media don't report on an event, it might as well not have happened.

The American public has been fully complicit in this reassignment of power to the unelected, and often unknown, masterminds of the media world. As long as the media cater to our voracious appetite for new stimulation—an appetite that itself was created by the media—we generally let them have their way, all the while contending that we have a democratic marketplace in which we can choose what to absorb and what to ignore and pretending that we can immerse ourselves in media content without it leaving a mark on us or distorting our view of reality. Perhaps there is no better indicator of how misinformed we are about the power of media than that most Americans believe they are not influenced by it.[1] That perspective, of course, flies in the face of the sales data and behavioral research that drives the efforts and messaging of advertisers and media production companies. In fact, our unawareness of the influence of media is a testimony to just how immersed in a media-driven culture we are: Like fish in water, we don't recognize the breadth and depth of the environment that has swallowed us whole.[2]

To better understand the weight of media impact on our lives, consider the sheer volume of content we consume per person each year. Reasonable estimates show that, on average, we ingest about 3,500 hours per year from various sources, which averages out to 67 hours per week. Such an extraordinary number is possible only because of multitasking—listening to music while surfing the Internet or reading a book or newspaper, or sending text messages on a mobile device while watching television or a DVD. Research finds that our favorite sources of media content are television (about 1,600 hours annually, which equates to almost 31 hours per week) and radio (750 hours annually),

To better understand the weight of media impact on our lives, consider the sheer volume of content we consume.

followed by listening to recorded music (about 200 hours), using the Internet (200 hours and increasing rapidly), reading newspapers (roughly 150 hours) and magazines (another 125 hours), playing video games (125 more hours), and reading books (100 hours), as well as another 125 hours or so for all other forms of media.[3] It would be difficult for a thinking person to argue that exposure to sixty-seven hours a week of carefully constructed input fails to make a lasting impression on the minds and hearts of the audience.

To understand the many facets of the media environment, let's touch on some of the most important components.

What's Happening with Music

It's easy to get the wrong impression about what has happened in the music world. You have undoubtedly heard that the "big four" music companies—Sony/BMG, Universal, Warner, and EMI—which produce an overwhelming majority of the music purchased (and pirated), have suffered huge financial and market share setbacks over the past decade. You may have seen reports describing the dramatic fall in the sales of music CDs. Most of the independent music shops around the nation have gone out of business in the last fifteen years. Even cable channels like MTV and VH1—once hallowed outlets for introducing new music or maintaining the profiles of popular acts—barely show musical content anymore. You might be led to think that music is diminishing in popularity.

Most of the independent music shops around the nation have gone out of business in the last fifteen years.

You'd be wrong.

Americans are responsible for one-third of all music sales on the planet.[4] Reliable estimates indicate that recorded music is more popular than ever. People are simply accessing it differently than they used to—and in more diverse formats than in years past. The importance of music should not be underestimated. It serves as more than a distraction from the pressures of the day. Each generation establishes its own pantheon of hallowed artists and adopts a particular sound as its own native language. The lyrical content of music affects the values of the generation that makes the music popular. The lifestyles of iconic musicians influence the behavior of their followers.

Other research shows that music can also be a tool that binds us together. A Pew survey discovered that significant majorities of people across all generations appreciate the music of several artists in common. At the top of the list are the Beatles, followed by the Eagles, Johnny Cash, Michael Jackson, Elvis Presley, the Rolling Stones, and Aretha Franklin. (Other musicians, whose popularity is more generationally defined, failed to bridge the gap: Such artists as Coldplay, Jefferson Airplane, Kanye West, Nirvana, and even the Grateful Dead remain largely unknown beyond their core audiences.)[5]

Here is a portrait of what has been taking place in the music world. Total music sales across all formats (albums, singles, digital tracks, CDs, vinyl records, cassettes, and music videos) have been flourishing, topping 1.5 billion units for the first time ever in both 2008 and 2009.[6] However, industry reports indicate that 95 percent of the music downloaded online in 2008 was done illegally. Estimates claim that for every unit of music purchased legally last year, thirty units were acquired illegally. That's an average of 2.5 billion music files stolen every month. Illegal music downloads are especially prevalent among teenagers. Music piracy is believed to have cost the music industry more than $5 billion in 2008 alone. With the total sales of recorded music worldwide registering around $16 billion that year, piracy was responsible for nearly one-third of the value of all music acquired by consumers. That's a huge loss to overcome for any industry.

But one inescapable point is that people want music—they just don't want to pay for it if they don't have to.[7]

People want music—they just don't want to pay for it if they don't have to.

The most popular form of music being purchased is digital tracks—individual songs sold in a digital format, such as might be used on an iPod or other MP3 player. Between 2007 and 2009 sales of these units jumped by nearly 40 percent, growing from 844 million units in 2007 to 1.17 billion in 2010. This means that digital tracks—a format that did not even exist twenty years ago—now account for more than three-quarters of all music sold.[8] Much of this explosion can be attributed to the enduring popularity of the iPod, which has now sold more than 250 million units since its debut in 2001, garnering in excess of $40 billion (not including the income generated through iTunes, Apple's online store for selling digital downloads and ancillary products).[9]

Digital tracks have replaced albums as the music resource of choice. Album sales peaked at 785 million units in 2000 and continued on a downward free fall, hitting just 326 million units in

2010—a decline of more than 50 percent in less than a decade. This is important because an album averages ten tracks of music. With digital singles replacing the higher-priced album format, artists and record companies lost massive portions of revenue through this transition.[10]

The magnitude of this loss can be seen in the unit sales decline of top-selling albums over the past decade. In 2000, boy band 'N Sync sold about ten million copies of their album *No Strings Attached*. Since then the top sellers have declined precipitously. After the big winner of 2004 sold eight million units (Usher's *Confessions*), sales figures dropped substantially each of the next several years, ranging from Mariah Carey's *Emancipation of Mimi* in 2005 (five million units sold) down to Lil Wayne's *Tha Carter III*, which topped the charts in 2008 with just 2.8 million units. Since then the top sellers have barely risen above three million units (Taylor Swift's *Fearless* sold 3.2 million units in 2009, and Eminem's *Recovery* reached 3.4 million in 2010). Tellingly, the number of albums surpassing the three-million mark dropped from eighteen in 2000 down to zero in 2008, with the slightest of recoveries since then (just two in 2009 and again in 2010).[11] It is doubtful that any future album will ever reach the heights achieved by Michael Jackson's *Thriller* or the Eagles' *Their Greatest Hits*, the best-selling albums of all time, at nearly thirty million copies apiece.[12]

Thirteen million songs are available for sale online, but last year, 90 percent did not register a single sale.

Making the scene even more confusing is the glut of music available. Approximately thirteen million songs are available for sale online, but sales-tracking data show that simply offering music for sale is no guarantee of finding an audience. Last year, 90 percent of all digital singles (more than ten million songs) and 85 percent of all digital albums available did not register a single sale. Eighty percent of all revenue was generated by roughly fifty-two thousand songs—that's just four-tenths of one percent of all the music waiting to be purchased. Making a living as a musician is not as simple as it might seem.[13]

People satisfy their need for music in various ways. Americans love a fun experience, which explains why concert tours have fared well even during the economic downturn. More than seventy million tickets are sold to concerts each year, with revenues topping $4 billion annually. At the top end are tours by giants such as U2, whose 2009 tour was described by lead singer Bono as "intimacy on a grand scale." That tour—which involved moving and setting up a 170-ton stage; loading, driving, and unloading two hundred trucks; managing some four hundred employees; and setting up more than 250 speakers and thirteen video cameras—cost the band $750,000 a day. In the end, though, the tour grossed more than $123 million in ticket sales alone, just for the North American leg. (Sales of ancillary merchandise at these concerts often eclipse ticket revenues.) At the other end of the spectrum—the more heavily populated end—many fledgling artists struggle to build a fan base. A growing number are going grassroots, developing their following by doing in-home concerts in the houses of ardent fans. In this mode, the artists perform in a relaxed setting (such as the host's living room), giving them an opportunity to build relationships with a more engaged audience while earning a modest amount from ticket revenue and sales of CDs and other merchandise. This approach appeals to many artists because it enables them to stay in touch with the tastes and views of their fans, often generates a buzz within their fan network, and they don't have to split the cash generated with managers, booking agents, marketing firms, or venues.[14]

Another sign of the popularity of music is its prevalence online.

Until recently, seven of the ten most popular channels on YouTube were music channels. That changed when three of the four major music companies realized what they were giving away without a return. They subsequently pulled the videos of their recording artists and formed their own channel, Vevo. Those companies—Sony, Universal, and EMI—hope that advertising revenue accrued from the viewings on Vevo will help cover some of the losses from music piracy and thus perpetuate the availability of online music for the public. But the Internet remains jammed with music videos, expanding the global reach of music far beyond the television channels such as MTV that ignited the video genre thirty years ago.[15]

Many fledgling artists struggle to build a fan base. A growing number are going grassroots.

Where is the music world heading? Much like the computer world, it is moving into "the cloud." "The cloud" is the phrase attached to computing that takes place on the Internet, where unimaginable amounts of content are stored on servers for immediate access by qualified users. Having failed to make money on the digital revolution by selling downloads of singles, the music industry is now moving toward stockpiling recorded music on servers that give subscribers continual access to any kind of music—and as much of it as they want—as long as they have access to a web connection (and, perhaps, a subscription). The music is then streamed to their connected device, which could be a computer, MP3 player, mobile phone, satellite dish, automobile, or other electronic device.

Among the early adopters of this strategy have been Rhapsody and MOG, which are fee-based subscription services (known to some as the "jukebox in the sky" model), and Pandora, an advertising-based, customizable online radio station. Although the revenue generation models differ, both services are similar in that users do not buy the music; they just listen to it on demand. Of course, the prerequisite for users is to have access to a broadband or robust wireless connection—but as I'll discuss later in this chapter, such access is around the corner. The primary benefit for consumers is that there is no longer a need to buy desired tracks and clutter electronic storage devices with megabyte after megabyte of content; now, countless terabytes of musical pleasure are archived in the cloud for unlimited access. The typical cloud-based music service currently offers customers more than six million songs.[16]

Streaming is clearly the wave of the future. It is already blossoming among the generations that will define the future of the industry: Two-thirds of all teenagers currently stream music regularly (and about half do so on a daily basis). That's important because it indicates they have already made the mental transition from the need to own the music (their parents' model) to a desire for instant access. Entrepreneurs and industry veterans

Streaming is clearly the wave of the future. Two-thirds of all teenagers currently stream music regularly.

are moving toward the streaming model as the way to generate revenue from music—in much the same way as people now pay monthly subscriptions for access to television programming. The biggest obstacles at the moment are figuring out the complexities of licensing music, overcoming format incompatibility, and building the broadband infrastructure, but those hurdles will eventually be surmounted. Some developing services (such as Lala and MP3tunes) promise to become a music locker for storing songs obtained in the past, thus adding further value and convenience to streaming.[17]

The emergence of online radio stations, such as Pandora, may be a harbinger of change in that industry, too. More than three-quarters of all Americans still listen to traditional radio stations on the AM or FM band—now termed *terrestrial radio*—but those numbers are on the decline. (Some radio professionals have suggested that the AM band may be either reassigned or replaced by other forms of broadcasting, ranging from satellite and Internet transmission to mobile devices and podcasts.) Not only are upstarts like Pandora (with more than fifty million users) stealing the conventional radio stations' market share, but so are satellite radio networks (e.g., Sirius XM, with its twenty million–plus subscribers) and MP3 players (such as the iPod), especially when the MP3 device can be played through an automobile or home sound system. (One-fourth of Americans twelve or older have accessed audio content from an iPod or other type of MP3 device that was connected to their car's stereo system.)[18] The future for terrestrial radio may hinge on providing its content to some of the new electronic devices, such as mobile phones. But it's a competitive marketplace: Even Pandora and other online broadcasters are now streaming their music to cars and energetically searching for new ways to reach consumers.[19]

Online broadcasters are now streaming their music to cars and energetically searching for new ways to reach consumers.

As for the musical artists, their world has been turned upside down too. In the future, they are not likely to release albums—that is, collections of songs based on a theme, or a combination of some songs with singles potential and others without such allure. As advances in recording technology enable amateur and semi-professional musicians to create recorded music that can be easily distributed digitally worldwide, the competition for listeners' allegiance has stiffened. Attracting an audience, though challenging, is possible through the Internet.

MySpace, once the talk of the media world, has gone through tough times in the past several years. News Corp. paid $580

million to acquire the site in 2005; by 2010, its value was estimated at roughly half that amount, and it is said to be losing close
to $100 million annually for its parent corporation. Formerly
the superstar of social networking, MySpace lost its supremacy to
Facebook (which now has more than 500 million registered users)
and now generates about one-third as much traffic as Facebook.
MySpace has retooled its raison d'etre and is once again focusing
on satisfying the needs of musicians and other creatives. It is estimated that MySpace presently serves as a base for some thirteen
million bands and solo artists—a massive crossroads for the intersection of artists and consumers that is likely to remain an important and active emerging-music hub for the foreseeable future.
News Corp. has embarked on a redesign and repositioning effort to
provide "social entertainment" rather than a true social network on
MySpace and to regain the trust and interest of its core audience
(twelve- to thirty-four-year-olds). As one industry analyst noted,
what MySpace needs to do is regain its former image of being
cool.[20]

What's Happening with the Internet

During the past century, there was arguably no single innovation
that changed the American way of life as dramatically as the
Internet. As this invisible but powerful
tool continues to evolve, it keeps altering the landscape of our lives.

No single innovation changed the American way of life as dramatically as the Internet.

According to Mary Meeker, the
esteemed Internet analyst currently at
Morgan Stanley, the world is in the
midst of the next great wave of tech-
nological advancement. The computing craze began back in the
1950s with the introduction of the mainframe computer. The next

revolution was the creation of the minicomputer in the 1970s, followed by the personal computer era of the 1980s and the rise of the Internet in the 1990s. Today's focus is the mobile Internet, with people no longer tethered to a desk in order to stay connected.

Almost three out of four American adults (72 percent) use the Internet at least once a month—63 percent from a home computer and 33 percent from a computer at a place of employment.[21] Those users invest an average of fifteen to twenty hours per week in Net engagement. Though younger adults have traditionally been the heaviest users, that balance has shifted substantially in recent years as usage has picked up among all generations, but especially quickly among people fifty and older. One reason for the increase in use by older, less tech-savvy people is the increased speed of interaction on the Internet. Recent estimates show that 84 percent of homes with Internet access have broadband connections.[22] There are differences by other demographics: The Internet is more likely to be used by college graduates than by those with a high school diploma (87 percent vs. 49 percent); and by Asians (73 percent) and whites (69 percent) than by blacks (51 percent) and Hispanics (48 percent).[23]

Perhaps most important, though, is the mindshare that the Internet is receiving these days. Television had been the medium of choice for Americans since the 1950s, but that has changed in the past few years, with little hope of reversal. The Internet is now considered the "most essential" medium in our society, selected by 42 percent of adults, compared to 37 percent who listed television, 14 percent who named radio, and only 5 percent who chose newspapers. As the Buster and Mosaic generations come of age and constitute a larger proportion of the adult population, that gap will grow, positioning the Internet as the most significant medium in our lives.[23]

The growth area in the Internet universe relates to the quest for wireless connectivity. The number of wireless Internet users in the United States has grown exponentially in the past decade, jumping from about twelve million users in 2003 to an estimated one hundred million in 2010. That represents one-third of adults and an even higher percentage of young people utilizing wireless services for computing. That growth is fueled by a voracious appetite for content (especially video content); expanding carrier

The number of wireless Internet users in the United States has grown exponentially in the past decade.

capacity that allows massive amounts of data to be sent wirelessly; households installing home networks; businesses and municipalities providing connection hot spots; and developments in mobile electronics, such as smartphones, that provide consumers with a means of instantly accessing and easily navigating a global library of information, images, and communications options on machines no larger than a pack of cigarettes.[24]

Identifying the breadth of uses for the Internet is like reciting names from the phone book (remember phone books?)—it goes on and on, touching on every dimension of our lives. Similarly, attempting to define how the Internet has become ingrained in our daily activities is like tracking blood flow in the human body: For most Americans, life without the Internet is unthinkable. Whether we are gathering information, conducting business, communicating, or seeking entertainment, the reach of this global network is breathtaking. But like a virus the Internet continues to change its shape and expand its reach, both in terms of the number of people using it (now approaching two billion internationally), the ways in which we use it, and the content we receive through its channels.

Predicting what the Internet will be like in the future is a fruitless task. Billions of dollars of research and development funding are spent each year on Internet applications and extensions as everyone tries to develop the next big thing—only to find that an idea hatched in a dorm room at Harvard or a garage in Silicon Valley takes the world by storm. But some emerging trends make the future a bit more clear than a UHF signal on a tube television.

Web 2.0 has been about dynamic engagement, allowing people to develop communities and interactive thinking.

For starters, the cloud will become the nation's central nervous system. From its inception, the Internet emphasized one-way communication through websites. The current iteration, Web 2.0, has been about dynamic engagement, allowing people to develop communities and interactive thinking. The next wave, Web 3.0, will be built on an infrastructure that offers richer utilization, regular and less overt upgrades of computing applications (e.g., word processing, spreadsheets, video editing), and even the ability to seamlessly move from one mobile device to another. People will store more than just music in the cloud: data, images, e-mail, and the application software used to operate our computers will be archived in the ether, enabling us to purchase skeletal computers and no longer fret about storage space and backup systems. Cloud computing will win people over by providing convenience, flexibility, and simplicity. Sharing and accessing files from virtually any location that offers a high-speed connection are benefits that presently outweigh people's concerns about their stored information being abused by the tech giants who store it for them.[25]

With so much of the nation's business, communications, and future riding on the storage and delivery of an invisible body of zeros and ones, increasing emphasis will be placed on data security. The master thieves of the twenty-first century will be less focused on penetrating physical bank vaults and more attuned to ways of breaking the cybersecurity codes and firewalls that protect our Internet transmissions and transactions.

Meanwhile, the explosion in user-generated content (UGC) will continue to grow, albeit at a slower pace in the years ahead. Dispersing editorial power from the elites to the public at large has redefined not only the media world, but even people's self-image. Whether it is through videos, blogs, ratings, reviews, or social network postings, the sources from which people get information—and which sources they enjoy or trust—will continue to morph. If nothing else, it will become more difficult to be a passive consumer of information: Almost everyone will have a hand in the sources they embrace as personally viable.

The future of television (which is discussed in greater detail later in this chapter) is inextricably linked with the delivery of video content through the Internet. More than sixty million people have watched television shows online, and more than ten million households regularly watch streamed television programs in place of traditional television viewing. To accommodate the

The future of television is inextricably linked with the delivery of video content through the Internet.

coming stampede, electronics manufacturers are tripping over themselves to make and market TV sets that carry streamed video; most of the flat-panel sets shipped to the United States by 2013 will be Internet enabled. With years of programming in the vaults and new programs constantly being produced, the growth of TV-program viewing through the Internet is currently limited only by fuzzy business models and licensing agreements; but pioneers such as Hulu are rapidly figuring out the equation. Interstitial advertising, the bane of traditional television, may well be replaced by other revenue-generating forms, enhancing the pleasure of the viewing experience. Expect to see a steady trail of people departing from cable and satellite TV in favor of streamed programming.[26]

The expansion of video content in general is moving like a

freight train down a hill: the quantity of streamed video content doubled between 2006 and 2009, and it is projected to double again between 2009 and 2013. Watching online videos is the most prevalent use of the Internet, surpassing even the ever-popular participation in social-networking sites. Nine out of ten Internet users in the eighteen to twenty-nine age group regularly watch online video; more than one-third watch streamed content on any given day. By early 2010, one-quarter of the people who purchased new TV sets had connected their TVs to the Internet for enhanced online viewing.[27]

Although a lot of the public's fascination with the Internet relates to its relational and entertainment capacity, the Internet has emerged as one of the most important channels for commerce, as well. The trends suggest that a growing share of the nation's commerce will be conducted online. As data security issues are satisfactorily addressed and as the Mosaic and Digital generations become a larger percentage of the consuming public, the buying and selling of consumer goods through the web will steadily increase, reshaping the nation's retail environment. This brings with it the likelihood of an entirely new form of underground economy, one that uses barter and other transactional currency to skirt taxes and other regulatory prohibitions.

The buying and selling of consumer goods through the web will steadily increase, reshaping the nation's retail environment.

Naturally, any growing entity brings with it serious legal issues as well, and the Internet is far from immune. The legal profession must consider the Internet a godsend, as continual battles over privacy, security, and intellectual property ownership will keep the courts tied up for years to come. Lobbying for the development of enforceable laws regarding the copying and sharing of content will become a profitable industry.

The final aspect of the Internet to consider is social networking. This category became a big deal in 2003 and 2004 when both MySpace and Facebook burst onto the scene. After MySpace captured everyone's attention, Facebook shot ahead to capture the largest audience, which today numbers more than 500 million active users worldwide (compared to MySpace's 125 million). The growth of this aspect of the Internet is astonishing. Started in a dorm room by four college kids in February 2004, Facebook spread to a few college campuses and caught on quickly before experiencing truly exponential growth in 2006. From twelve million active users at the end of 2006, it quadrupled to fifty million by the following October, doubled to one hundred million by August 2008, doubled again by April 2009, and doubled yet again by February 2010. Perhaps more than any other site on the Internet, Facebook links the world together: About 70 percent of Facebook's current users live outside the United States, with nations in the Middle East, as well as emerging economic powerhouses such as Brazil and India, among the fastest growing. Other social-networking applications have driven to the forefront services such as Twitter (more than one hundred million users) and LinkedIn (more than seventy million users who rely on it for professional contacts).[28]

About half of the adult population visited a social-networking site in the past year.

Nielsen's research finds that about half of the adult population visited a social-networking site in the past year. Social networks and blogs are the fourth most popular online activity and are responsible for 10 percent of all time logged on the Internet. Another study, by Arbitron/Edison Research, revealed that 48 percent of all Americans twelve or older have a profile on one or more social networks, double the percentage who had one two years earlier.

Even though Facebook has garnered the largest share of online

time and more than its fair share of media buzz—it is the most
trafficked site, averaging about 150 million unique visitors per
month in mid 2010—it does not represent the full extent of the
social-networking world. There are many other social-networking
sites, ranging from those serving the business community (e.g.,
LinkedIn) to those geared to retired people (AARP's network), and
a multitude of affinity-based networks. Though many people chide
sites such as Facebook and MySpace for the self-focus they facilitate among users, many other sites have been established primarily
to facilitate an other-orientation, spawning new relationships or
robust conversations among people with shared interests.[29]

Where is this aspect of the Internet headed? Probably toward a
more diverse population of networks, serving ever more targeted
niches; toward a shakeout of older users as they figure out how
to maximize their use of this tool; toward greater commercializa-
tion of these digital gold mines that allows marketers to reach the
kind of consumers most likely to resonate with their products; and
toward increased reliance by Americans upon multiple networks to
meet their relational and communication needs.

What's Happening with Television

Besides the changes already described that threaten the way we have
experienced television in the past, the shifting audience will affect
other aspects of television programming besides the delivery system.

The migration of audiences to other media has affected advertising revenue, which, in turn, affects programming. The recession severely affected ad revenue for broadcasters, dropping total
income to about $70 billion in 2009 (about 60 percent of which
went to the broadcast networks and the other 40 percent to cable).
Although television revenues still constituted about one-quarter
of all advertising income generated in the United States in 2009,

the decline in total revenue meant that production budgets continued to suffer. The advent of reality shows has been a blessing for the networks. Their production costs (approximately $1 million per hour) are substantially lower than those of original dramas (approximately $3 million per hour). There is a persistent fear in the industry, however, that reality shows may well run their course within the next few years, requiring the networks to produce higher-quality, original programming or lose even more viewers.[30]

The migration of audiences to other media has affected advertising revenue, which, in turn, affects programming.

Technological advances have also created a glut of competition in an already competitive field. Hundreds of networks are now producing shows and vying for airtime on cable and satellite-delivery systems. As the marketplace becomes ever more splintered, we can expect to see networks competing for increasingly limited space and audience share. These emerging niches will likely include additional international programming, foreign-language programming, and local origination offerings. Of course, much of the content produced for traditional broadcast networks and cable channels also finds its way onto streamed Internet sites (e.g., Hulu), which garner larger audiences for the content but make recouping production and transmission costs more difficult for the networks.

The days of blockbuster ratings for any particular program, other than special events (such as the Super Bowl), are long gone. Drawing an audience of fifty-two million viewers (as the final episode of *Friends* did in 2004) is unlikely. Even the top-rated shows these days attract audiences that would have been solid but middle-of-the-road when the media universe was more contained and the three broadcast networks ruled the television roost.

Among the most significant changes in the television universe in coming years will be advances in TV technology. During the past decade, millions of households swapped their old sets for flat-panel LCD sets. More swapping is likely in the coming decade as people purchase sets designed for 3-D viewing and for easy connection to the Internet, thereby converting their TV sets into giant computer monitors that allow them to view any and all video streamed online as well as static web pages of interest.

Among the most significant changes in the television universe in coming years will be advances in TV technology.

One of the fears currently stalking TV executives is the potential for consumers to engage in "cord cutting"—the term used to describe households that drop their cable or satellite television subscriptions in favor of viewing programs via video streaming from a potpourri of free online sources. Though the feared exodus has not yet begun to a substantial degree—through the end of 2009 less than a half-million households had abandoned cable and satellite for online-only programming—studies show that significant numbers of younger, tech-savvy adults are already contemplating the move. The switch will be made even more attractive with the availability of web-connected television sets, which various manufacturers are now developing and testing. Though television producers have already begun to implement business models designed to protect their investment in the programming they create, it remains likely that within the next decade cord cutting will be the norm for millions of households.[31]

What's Happening with Movies

Movies remain one of the nation's favorite forms of entertainment. Despite the recession, the movie industry broke box office records in 2008 and 2009 for attendance and revenue (though some of that can be attributed to higher ticket prices). International box office revenues also continue to climb. The solid performance of first-run films in theaters has helped to offset the plummeting revenues from DVDs in recent years as that sector of the industry has matured.[32]

As the media environment changes, studio executives are working hard to understand those shifts and capitalize on the opportunities they present. The studios have only so many variables they can control. One of those is the number of movies they release each year. As studios seek to enhance their profit margins, look for a slight reduction in the number of films released, moving downward from the six hundred or so released annually in recent years. Theater owners confess that having five or more new, significant films released on the same weekend is often too much for consumers to absorb.

Another variable concerns formats. One of the growth areas of the future relates to 3-D films. *Avatar* broke all box-office records, and other 3-D movies (e.g., *Monsters vs. Aliens*) have used new graphics and motion techniques to thrill audiences worldwide. Expect to see more theaters outfitted with the necessary equipment (less than one-third were equipped by the end of 2009) and more films created in 3-D. Audience response to the remarkable quality of the initial group of 3-D releases has encouraged the six major studios to invest more resources into developing 3-D titles. The key to success, of course, is a compelling story; but if the creative teams on the Hollywood lots can craft a moving tale, audiences will flock to see it.

The studios have only so many variables they can control. One of those is the number of movies they release.

Perhaps the most perplexing challenge facing the movie industry relates to the management of their properties after they have hit the theaters. Movies typically run the gauntlet, shifting from theaters to video shops, to pay-per-view, to premium cable channels, and finally to basic cable and the broadcast networks. At each stop along the way, the studios reap a good return on their initial investment. But the challenge is to know how long the window at each stop should be. Studios are now tinkering with their formula for three reasons: changes in the rental business, the onslaught of streaming on the Internet, and fear of making the wrong decisions and torpedoing their industry, as happened when the music industry misread market signals.

Have you noticed that thousands of video rental stores have closed down in recent years? Part of the reason is the explosive growth of two newcomers to the field: Netflix and Redbox. Netflix is the premier DVD-by-mail subscription service, offering its ten million–plus customers a choice of one hundred thousand movie titles. The company's sales topped $2 billion in 2010. But in order to stay healthy, Netflix is already testing new ways of delivering movies—including a streaming model. Their biggest obstacle is getting the movie studios to agree to give them the same content that has historically been reserved for other partners in the studios' network of sellers. However, the company has no trouble getting the ear of Hollywood executives; after all, it buys a quarter-billion dollars' worth of DVDs for inventory every year. (Fascinating fact: Netflix spends some $600 million annually on postage for shipping its DVDs.)[33]

Mastering the technological challenges won't matter if a deal cannot be struck with the content suppliers.

Many industry analysts, however, contend that the winner of the streaming wars will be whichever company—Apple, Amazon, Google, Verizon, News Corp., etc.—is most successful at negotiating a win-win deal with the movie studios and independent production houses. Unlike previous battles for consumer attention and loyalty, mastering the technological challenges of movie delivery—such as streaming in ways that provide content without a glitch on numerous platforms, including touchpads and smartphones—won't matter if a deal cannot be struck with the content suppliers.

Meanwhile, Redbox has championed a low-maintenance, low-cost strategy. Begun as an experiment by McDonald's—yes, the burger giant—Redbox tried selling various products in vending machines until they discovered that the only product with sufficient potential was DVDs. They rolled out the Redbox system and eventually sold the rapidly expanding division to Coinstar, which has aggressively pushed its machines into supermarkets and other retailers. In 2009 and 2010, a new kiosk was installed somewhere in North America every hour of every day. The machines hold about seven hundred discs of roughly two hundred current and classic titles, costing the renter just one dollar per day. (Part of the secret to Redbox's success is that most renters wind up paying for two or three days.) The low cost attracts enough people that nearly four million people rent Redbox DVDs in an average month. Their strategy has been so successful that it not only threatens Netflix, but also Blockbuster, the longtime industry leader. Blockbuster has begun testing its own rollout of kiosks in a different network of retail channels, but the company also filed Chapter 11 bankruptcy in September 2010, leaving its future even more uncertain. Redbox, too, is wary of the vicissitudes of the marketplace and has been pushing the envelope regarding how quickly it can make new movies accessible to its customer base.[34]

Studio chiefs are moving judiciously on the release-window dilemma. As one former studio head noted, nobody wants to be the first to make a mistake in this corner of the business; it is widely agreed that such a mistake would be a career killer. The model the studios use is working fine—for now. Their fear is that the failure to anticipate and deftly respond to the changing expectations of the audience could scuttle one of the most profitable elements of their business. (DVD sales and rentals typically generate about 70 percent as much income as a movie's theatrical run, which accounts for about half of a film's gross earnings from all sources.)[35]

Studio chiefs are moving judiciously on the release-window dilemma. Nobody wants to be the first to make a mistake.

In the meantime, expect the marketplace to be flooded with independent, low-budget movies, some of which the studios will purchase to give wider distribution (e.g., *Fireproof*), but most of which will never receive a theatrical showing. Instead, they will rely on Internet marketing and viewing strategies. Those films will help to meet the seemingly endless demand of the video-on-demand and pay-per-view capabilities of today's cable and satellite systems.

Hollywood is responsive to the changing tastes of its customers. Recent research indicates that the preferences of the moment are for more comedies (30 percent chose that genre as their favorite) and dramas (28 percent). The least favorite genres are horror (6 percent) and musicals (3 percent). In the future, the nature of the films produced—at least the six hundred or so releases from the major studios each year—will reflect both the audience's preferences and the typical return on investment for movies in a given genre. The industry will still produce a wide variety of films, but movies in less popular genres will be made largely under exceptional circumstances, such as low budget requirements or a major star signing on to carry the movie. The studios, all of which are publicly owned corporations, are not as much about art as they are about making a profit for their shareholders. Whatever sells is what they'll produce.[36]

What's Happening with Books

To walk into a bookstore these days, or to browse through the voluminous catalog of Amazon.com, you would never suspect that the book industry is in utter turmoil. But it is, and for some very peculiar reasons.

Some reasons are easily understood. For instance, with all the intriguing new technologies available these days, people are drawn to products other than books. These competitive products chip away at the time and money that might otherwise have been invested in books. Another reason is that one of the competitive products is e-books: digital versions of books that people download on electronic book readers like the Amazon Kindle or the Barnes and Noble Nook. Preliminary research has found that digital versions of books are not expanding the universe of book buyers, but simply rearranging the existing population of bibliophiles.

Preliminary research has found that digital versions of books are not expanding the universe of book buyers.

Perhaps the strangest reason for the book industry's hardships is that there are simply too many books being published. If you're thinking that's a variable that publishers control, you're right, but that has not stopped the industry from overwhelming itself with new titles. To wit: More than a half-million new titles are published every year. That amount has more than doubled since 2003. To be fair, a substantial share of that growth is attributable to print-on-demand and special limited print runs of books. But the point remains that the market is glutted with an unsustainable quantity of books.

That wouldn't be such a bad thing if sales were able to keep pace with the host of new offerings; but they haven't, and they probably can't. One publisher estimated that the average book in the United States sells fewer than 250 copies per year, and fewer than 3,000 copies over its life span. Nielsen Bookscan, which tracks book sales for the 1.2 million books in print, determined that almost one million of those books sold fewer than 100 copies in the past year; 200,000 titles sold fewer than 1,000 copies; and only 25,000 titles sold at least 5,000 copies during the prior twelve months. We read about the success of mega-selling authors like John Grisham, J. K. Rowling, Dan Brown, and James Patterson, but their stories in publishing are aberrations. As several studies have convincingly shown, very few people actually earn a living by writing books. [37]

Part of the answer to selling more books, of course, is better marketing. But again the realities paint a different portrait than most people imagine. For most books, the relatively few copies that sell typically wind up in the hands of people who are part of the author's relational network or community. In other words, if a book is going to sell, it is up to the author to sell it. This is a sad truth that publishers recognize and authors grudgingly come to realize. For most books, the publisher cannot afford a marketing campaign that will effectively cut through the clutter in today's saturated and diverse media world. If authors cannot effectively use their platform and contacts to sell their books, chances are the books will sit in the warehouse until the publisher disposes of them.

Discouraging as this information may seem, books are not about to leave the scene. Changes will occur—there might be greater reliance on instant publishing (i.e., books on demand), publishers might wise up and publish fewer titles, creative pricing and bundling strategies might bump the sales curve, and new distribution channels might make the industry more efficient. E-books are not likely to raise the tide. They represented about 8 percent of total book sales in the first half of 2010, and even though that number will climb, it will be a long time before e-books attract a significant number of people who would not otherwise have bought books. And, as author Stephen King and others have adroitly noted, a substantial shift to e-publishing would be detrimental to the quality of books because fewer resources would be available to invest in editing, author advances, and marketing.[38]

Make no mistake about it, though: E-books are here to stay. Increasing numbers of parents and educators see the potential for getting children more interested in reading by providing content through the technology that already appeals to them—such as computers

Publishers might publish fewer titles, and new distribution channels might make the industry more efficient.

and mobile devices, as well as dedicated e-readers. Currently, more than one-quarter of all American children ages six through seventeen say they have read one or more books on a digital device, while six out of ten young people admit to being very interested in doing so, and more than four out of five parents of such youths say they would permit or even encourage their young ones to use an e-reader. Manufacturers of those devices will certainly promote the devices, and the content purchased for them, and thus maintain a high profile for digital books. But the studies also emphasize that digital devices can provide distractions for young people, who are more prone to use them for video games, web surfing, or social networking. Parents and teachers still have a role to play in introducing interesting reading material to young people and enforcing boundaries on how much time is spent on other pursuits through those devices.[39]

But one player has created a controversial solution of its own. Enter Google, nascent publisher.

Around the turn of the millennium, Google began scanning books. I mean, they *really* got busy scanning a lot of books. Today, they have completed scans of more than fifteen million books, three million of which were released to the public in December

2010 as part of Google eBooks. This activity has not been without conflict. A major class-action lawsuit was lodged against Google by authors and publishers, but with a settlement pending and agreeable terms in place, Google will make the scanned content available online in the form of e-books as well as search content. Google plans to continue scanning more books for its archive and will partner with the copyright holders to provide physical editions of out-of-print books for those who desire a copy.[40]

If you walk into your favorite bookstore and cannot find a book you are seeking, don't be surprised. The average bookstore carries fewer than ten thousand unique titles; even the megastores shelve only about fifty thousand titles. The rule of thumb in book retailing these days is to carry a deeper inventory of fewer books, stocking those most likely to sell through quickly. But with the advent of Google eBooks, online booksellers such as Amazon.com, megastores like Barnes & Noble, and a multitude of online sources from which both new and used books can be acquired, any book is within your virtual reach.

Google will make scanned content available online in the form of e-books as well as search content.

What's Happening with Other Media and Entertainment Vehicles

What else is happening in the media world? Here are some quick hits about what's going on in other dimensions of the media and entertainment sectors.

News Media

How Americans get their news has shifted dramatically in the past decade. A study by Pew Research found that most Americans (92 percent) now get their news from multiple platforms (a combination of television, radio, newspapers, magazines, and online).

Half of all adults (46 percent) rely on at least four different sources, and six out of ten adults (59 percent) turn to a combination of online and offline sources.[41]

Further changes are occurring in the news industry because of concerns about content bias. Additional research shows that people don't trust the objectivity of the journalists providing the news. By interviewing a national sample of journalists and media executives, Pew discovered that while 36 percent of the public declared themselves to be conservative, only 6 percent of national journalists did so, and 32 percent of journalists described themselves as liberal, which was double the proportion among adults in general.[42] In fact, increasing numbers of people are worried that the news media exert too much influence on government action, political elections, and people's views of reality.[43] The public's concern about media spin has caused people to seek out sources they perceive to be objective or that better reflect their own ideological perspectives, resulting in a fragmentation of the news universe.

Competition in the news business has changed as well. In the old days, the competition came primarily from a cross-town rival—another newspaper that tried to appeal to the same population base in a head-to-head marketing battle. (Think *New York Times* vs. the *Daily News, Los Angeles Times* vs. the *Herald,* and *Chicago Tribune* vs. *Sun-Times.*) Now the competition is not only over format (online vs. offline), but also between originators and aggregators. It is very expensive for a typical local or metropolitan newspaper to maintain a staff of reporters and editors who physically collect information and identify news. The new warriors in the news field are those who gather information from a variety of sources—newswires (e.g., AP and Reuters), marketing firms, personal contacts, online

> *Research shows that people don't trust the objectivity of the journalists providing the news.*

sources—and mix them together. This has further challenged the supremacy of the legacy news entities, many of which are big-city newspapers.

Fewer people are turning to hard-copy newspapers for their daily dose of current information. Because subscriptions and newsstand sales have been dropping for several years, advertising revenue has also plummeted. Newspaper organizations have been trying to cash in on the Internet, but the increase in online ad spending on those sites has not compensated for the decline experienced in the traditional print format.

Increasing numbers of newspaper entities will limit the free information they publish online and try to market online subscriptions. However, early attempts at promoting such offers, along with data from consumer surveys, indicate that online subscriptions will not be the magic bullet for the industry. Another trend is toward daily newspapers producing their pages less frequently—switching, for instance, to a weekly or every-other-day schedule. This less frequent availability will coincide with a shift in the depth of the reporting provided, as newspapers become more like magazines, with longer stories on topics that are less time sensitive.

> **Fewer people are turning to hard-copy newspapers for their daily dose of current information.**

Over the last few years, as we have become more of an ADD society, people have shown more interest in a breadth of awareness than in a depth of understanding when it comes to news. Consequently, many people now use Twitter and RSS feeds to alert them to headlines—tidbits about new and emerging events—rather than taking the time to drill deeper to comprehend the substance of those events. Some analysts have suggested that this is at least partially due to the overwhelming amount of information now presented to people every day. Others have identified a public boredom with news—the result of having so many talking heads filling time on televised news programs. Pew's extensive studies in media usage also point out that users now treat information differently. They suggest that users now need their news to be *portable* (accessible through a variety of tech devices); *personalized* (providing users the ability to identify the types of news they want, without having to wade through reportage they deem irrelevant); and *participatory* (giving users the ability to respond through comments, blogs, etc.).[44]

Video Games

Video gaming has become mainstream media—and big business. Almost half of all adults play video games, with one in five playing on a daily basis. The universe has broadened considerably over the years, with the profile of gamers reflecting national norms in terms of gender and ethnicity. Younger adults (among whom more than four out of five play) and preadults (better than nine out of ten teens play) are much more likely to actively participate than are Boomers (roughly one-quarter play) and their elders, but the growth of this industry has been remarkable. Americans spend about $20 billion annually on video gaming (including games, equipment, and accessories). In fact, more than twenty million video game consoles have been sold in the United States alone since 2005. It is not unusual for popular video games to sell more than two million copies each.[45]

Expect continued interest in this genre as time rolls on, with Microsoft, Sony, and Nintendo, the big-three gaming companies, continuing to push the limits of computer graphics—and community standards. As the games become more supercharged and violent, expect increased public controversy about the current ratings system, the addictive nature of these games, and the impact of the moral content on players' personal lives.

And don't be surprised if your son or daughter expresses a desire to become a professional gamer. There are now professional competitions run in arenas, where thousands of spectators assemble to watch the best gamers compete head-to-head. With major corporate sponsors climbing on board, live competitions are poised to become a significant entry into the live entertainment world. Some of the events are solo, and others are team contests. Before you snicker, consider this: The field hasn't even revved up to full

More than twenty million video game consoles have been sold in the United States alone since 2005.

bore yet, and already some contestants are making a decent living by playing games. If young athletes can earn tens of millions of dollars playing baseball and basketball, why can't a bunch of competitive gamers make a living showcasing their video game skills?[46]

Mobile phones

While the major mobile providers fight over market share and coverage, the real intrigue concerns the evolving uses of cell phones. With the widespread acceptance of smartphones (more than one-quarter of the population now has one) and the introduction of 3G and 4G units (which a majority now possess), users have a growing bevy of options at their disposal.

The most popular use, of course, is texting, especially among young people. Most Americans own cell phones, but their original use is no longer their most prevalent use. These days, texting is king. Americans send more than seventy-five billion text messages every month. Texting is especially common among young people; the typical teen sends more than three thousand text messages every month, and children twelve or younger send an average of more than one thousand texts every month. Though some studies suggest that the majority of the content is meaningless drivel, texting has become the dominant form of interpersonal communication among people under thirty.[47]

How much do we rely on our mobile phones? Consider this: In the past ten years, we have gone from no households relying solely on a mobile phone to more than one-quarter of all households eliminating their hardwired telephones and using only mobile units. This is partially a financial consideration: Eliminating a hardwired phone saves households an average of more than $400 per year. But it is also a testimony to people's comfort with their handheld units and the services provided through them.[48]

The future will produce an ever-growing percentage of households that go cell-only; a growing proportion of people who shell out the money for unlimited service plans; and increased volume once the new fourth generation (4G) units are widely available—which, among other benefits, will enable people to make free international calls. A mushrooming industry of tech experts creating new applications for smartphones will also flourish as young people create buzz around the latest and greatest apps.

> *Texting has become the dominant form of interpersonal communication among people under thirty.*

New Technologies

As always, the consumer electronics world will be excited by the newest advances in technology. Here are just a few of the advances that will either be introduced or hit critical mass in the coming decade:

- *Touch-screen devices.* Powered by positive experiences with touch screens such as ATMs, airport kiosks, GPS devices, and smartphones, consumers will expect these displays to proliferate—and will expect innovations to enhance the experience they provide.

- *Pico projectors.* These pocket-size, rechargeable projectors give the user the ability to flash six-foot-high images on any available surface—walls, ceilings, bedsheets, whiteboards, etc. This capability will be built into other devices, such as cameras, cell phones, and MP3 players.
- *Gesture commands.* We will be able to change TV channels or shift the location of documents on a computer with hand gestures. This technology, which has been in development for years, is not yet at a stage where it is likely to replace the computer mouse or the TV remote as indispensable interface devices. The video game industry will be the first to bring these devices to market, but expect an avalanche of similar introductions for other media soon thereafter.
- *Internet-connected dashboard computers.* Though recent surveys show that Americans are a bit skeptical about the safety of dashboard devices, the tech industry is now prepared to install computers in front of the front-seat passenger. After the initial resistance dissipates, a greater share of new cars will feature this new form of computing power, enabling passengers to call up directions, send text messages, place phone calls, gather information, and play videos.
- *Disposable computers.* Relying on the cloud or network servers for their computing power, more and more companies (and individuals, eventually) will use cheap, basic computing machines whose primary function is to connect them with application software and stored data that resides elsewhere. Sometimes called "thin clients," these stripped-down units will not have hard drives or other input capabilities. Companies using these machines have thus far found them to be more efficient: Defective units are simply discarded, and new ones are plugged in and working in a matter of minutes.
- *Media tablets.* The trend ignited by the iPad will catch fire

well beyond the hallowed Apple product. Once Apple proves there is sufficient interest in the marketplace, myriad competitors will begin providing and aggressively marketing a wide range of alternative tablets, incorporating innovations and applications now in development. A growing number of schools will expect students to have these flexible and useful devices in the classroom.

Reflections

Several unmet needs will help to further define the direction of the media and entertainment worlds. One of these needs is for new and efficient business models. No matter what dimension of the media world we discuss, the old rules are clearly outdated, and a new set of rules—largely undetermined—is needed to produce order and customer satisfaction, along with a reliable profit stream. This may well be remembered as the decade of the CFOs and business strategists—those who were able to mastermind new structures and methods of satisfying demand while generating a healthy bottom line.

Immediacy is rapidly changing from being a consumer benefit to a customer expectation.

Another pattern is that immediacy is rapidly changing from being a consumer benefit to a customer expectation. The promise of new technologies is to place the world at our fingertips, thus eliminating the time gap between desire and fulfillment. Expect on-demand technologies and processes—whether they provide books, music, or video content—to redefine our schedules, our budgets, our entertainment and information diets, and the identity of the leading media providers of the near future.

And don't overlook the passing of the generational baton. As Boomers nestle into their retirement estates, surrounded by the media with which they are comfortable, it won't take long for their successors—especially the Mosaic and Digital generations—to redirect the flow of the media universe in new and exciting ways. That means more opportunities for user-generated content, a new language about information and media, new chieftains in the media universe, and redefined expectations regarding quality.

It seems inevitable that there will be serious battles over the limitations on speed and capacity in the wireless world. The Internet has now transitioned from a fun and profitable luxury that adds adventure and value to being the heartbeat of our economy and social connections. It is quickly being established as the only indispensable, universal, all-generational technology of choice. Enabling the public to have unlimited, instantaneous, and reliable access to the Internet and all that it harbors will be one of the great challenges in the coming years.

> *Americans are comfortable experiencing reality through their media screens and are now morphing into a "six-screen society."*

Americans are comfortable experiencing reality through their media screens and are now morphing into a "six-screen society," with televisions, computers, mobile phones, and LCD displays at church, at the movies, and on the car dashboard. The newest screen to enter the fray, of course, is in the car—either a GPS screen, an in-dash mobile-phone screen, or a personal computer screen (currently being tested by several automakers). The expansion of our screen addiction reflects the inescapable interconnectedness of modern life—for better or worse.

But amid the discussion about new media tools and technologies and evolving forms of content, we have to ask ourselves what difference it makes being a Christian in a media-saturated world. We can also ask what difference it makes to the future of the world if the love of Christ and the beauty of God's truth are buried in Christian media vehicles that generally do not penetrate the mainstream of society. Having media that primarily, if not exclusively, offer Christian content is fine, and even potentially useful. But if we know that media and technology are what will drive the values, beliefs, relationships, and dreams of society, then isn't the bigger challenge to figure out how to avoid having Christian truth and values marginalized? Should we not instead learn how to pleasingly and powerfully incorporate a biblical worldview and godly leadership into the mainstream of the media universe?

Based on years of surveys examining and analyzing Christians' behavior, it seems that we have largely missed the boat with media use and development. We train relatively few young Christians to make their mark in the secular media world. Many churches and families flat-out discourage their young people from even considering such an option. But in today's marketplace, isn't a first-class media professional with Christian beliefs, ethics, and behavior the ultimate missionary? With American media exported around the world, as well as invading every corner of our lives in this country, wouldn't it be a blessing to have an industry whose creative and productive superstars deftly used media tools as a way not only to do a world-class job of entertaining and informing the public, but also to elevate the moral and ethical standards of society? If all things are possible with God, then it stands to reason that we must be able to shape the moral character of the nation through media and technology without blunting the edge in humor, drama, story-telling, artistic expression, etc.

We train relatively few young Christians to make their mark in the secular media world.

Everyone pretty much knows what Christian leaders oppose in media content, but too few of the Christians they represent back up those statements through their media consumption patterns. Families fail to monitor the content in the movies, TV shows, music, and video games their children absorb—media the parents themselves pay for. Parents tend to have a different standard for the media content they embrace and that which they allow their children to enjoy. The research shows an embarrassing gap between what the Christian public describes as morally acceptable media fare and the media content they personally consume. At some point, we have to abandon the notion that we are not influenced by media content. Let's admit that it makes a big difference in how we perceive the world, the values and beliefs we embrace, the ways we live, and the goals we set for the future. If we do not like the direction the nation is moving, both morally and spiritually, then we must do something about it. The substance of media content is a plausible element to redirect. Yes, prayer is one weapon in the battle to return America to a more godly society, but prayer alone is not enough. God has provided us with more weapons than that, and we should not be reluctant to use them.

As consumers, we have the ultimate sway over what Hollywood, New York, and Silicon Valley produce and distribute.

As consumers, we have the ultimate sway over what Hollywood, New York, and Silicon Valley produce and distribute. Take that authority seriously; make the most of it! Media moguls may not fear Satan, but they do fear you, because you wield what to them is the ultimate weapon: your wallet. Through the way you spend money on media and entertainment options, you control their destiny. If the church would stand up and boldly back its theology with media choices that are consistent with the beliefs we claim to hold, things would change yet again in our society. I'm not suggesting a media boycott strategy, but rather a consistent series of choices, across all media platforms, to send a clear message about what is acceptable and what isn't. It's time we refused to settle for content that is beneath our standards.

We cannot blame "secular media executives" for the mediocre content they serve us or complain that the Internet has become a moral cesspool. Until we exert our influence in terms the world understands, respects, and responds to—specifically, economic and behavioral choices rather than mere verbal jousting—we can expect the media providers to continue to lead the nation down an inglorious path. Until we champion new technologies for the uplifting and positive applications they can introduce into our lives, we will be victims of alternative uses that do little to enhance our lives or advance the Kingdom of God. It's our choice.

CHAPTER 5

AMERICANS' RELIGIOUS BELIEFS

The New Train of Thought

AMERICANS HAVE A passing interest in what other people believe, but we are likely to assert that one's beliefs are a private matter and that our own religious beliefs have a limited influence on our lives. Years of study, however, have shown that this is simply not true: Our most cherished beliefs fit together, usually without much premeditation, into a mental filter that we sometimes refer to as a worldview. That worldview is the lens through which we see our surroundings, and it therefore affects the ways in which we interpret reality and respond to that perceived reality. In other words, actions follow beliefs; we do what we believe. Not only is perception reality, but our perceptions and the worldview they lead to shape our response to reality.

Among the most important beliefs we possess are views about religious matters that help to determine our core values, dominant attitudes, lifestyle choices, self-image, and personal goals. We all have a worldview, even if we are not aware of it. Religious spectives are a crucial foundation in the formation and constant refining of our worldview.

What's Happening with America's Religious Self-Perception

Abraham Lincoln had a great ability to challenge people through clear thinking and the clever turn of a phrase. On one occasion, frustrated that those with whom he was negotiating failed to see conditions as they were, he posed what seemed like a stupid question with an obvious answer: "How many legs does a dog have if we call its tail a leg?" After his companions dismissively pointed out that of course the answer was five, the president made his point: "No, it has four. Calling a tail a leg doesn't make it a leg."

There must be a connection between claiming the name of Jesus and one's lifestyle and choices.

People's self-perception regarding their faith is similar to the dilemma pointed out by Honest Abe. Calling yourself brilliant doesn't mean that you are. In the same way, one might cast a skeptical eye toward those who claim to be Christians. The term, based on being a follower of Jesus Christ, must relate back to what following Jesus means—in other words, there must be a connection between claiming the name and one's lifestyle and choices. Yet it appears that millions of self-described Christians are more like Lincoln's five-legged dog: They embrace the title without backing it up with visible proof of their allegiance.

Throughout the past twenty years, people's general religious self-identification has remained remarkably stable. In 1991, 84 percent of adults in the United States called themselves Christians. In 2010, the number was 85 percent. During the intervening two decades, all kinds of events arose that might have challenged people's willingness to be publicly aligned with the Christian faith—everything from sex scandals among the clergy to proposed shifts in morality (e.g., gay marriage) to "Christian lite" churches. But the survey data demonstrate that most Americans consider themselves Christians, consider the United States a Christian nation, and are cognizant that the Christian faith is taking a beating in the media and in the political sphere—and are uncomfortable with that disrespect toward their chosen faith.

The public is not unaware that things are changing on the spiritual front. We recently learned that half of all adults (50 percent) agree that Christianity is no longer the default faith of most Americans, even though they and their family members continue to embrace it as their own. In that same vein, people are more likely than not to acknowledge that Americans are becoming more hostile and negative toward Christianity (47 percent say we are; 45 percent say we aren't). A significant motivation for that sense of growing hostility is that so many people have had a personally significant negative experience with a Christian church or individual that left them with a negative image of Jesus Christ. In fact, three-quarters of the one out of five Americans who admit to such an experience are self-identified Christians. If you add on the proportion of Americans who are generally dismissive, if not hostile, toward any faith tradition at all, as well as those who believe in a faith other than Christianity, you have one-third of the population that has either theological or emotional issues with the Christian faith.

People are more likely than not to acknowledge that Americans are becoming more hostile and negative toward Christianity.

And yet more than four out of five Americans consider themselves Christians. To understand why that bond is so durable, you have to explore our full slate of religious beliefs more carefully—and understand which of those views are changing.

There are many ways to categorize people spiritually.[1] The most general of those is by creating a Christian/non-Christian dichotomy. But you can get more specific by looking at people's more closely held beliefs, combining both the labels they embrace (Protestant, Catholic, Jew, Hindu, Buddhist, no faith, Mormon, etc.) and their beliefs about the role of Jesus Christ and the Bible in their lives. Based on a national survey we conducted in early 2010 among a representative sample of 2,006 adults, we created the following spiritual map of the public:[2]

- 6 percent are Protestant evangelical Christians[3]
- 26 percent are Protestant, non-evangelical, born-again Christians[4]
- 20 percent are Protestant notional Christians[5]
- Less than one-half of one percent are Catholic evangelical Christians
- 6 percent are Catholic, non-evangelical, born-again Christians
- 15 percent are Catholic notional Christians
- Less than one-half of one percent are nondenominational evangelical Christians
- 6 percent are nondenominational, non-evangelical, born-again Christians
- 5 percent are nondenominational notional Christians
- 10 percent are atheists, agnostics, or people who claim no faith alignment
- 1.5 percent are Mormons
- One percent are Jehovah's Witnesses
- 1.5 percent are Jews
- 1.5 percent are aligned with Eastern faiths (Buddhism, Hinduism, etc.)
- One-half of one percent are Muslims

What do these numbers tell us? About half the country (52 percent) is associated with Protestant Christianity; about one-fifth (21 percent) align with Catholicism; and another one-tenth (11 percent) see themselves as Christians without association with either Catholic or Protestant traditions. One out of every ten adults (10 percent) claims to have no religious faith. Very small numbers are associated with Eastern, pantheistic faiths (less than 2 percent); Judaism (less than 2 percent); faith groups that believe they are Christian but are not accepted by the mainstream Christian body (slightly more than 2 percent); and Islam (about one-half of one percent).

> *One out of every ten adults claims to have no religious faith.*

Broken out differently, the numbers show that about 7 percent of the public can be considered evangelical Christians. Almost two-fifths (38 percent) are born-again but not evangelical Christians, and two-fifths (40 percent) think of themselves as Christians, but their theological views do not place them in the born-again segment. The total proportion of born-again Christians—based on what they believe, rather than what they call themselves—has grown from 32 percent in 1982 to 45 percent in 2010. Interestingly, though the Baptists produce the greatest number of born-again Christians, the denomination that delivers the second-largest number of born-again adults is the Catholic church—a fact that would not have been imaginable a quarter century ago.

The only other faith segment that has shown significant growth during that time is the "none of the above" group: atheists and agnostics. Their numbers have doubled in the last three decades, from 5 percent in 1982 to 10 percent in 2010.

Into this mix, we could throw the notion of being charismatic (or, as described in some circles, Pentecostal). In total, one-quarter of all self-identified Christians also describe themselves as charismatic. Over the past three decades, the big growth in this area has been among Catholics. (Two out of ten Catholics today self-identify as charismatic.) As you might expect, given the foundational theological teachings of charismatic bodies, a larger-than-average share are born again (61 percent). We also found that charismatic Christianity is especially appealing to blacks (30 percent of whom are charismatic) and Hispanics (also 30 percent).

Be careful when reading media reports that describe "born-again" and "evangelical" Christians. First of all, most journalists do not distinguish between those two groups; as far as they're concerned, or based on the research their organizations produce, the terms are interchangeable. A lot of misinformation is tossed about—particularly regarding political influence and preferences—as if it were authoritative, when in fact it is based on superficial labels that do not have the meaning ascribed to them.

Almost all news organizations rely on self-reporting as to whether someone is born again or evangelical.

Second, almost all news organizations rely on self-reporting as to whether someone is born again or evangelical. When The Barna Group asks people in surveys whether they adopt those terms for themselves and then study their beliefs, we find huge differences between their self-reporting and the belief-based categorization used in Barna analyses. For instance, our studies show that 40 percent of adults say they are evangelical. However, more than one-quarter of those individuals (28 percent) do not believe that their eternal salvation is based upon full reliance on the forgiveness of sins by Jesus Christ. In addition, more than three-quarters of those who fit the born-again classification (78 percent) do not meet the other criteria we use to classify evangelicals (such as their beliefs about the Bible, God, Jesus Christ, Satan, and the role of faith in their lives). The so-called evangelicals tracked by the media generally do not buy into the reliability of the Bible, the existence of Satan, the need for God's grace to attain eternal life, or a personal responsibility to share their beliefs with others who believe differently. You can imagine how misleading it is to associate evangelicals as we define them with a faith of that nature. (For a description of how self-reporting evangelicals differ on core beliefs from beliefs-based evangelicals, see the "Faith Segments" section in appendix A.)

A similar gap is revealed when we compare the people who call themselves born again and those who are classified that way according to their beliefs. When we ask people if they consider themselves to be born-again Christians, about 45 percent say they do. But once again, there are massive differences between how people categorize themselves and how their beliefs categorize them. For example, more than one-quarter (28 percent) of those who have a personal commitment to Jesus that is important to them and also believe that their salvation is wholly dependent upon God's forgiveness do not call themselves born again, even when asked to do so. On the other hand, among those who adopt that label, almost one-quarter (23 percent) do not claim the commitment to Christ and full reliance on grace as their means to salvation necessary for being identified as born again. Stated differently, when you read about people who say they are born again according to surveys, many of them probably are not, and many who probably are born again are absent from the analysis. When we examine all of the people who fit at least one of the two ways of categorizing born agains, 42 percent fit one category but not the other. That's a lot of room for misrepresentation.

What does this have to do with making sense of faith in America and where our faith is headed? Very simple: Be careful what you believe about what others believe! Organizations that specialize in political or business research sometimes use shortcuts to estimate the opinions and behavior of segments of the population about which they have limited understanding. But consider this: When we compare self-reported evangelicals and beliefs-based evangelicals on the most basic of political indicators, the differences are huge. At the time of the surveys, self-reported evangelicals were almost evenly split between registered Republicans and Democrats. Beliefs-based evangelicals, however, were two-and-a-half times more likely to be Republicans. Ideologically, self-reported evangelicals were more likely to describe themselves as conservative than liberal by a 5:1 ratio. But among beliefs-based evangelicals, the ratio was 16:1. If we examine the implications of these differences in a real situation—the 2008 presidential election between Barack Obama and John McCain—we can again see the importance. The self-reported evangelical voters preferred Mr. McCain by a sixteen-point difference. However, the beliefs-based evangelical voters favored Mr. McCain by a seventy-point margin. The self-reported born agains supported Mr. Obama by a six-point margin, while the beliefs-based born agains gave Mr. Obama only a two-point margin. You can begin to see how these distinctions can provide completely divergent interpretations or explanations of history.

When we ask people if they consider themselves to be born-again Christians, about 45 percent say they do.

The differences may be difficult for a casual observer to recognize. After all, among American adults, 46 percent are self-reported born agains; 45 percent are beliefs-based born agains; and 40 percent are self-reported evangelicals. Because the percentages are all similar, many people assume they must be measuring the same thing. But as the political example above shows, they don't! Don't let a researcher's or an analyst's lack of experience with the nuances of faith segments lead you astray.

Let's circle back to the original focus of this section: How do people see themselves spiritually? Apart from their labels and whether those characterizations fit snugly, here's another view that people give us of how they're doing spiritually. Nine out of ten adults argue that their faith is very important in their lives (71 percent strongly believe this). More than eight out of ten boast that they are spiritually mature. Half of all Americans—including three-quarters of born agains and nine out of ten evangelicals—contend that their faith has "greatly transformed" their lives. In a way, one gets the sense that most individuals who are pursuing the Christian life believe that they are on track and do not need any significant upgrades to their spiritual regimen.

One of the latest twists on our religious identity is the growing segment who say they are "spiritual but not religious." This characterization has been adopted by about one-quarter of all adults, but it is normative among people under the age of thirty. This concept means different things to different people, but for many it reflects their general indifference toward the usual church programs and events and a distinct distaste for the politics and traditions of the conventional church world. For a generation that esteems relationships, shared experiences, adventure, and tolerance above all else, the restrictions confronted in a conventional church environment are unappealing.

Don't let a researcher's lack of experience with the nuances of faith segments lead you astray.

What's Happening with the Bible

The foundation of what we know and believe about the Christian faith is contained in the Bible. By any measure, Americans love the Bible. Year after year, it is the best-selling book in the country, with an estimated twenty to twenty-five million copies sold each year—which doesn't include more than twice that number distributed free by evangelistic and missions organizations. Although the top ten editions sell more than 90 percent of the total copies in any given year, Americans cannot complain about a lack of access to God's Word. It is ubiquitous. Organizations that publish lists of best-selling books simply leave the Bible off their lists because of its perennial bestseller status.[6]

Bibles come in an amazing variety of styles and formats—more than five hundred translations, versions, and editions are available in English alone. The Bible (or at least a portion of it) has also been translated into more than 2,200 languages and dialects. If you're not a traditional reader, that's not a problem: You can get an audio Bible, video Bible, or digitized Bible (for mobile access)—just about any form, format, color, size, shape, or language you want.[7]

The Bible has been translated into more than 2,200 languages and dialects.

The typical American household owns four Bibles. It is the most widely read book in the country, year after year. And no text comes close to the hallowed view that Americans have toward the Bible: 84 percent consider it a holy or sacred book. For the sake of comparison, just 4 percent accord such status to the Koran. At the same time, nearly half of all adults argue that the Bible, Koran, Book of Mormon, and other holy books essentially communicate the same message using different stories, teachers, and languages. So while the Bible is clearly a popular and revered book, a growing percentage of the population contends that its message is not unique. That view is particularly prevalent among young people.

Just less than half of all adults (45 percent) strongly believe that the Bible is totally accurate in all of the principles it teaches. That sense of reliability has increased by a few percentage points over the past fifteen years, showing the stability of people's notions of the Bible. That consistency may well change within the next two decades, however, as early indicators show that the Mosaic generation is far less likely than the preceding pair of generations to accept the accuracy of biblical principles. Even though the tendency is for young adults to be less accepting of virtually everything related to the Christian faith when they are teens and in their twenties, history shows that they later move closer to the norms of the prior generation. However, the starting point of Mosaics is so distinct from the current views of Busters and Boomers—less than 30 percent of Mosaics firmly state that the Bible is totally accurate in all of the principles it teaches—that we expect to see substantial decreases in the national average regarding people's trust in the Bible. Other groups that are considerably less likely than average to accept the Bible's teaching as accurate are men, Catholics, and people who have a college degree.

One of the ongoing debates in theological circles concerns just how much we can trust the text of the Bible. One measure reveals how people perceive the Bible. Nationally, people are about equally likely to view the Scriptures as the actual Word of God that can be taken literally, word for word (26 percent), and to describe it as the inspired Word of God and agree it has no errors but argue that it cannot be taken literally because some of the content is symbolic (30 percent). Together, nearly six out of ten adults agree that the Bible is accurate and without error. They are joined by almost one-fifth (18 percent) who believe the Bible is the inspired Word of God but that it contains some factual and historical errors. The remaining population is split between saying the Bible is not the inspired Word of God but is simply a narrative of how human writers understood and interpreted the ways and principles of God (11 percent) and those who pass it off as just another book of teachings by men, one that includes stories

Nearly six out of ten adults agree that the Bible is accurate and without error.

and advice (11 percent). These perspectives have not budged in the past decade, but as the Mosaics become a greater share of the adult population, we are likely to see a weakening of a "high view" of Scripture—that is, trusting it to be an accurate representation of God's actual or inspired words for people to follow.

The respect that Americans have for the teachings of the Bible is well reflected by the numbers who believe that the various stories in the Bible actually happened. We quizzed adults about a dozen different Bible passages and asked whether they believed that the event described in that passage actually took place and if it happened as described in the Bible. For the most part, people accept what the Bible says as an accurate depiction of history. Support for these events ranged from a low of half the nation (49 percent, a number that includes non-Christians as well), who believe that Samson lost his strength when Delilah shaved his head, to a high of three-quarters (75 percent), who believe that both the Virgin Birth and Jesus' resurrection from the dead happened.

The information displayed in the accompanying table shows a couple of important patterns. Catholics are quite different from Protestants in their relationship with the Bible. Not only do they read it less often, but they are less likely to embrace its content. Protestants are 48 percent more likely to believe that the Bible is totally accurate in all of the principles it teaches. Protestants are twice as likely to say that the Bible can be taken literally, word for word.

> **Protestants are twice as likely to say that the Bible can be taken literally, word for word.**

Their high view of Scripture gives them greater confidence that the stories contained in the Bible are believable. For instance, in relation to the dozen Bible stories studied, Protestants were twenty percentage points more likely to believe those stories, on average, than were Catholics. The biggest issue for Catholics

Bible story	All Adults	Catholic	Protestant	Born Again	Not Born Again
Jesus Christ was born to a virgin	75%	80%	87%	96%	62%
Jesus was physically crucified and buried and then was raised from the dead	75%	82%	89%	98%	61%
Jesus turned water into wine at the wedding in Cana	69%	68%	80%	94%	49%
Jesus Christ fed 5,000 people with 5 loaves of bread and 2 fish, and had 12 baskets of leftovers	68%	64%	82%	93%	53%
Daniel survived being left in a den with lions	65%	51%	81%	90%	47%
Noah built an ark and survived a flood that wiped out the earth	64%	49%	78%	89%	45%
Moses parted the Red Sea; Israel escaped the Egyptians	64%	60%	79%	90%	48%
God created the universe in six days, as we know them	63%	58%	76%	86%	47%
David killed a giant, Goliath, with just a slingshot and stones	63%	46%	79%	85%	47%
Peter walked on water with Jesus	60%	53%	75%	86%	44%
Satan, disguised as a serpent, tempted Eve in the Garden of Eden	56%	56%	69%	82%	39%
Samson lost his strength when Delilah cut his hair	49%	31%	63%	72%	31%

PERCENTAGE OF ADULTS WHO BELIEVE THESE BIBLE STORIES ARE LITERALLY TRUE

relates to trusting the Old Testament. Of the seven Old Testament stories evaluated, Catholics were twenty-five percentage points less likely than Protestants to accept those narratives as true. In contrast, Catholics were only thirteen percentage points less likely to accept the five New Testament stories as true—still a big gap, but not nearly the chasm found in relation to the Old Testament events.

Take note that the average difference between born-again and non-born-again adult respondents is forty percentage points! For nine of the twelve stories, less than half the non-born-again population believes those stories are true—yet three-quarters of the non-born-again population are people who describe themselves as Christian. In contrast, the least believable story in the eyes of born-again adults—Samson losing his strength when his hair was cut—was considered credible by 72 percent. There was not a single story among the twelve tested that reached that level of credibility in the eyes of the non-born-again segment—not even Christ's resurrection.

Truth is the ultimate question when it comes to the Bible. A related research finding will help us to better understand the struggle that many people have with the Bible. As postmodernism has become the predominant worldview for most Americans under thirty-five—and for a surprisingly large share of those over thirty-five—the idea that absolute moral or spiritual truth exists is widely dismissed. Presently only one-third of the adult public (34 percent) believes that there is any absolute moral truth. Among those who say such truth exists, only 39 percent argue that the primary tangible source of truth for us is the Bible. In other words, among all American adults, just 13 percent believe that absolute moral truth exists and is primarily given to us through the Bible. That number is actually a bit higher than it was a few years ago, but we are on the precipice of seeing it decline once again with the coming of age of the Mosaics. Only 3 percent of Mosaics believe that absolute moral truth exists and comes primarily through the Bible. Even though that number is likely to increase in the next two decades, it is not likely to grow enough to allow the national proportion to remain static.

Our ongoing research regarding worldviews has consistently found that relatively few people have a biblical worldview. Such a broad concept can be measured in myriad ways. Our efforts are undoubtedly incomplete, but they offer an anchored, defined perspective on how Christians incorporate the Bible into their understanding of and response to the world. For survey purposes, we have had to narrow the field of questions to a half dozen—a manageable quantity that can be replicated in various national studies without fatiguing respondents or excluding other questions that place the role of worldview in context. Consequently, we have defined a biblical worldview as one that includes the following six points:

Our ongoing research regarding worldviews has consistently found that relatively few people have a biblical worldview.

- absolute moral truth exists;
- the Bible is totally accurate in all of the principles it teaches;
- Satan is a real being or force, not merely symbolic;
- people cannot earn their way into heaven by trying to be good or by doing good works;
- Jesus Christ lived a sinless life on earth; and
- God is the all-knowing, all-powerful creator of the world and still rules the universe today.

I would be the first to say that a truly biblical worldview would contain much more than this handful of beliefs. At the very least, then, we can agree that our approach undoubtedly overestimates how many people have a robust, Bible-centered view of the world and their role in it.

Even with that caveat in mind, the results we get are discouraging. Overall, just 9 percent of American adults possess such a worldview. While born-again Christians are twice as likely to possess a biblical worldview, that still represents less than one out of every five born-again adults (19 percent). The proportion of all adults who have a biblical worldview (as defined here) has remained relatively consistent over the past fifteen years. Seven percent had such a worldview in 1995, compared to 10 percent in 2000, 11 percent in 2005, and 9 percent in 2010. Even among born-again adults, the statistics have remained flat: 18 percent in 1995, 22 percent in 2000, 21 percent in 2005, and 19 percent in 2010.

The specific components most likely to keep born-again adults from having a biblical worldview are belief in the existence of absolute moral truth (54 percent of born agains dismiss the idea), the existence of Satan (60 percent of born agains are not sold on this), and the belief that it is impossible for people to earn their way into heaven through good behavior (53 percent fail to meet this criterion). These measurements do not bode well, theologically or sociologically, for the future of orthodox Christianity. Indeed, the aggregate statistics are alarming enough, but the fact that less than one percent of adults in the Mosaic generation (i.e., adults born between 1984 and 2002) have even this truncated form of a biblical worldview is truly frightening.

This is not simply a matter of academic speculation. Over the years, we have examined the relationship between worldview and behavior and learned a very powerful insight: People do what they believe. Your worldview, whatever it may be, is your decision-making filter, enabling you to make sense of the complicated array of facts, experiences, relationships, and opportunities you encounter every day. By helping to clarify what you believe to be important, true, and desirable, your worldview dramatically influences your choices in any given situation.

We have uncovered unusually large differences in behavior—based on a person's worldview—related to matters such as media use, profanity, gambling, alcohol use, honesty, civility, and sexual choices. And we have also discovered that a person's worldview is primarily shaped and firmly in place by the time he or she reaches the age of thirteen. Perhaps today's parents are ineffective at raising their children with a biblical worldview because they themselves do not have one. You cannot give what you do not have.

> *By helping to clarify what you believe to be important, true, and desirable, your worldview dramatically influences your choices.*

What's Happening with Beliefs Regarding the Supernatural

When we probe into beliefs regarding supernatural forces, things begin to fall into place.

More than nine out of ten adults believe in some kind of divine being or power. But that does not mean they accept the Christian idea of God as the creator and sustainer of the world. Once again, stability in beliefs has been the norm over the past twenty years. Here is what Americans' belief patterns look like with regard to supernatural beings:

- Seven out of ten adults believe in the biblical concept of God: the all-knowing, all-powerful creator of the universe, who still rules that world today. The other 30 percent—a group that represents almost seventy million adults—is fragmented into six primary camps. One niche, attracting one out of fourteen adults, describes God as the "total realization of all human potential." Another group, roughly the same size, believes that "God" refers to a "state of higher consciousness" that human beings may achieve. One out of twenty adults admit they have no idea who or what God is, or if God even exists (agnostics), while the same number argue that there is no such thing as God. The remaining niches are made up of people who believe that everyone is God (about 3 percent) or that many gods exist, each with a different level or sphere of authority. The people least likely to possess an orthodox, biblical concept of the nature of God are young adults, men, college graduates, and people who are less engaged in the political process (people not registered to vote and independents).

• More than nine out of ten Americans believe that Jesus Christ was a historical figure. Similar numbers believe He was a great teacher. But fewer people believe He was a divine presence on earth. In fact, shockingly close to half of all adults (41 percent) believe that when Jesus was on earth, He sinned. However, Jesus remains the most beloved historical figure we have been able to identify at the same time that many individuals question His deity.

• For a faith built on the notion that we are sinners tempted by God's enemy, Satan, it is perhaps surprising to find that a majority of Americans do not believe that a living entity known as Satan exists. Nearly six out of ten adults (59 percent) suggest that Satan is just a symbol of evil. The types of people most likely to write off Satan's existence are adults who attend mainline Protestant churches and African Americans.

• Like Satan, the Holy Spirit gets little respect from Christians these days (except, notably, in Pentecostal churches). The Holy Spirit is most commonly thought of as a symbol of

God's power or presence, but He is not generally accepted as a living spirit or entity. (Americans struggle with the notion of the Trinity.) A majority of adults (56 percent) contend that the Holy Spirit is merely symbolic. Most significant, even half of born-again adults maintain that view. And one of the most eye-opening realizations is that two-thirds of Catholics (67 percent) deny the existence of the Spirit.

- At the same time, half the public (51 percent) claims to consistently allow the Holy Spirit to guide their lives. How can we reconcile this with their overall dismissal of the Spirit? It may well be that they do not accept the idea of an actual, godly being as much as they embrace the notion that God's Spirit can affect our thinking and feelings. Given their perplexity over the Trinity, many adults seem to accept that God has three unique functions, one of which is to influence people through His presence and nudging. That, it seems, is what people consider to be the Holy Spirit—not a unique (though integrated) person of the Trinity as much as a unique function of God Himself.

- Only one-third of adults (36 percent) are firmly convinced that a person can be under the influence of spiritual forces such as evil spirits or demons. Another one out of five (21 percent) believe that it is possible such forces may exist and hold such influence. In general, we love movies in which such powerful spirit-natured foes are involved, but we consider demons and evil spirits to be akin to comic book villains: powerful and wicked, but not real. Perhaps our steady diet of such movies over the course of time has eroded our sensitivity to the breadth of the supernatural world.

None of these views has changed discernibly in the past twenty years. Americans have placed tight limits on the spiritual world:

We allow for God, but little else. For those who believe that Satan exists and is committed to attacking God through humanity, it is important to recognize that theirs is a minority view in the United States; the notion of continual spiritual warfare between God and Satan, involving people on earth, is not a widely held perspective.

The notion of continual spiritual warfare between God and Satan, involving people on earth, is not a widely held perspective.

What's Happening in People's Relationships with God

One of the most striking results from recent years' surveys has been the finding that four out of five adults agree that "the single most important purpose in life is to love God with all your heart, mind, strength, and soul." Overall, about two-thirds of adults strongly agree with that sentiment, while another one-fifth agree somewhat. This concept receives nearly universal, fervent support from evangelicals and very strong agreement from non-evangelical born-again adults (81 percent) as well. Certainly, Americans buy into the idea; knowing how to actually put it into practice appears to be a challenge that many have not yet mastered.

One way to love God, of course, is to live a life fully committed to Jesus Christ. Again, most Americans would argue that they've already made such a commitment: About seven out of ten adults claim to have made an important commitment to Jesus that is active in their lives. Further, two out of three adults say they have a personal relationship with Jesus and that it is an active influence in their lives. But at the same time, we also found that, among adults who are associated with a Christian church, barely half contend that they are "absolutely committed to the Christian faith." That's quite a drop-off from seven out of ten saying they have made a significant and active commitment to Jesus.

When it comes to Christian commitment, where does the linkage between intellectual assent and actual follow-through break down? Perhaps the first cracks in the armor have to do with a person's willingness to relentlessly side with God in all matters and all situations. For instance, only slightly more than half of all adults—including about six out of ten self-identified Christians, three out of four born-again adults, and more than nine out of ten evangelicals—firmly agreed that life is that black-and-white, that simple. Barely half of all Catholics and mainline Protestants buy this line of reasoning. We live in a complex world, and people are used to juggling mountains of information and behavioral menus packed with options. It's a tough mental adjustment to look at the choices we make and see them as either aligning with God's ways and purposes or with His adversary's. It's especially difficult when we compartmentalize our faith and fail to see its relevance to many, if not most, of the decisions we make.

We live in a complex world, and people are used to juggling mountains of information.

Christian commitment also relates to our perceptions of success. Fewer than one out of three adults concur that success is simply obedience to God—no more, no less. In our achievement-driven society, accepting such a radical idea is, well, radical. Yet, if the ultimate purpose of life is to love God with heart, mind, strength, and soul—as most Americans say—then defining success in terms of our obedience to God's will and principles makes logical sense. But the gap between avowed commitment and actual obedience indicates that half of all adults either do not see the connection or do not want to acknowledge it.

Further evidence of the breakdown between our good intentions and our follow-through comes from research concerning our ideas about the things that give us the greatest pleasure and meaning in life. First, when asked to identify their most fulfilling relationship, not quite one out of five adults listed their connection with God or Jesus Christ as tops. (The winners, by the way, were relationships with family, spouse, and children, which together reflected 71 percent of the relationships mentioned.) Second, when asked to identify the group that is most significant in their lives, slightly less than three out of ten listed their churches. Third, when asked to describe the single most important choice or decision they had ever made in life, a mere one out of six stated that it was their determination to accept Jesus Christ as their Savior. (Placed in context, that constitutes a bit more than one-third of all born-again adults—still a disappointingly low proportion.) Next, only about one-third submit that they consistently and completely cooperate with what they believe God wants them to do. Finally, less than one out of five adults (including only one-quarter of born-again Christians) note that they have made a total commitment to their spiritual development.

We cherish the idea that we are good people and that God wants to bless us.

Nobody wants to be—or even think of being—disloyal to God. We cherish the idea that we are good people and that God wants to bless us. For the most part, Christians believe it is possible to have a relationship with God. But it seems that we still struggle to know exactly how to do that, beyond praying for His blessings, calling ourselves by His name, and associating with people who are also involved in the struggle to make sense of it all. Journalists can pontificate that America is the most religious nation in the world, but the jury is still out as to whether we are truly the most Christian population on the planet today.

What's Happening in Church Life

Studies conducted by Gallup and others a half century or more ago confirm that church involvement was a given in those days. During the tumult of the 1960s, people began to seriously question the value of all institutions and cultural norms, including the value of church life. Americans continue to question the value of many traditional institutions and lifestyle habits, one of which is how best to further their spiritual objectives.

Take a look at the progression of people's commitment:

- Half (54 percent) are "totally committed" to developing a deeper connection with God, no matter what it takes.
- Half (54 percent) firmly assert that their religious faith is becoming more important than ever as a source of objective and reliable moral guidance, with an additional 20 percent leaning in that direction.
- Not quite half (45 percent) strongly affirm that God is moving them and others to remain connected to Him in different ways and through different types of experiences than was true in the past.
- Two-fifths (44 percent) are "completely committed" to personally making the world and people's lives better.
- One-third (34 percent) strongly agree that Christian churches unconditionally accept and love people regardless of their looks or behavior.
- Less than one-fifth (18 percent) believe that belonging to a community of faith is necessary to become a complete and mature person.
- Less than one-fifth (17 percent) believe that their faith in God is meant to be developed primarily through involvement in a local church.

Do you get the drift? Americans are not so much giving up on God as they are wondering about the viability of the channels they have habitually relied upon to advance their relationship with Him. One of the most revealing discoveries from this research is that the same proportions of evangelical, non-evangelical born-again, and non-born-again self-identified Christians believe they are missing out spiritually. That is striking because the typical pattern is for evangelicals to be the group most committed to the spiritual journey, followed at a distance by non-evangelical born-again adults, and distantly trailed by notional Christians. But that's not so in this case.

Even though Protestants exhibit more ardor for spiritual development and engagement than Catholics, both groups possess a nagging sense that they are not making the most of their spiritual potential. The underlying desire to optimize one's spiritual journey is a refreshing sign of spiritual hope and yearning that can lead to a renaissance of Christian life.

Undoubtedly, for some adults, their spiritual quest is fueled by the same hyper-individualism that drives pop culture. But clearly, for many Americans, the thought of continuing with what they've been doing with the hope of different results is not a sane alternative. Rather than accepting that the only way to God is by attending Sunday morning church services and Sunday school classes and by giving their donations to a church for distribution, growing numbers are seeking to connect with and honor God in new, more meaningful ways.

The underlying desire to optimize one's spiritual journey is a refreshing sign of spiritual hope and yearning.

Americans are certainly not anti-God, nor are they antichurch. However, more people have begun to question both the value that conventional church practices add to their lives and the degree of value they can add to the lives of others through those same channels. At the same time that many people are wondering if church life is for them, others are taking matters into their own hands in order to make progress—addressing their frustrations by no longer accepting a predetermined slate of beliefs and activities from institution in which they feel they have no dynamic input. That's how three-quarters of adults (71 percent) now view the situation. In the process, most people admit to being open—one-third (36 percent) strongly so and another one-quarter (28 percent) more timidly so—to experiencing and expressing their faith "in an environment or structure that differs from a typical church." That is why alternative church models—house churches, cyberchurches, marketplace ministries, and all the other new forms described in the previous chapter—are eliciting interest and gaining traction.

Some analysts have concluded that Americans are simply carrying their selfishness and consumer mind-set into the church. But I believe a more accurate perspective is that people have invested in and gotten what they can from the conventional approach to spirituality and are now seeking ways to build on that and go beyond it. In other words, they've had a taste of God, but now they want the whole meal, and they are willing to make some changes to get it. Because many of them do not know what that means, after they explore their options they might return to the safe path of what already exists. American Christians have a poor track record of pushing forward when sacrifice and surrender—of self, resources, and personal dreams—are involved.

What is driving them forward? After all, for years people settled for whatever was available to them through the only game in town: the conventional church. Today, however, the onset of new communications technologies has alerted millions to possibilities they never knew existed. A majority of Americans have a gnawing sense that there is more to the spiritual life than they are experiencing. In fact, almost half of the adult public (45 percent) strongly feels a sense of loss, with another one-quarter (27 percent) in moderate agreement. These people are not rebelling against God; they want *more* of Him. Do they want Him on their terms? Undoubtedly some do, but it seems that most are honestly seeking to figure out the best way to know and enjoy God. The fact that they realize that getting closer to God may require new forms and functions is a healthy sign. Rather than passively accepting what is handed to them, millions of Americans are now seeking to engage in a faith quest at a deeper level.

For years, people settled for whatever was available to them through the only game in town: the conventional church.

There's even a bit of desperation for millions of Americans, as witnessed in that about one-third of regular churchgoers now visit multiple churches—not so much as an exercise in church hopping, but to see if they can find God moving somewhere in their community.

Reflections

This is clearly a time of ferment in American spirituality. Whereas the challenges of the 1960s were reflected in the notion that "God is dead" and in a blatant disrespect for religious tradition, clergy, and ways of thinking, the challenges today are no less intense. And in some ways, the challenges are no different. Young adults, looking for but not finding examples of vibrant Christianity, are questioning the underpinnings of faith itself. Longtime adherents of Christianity are exploring the value of church traditions and assumptions; many are emerging with a desire to discover new habits that facilitate greater peace and spiritual maturity. Clergy, who have been trained to help people through specific procedures and channels, struggle to understand how people can grow close to God outside the boundaries of what church leaders have been trained to offer. Religious institutions, such as denominations and seminaries, are fighting for their survival. Still, they accept incremental changes without seeing or embracing the need for a fundamental rethinking of their purpose and process. As congregants become more aware that they need not be bound to the way things are—most of what we do in conventional church settings is not how the early church did things; instead, it represents preferences and traditions that were added over the past nineteen hundred years—that sense of freedom clashes with the reality of having to both create and sustain something different and more productive.[8]

Young adults, looking for but not finding examples of vibrant Christianity, are questioning the underpinnings of faith itself.

Where will all of this take America spiritually? What will become of the conventional churches that now exist? How will this affect the infrastructure that has been built to support those institutions? These questions, and others like them, are valid and important, though no one has the answers at this stage. We do know this:

- The protectors of the status quo will criticize attempts to reach new levels of spiritual maturity through nonconventional means.
- Spiritual questers will feel uncomfortable as they blaze new trails and encounter unforeseen obstacles.
- Genuine spiritual leaders—people with a calling from and a heart for God and who are dedicated to pursuing a God-given vision—will never have a greater moment of opportunity to bless the nation and advance the Kingdom of God in the United States.
- The media will emphasize idiosyncratic attempts to reshape the religious realm, elevating random examples to the status of trends.
- The organized church at large will undergo a period of instability as new structures and behavioral patterns are tested.

- Many people—perhaps millions—will either stagnate or abandon the journey altogether as they assess the costs and benefits and conclude that they are not making enough progress to justify the resources expended.
- Millions of Americans will tepidly experiment with new faith forms and structures; some will return to what they knew in the past, while others will continue forward with the unique possibilities they have discovered.

Don't assume that this spiritual ferment is all negative. We can expect to see a growing percentage of Americans become born-again Christians. We will also see growing numbers of atheists. It will be a confusing time theologically, but with the continued influx of immigrants from Latin America and the shift of millions of Hispanics from the Catholic church to Protestant churches— and especially to charismatic congregations—the numbers of born-again Christians will grow.

A few more words about the coming theological confusion. The marketplace of spiritual ideas has exploded along with all the recent innovations in communications technology. The advent of postmodernism has actually made it more likely for people to have conversations about matters of faith, even if the postmodernists who proclaim the virtue of tolerance are often decidedly intolerant of conservative Christian beliefs. The coming decade will be a fertile period for reasonable, unemotional dialogue about matters of faith. The emergence of those discussions is healthy for Christianity. We cannot get bent out of shape by the fact that Americans do not automatically accept the doctrines preached by a given church; after all, Protestant Christians themselves cannot agree on what the Bible teaches, which is why we have more than two hundred denominations. Yes, there is a corpus of scriptural truth that we can all embrace, but the best news might be that millions of Americans are now trying to discover for themselves just what that truth is—and how to apply it to their lives. Teaching people how to integrate those newly discovered religious insights will be one of the great challenges of the coming era.

The marketplace of spiritual ideas has exploded along with all the recent innovations in communications technology.

Next Sunday, as you drive through your community, if you observe all the cars in the church parking lots and breathe a sigh of relief, deciding that all is well—you're just fooling yourself. If you are not examining the *why*, *what*, and *how* of your spiritual life, you are in the minority. The cumulative outcome of those ruminations will produce a religious landscape—and even a Christian church—that bears a surprisingly limited resemblance to the church world of 2000.

CHAPTER 6

AMERICA'S RELIGIOUS BEHAVIOR
Practicing What We Think We've Preached

OFTEN THE MOST closely watched signs of religious vitality are matters such as church attendance, Bible reading, and financial giving.
These are certainly useful indicators because behavior is a much
more stable reflection of what we truly value than what we say we
value. Remembering, though, that beliefs stimulate behavior, it is
important to assess both sides of the coin—what we believe and
how we behave—to get a full read of the situation.

But we can build on a simple and profound realization from
the start of our analysis of religious behavior in the United States:
Despite all the agitation about new faith structures and perspectives, the general picture is one of consistency. Let's dig into what
that consistency looks like and where things are headed.

What's Happening Regarding Faith Expression

More and more people are finding new and different ways to experience God and express their faith. Sometimes those expressions are more satisfying than what they had previously experienced. An example is house church participation. One of our studies showed that people attending a house church were significantly more

More and more people are finding new and different ways to experience God and express their faith.

likely to be "completely satisfied" with their experience in each of the four dimensions examined. Two-thirds of house church attendees (68 percent) were "completely satisfied" with the leadership of their church, compared to only half of those attending a conventional church (49 percent). Two-thirds of the house church adherents (66 percent) were "completely satisfied" with the faith commitment of the people involved in their gathering. In contrast, only four out of ten people attending a conventional church (40 percent) were similarly satisfied with the faith commitment of the people in their congregations. Three out of five house church adults (61 percent) were "completely satisfied" with the level of community and personal connectedness they experienced, compared to only two out of five adults involved in a conventional church (41 percent). Finally, a majority of those in house churches (59 percent) said they were "completely satisfied" with the spiritual depth they experienced in their house church setting. In contrast, a minority of the adults involved in a conventional church were "completely satisfied" (46 percent).

This does not mean that house churches are better than conventional churches. It simply suggests that the kind of people who choose a house church over a conventional church are more likely than those who are in conventional churches to feel pleased with their experience. Notice that even a substantial share of house church people—typically about one-third—are not fully satisfied with what they experience in the organic model. Several adages that come to mind seem appropriate reactions to such findings: different strokes for different folks; you can please some of the people some of the time, but you can't please all of the people all of the time; one man's dream is another man's nightmare.

But another bit of well-traveled wisdom also serves us well: The church is a collection of people who are committed to God and each other; it is not simply a collection of people who worship in a given style, receive sermons preached in a particular manner, or attend churches aligned with certain denominations. Jesus died on the cross for everyone who comes to Him humble and broken, ready to be healed by the Great Physician. His sacrifice was not about methods or numbers.

Jesus died on the cross for everyone who comes to Him. His sacrifice was not about methods or numbers.

So how do Americans experience God's presence and express their faith in Him? One of our surveys revealed some of the ways in which people do so in a typical month:

- 56 percent attend a service or event at a conventional Christian church
- 37 percent watch a religious TV show
- 33 percent attend a house church or cell group gathering
- 32 percent listen to a religious radio program
- 21 percent attend a special ministry event such as a concert or a community service activity
- 11 percent spend time on a faith-oriented website
- 9 percent attend a ministry that meets at a place of employment

Still others reported that they interact with God and His people through in-home, family faith experiences; by participating in a live, real-time Internet event; or through gatherings with friends in which they talk about faith matters and engage in other spiritual practices (such as prayer).

Americans are becoming more skilled at distinguishing between being present at a religious event and experiencing a spiritual moment. That distinction is important as it speaks to the difference between being active and being changed by the presence of God or to the gap between attending church and being the living body of Christ.

What's Happening Regarding Church Attendance

The numbers go up, the numbers go down, but adult church attendance statistics tend not to stray much from the average. For the past twenty years, the attendance norm has generally been in the 40 to 45 percent range. For the decade from 2000 to 2009, the average was 43 percent. Add another 5 percent to account for people who participate in a house church rather than a conventional congregation,

Adult church attendance statistics tend not to stray much from the average: 40 to 45 percent.

and we're closing in on half the adult population who claim to be involved in a church gathering on any given weekend.

Measuring church attendance using national surveys has been a common practice undertaken by dozens of national research firms since the beginning of the survey research field back in the 1930s. In recent years, this means of measuring church attendance has become somewhat controversial. Doubting the survey totals, several groups of researchers have conducted studies in which they tried to physically count how many people in some relatively small, isolated communities actually showed up in church on a particular Sunday. Though those efforts have some methodological flaws and limitations, the results—which have usually shown that only about half the proportion claimed in national surveys were physically accounted for in target area churches—have raised questions about the reliability of sample surveys to measure church attendance. Critics of the survey approach suggest that respondents have various reasons for telling researchers they attended a church service even if they did not: the social desirability of being thought of as a churchgoer; they meant to attend or usually attend even though they didn't during the week of the survey; or they believe it is the answer the interviewer wants to hear. Though it is not likely that actual church attendance is only half as much as the survey approach estimates, there is a reasonable probability that some people "misstate" their religious behavior of the weekend in question.[1]

What the surveys do point out is that some types of people are more likely than others to attend church services: Women are more likely than men; upscale people more than downscale; blacks more than whites, Hispanics, or Asians; residents of the South and Midwest more than those of the Northeast and West; married adults more than singles; and political conservatives more than political liberals (by a two-to-one margin).

A different angle on church attendance is to examine those who are often referred to as "unchurched."

A different angle on church attendance is to examine those who are often referred to as "unchurched." In Barna surveys, these are defined as individuals who have not attended a church service or church-related event, other than a special occasion such as a funeral or wedding, in at least six months. About three out of ten adults do not attend any church activities, including services, within a consecutive six-month period. That translates to nearly sixty-five million adults. When children under the age of eighteen who live with them are added to the picture, the number swells to more than one hundred million people.

The total proportion of unchurched adults has hovered in the 28 to 34 percent range for the past fifteen years. One of the biggest surprises to some people, however, is that a large majority of the nation's unchurched population is drawn from the sector comprised of people who consider themselves Christians. Among unchurched adults, self-identified Christians outnumber those who do not embrace Christianity by a 3:2 margin (61 percent vs. 39 percent).

Some of the traditional measures of church health are outdated and need to be refreshed.

With Americans pursuing a growing number of church options, some of the traditional measures of church health are outdated and need to be refreshed. New forms of faith community and experience, such as house churches, marketplace ministries, and cyberchurches, must be taken into account. People who engage in these new forms of ministry should not be counted as unchurched, although according to the standard definition that's where they fit. Further, millions of people are now involved in multiple faith communities—for instance, attending a conventional church one week, a house church the next, and interacting with an online faith community in between—which has rendered standard measures of "churched" and "unchurched" less useful. (If you want to get really radical, the New Testament definition of "church" has nothing to do with attending services or being present in the buildings of a religious organization; it's about multiple people of like mind and passion coming together to worship God, grow in their faith, serve community needs in tandem, and enjoy each other's company. Calculating statistics for those types of gatherings would really introduce chaos and controversy into the present measuring process.)

Instead, if we examine participation in widely accepted forms of faith communities by exploring the types of corporate faith engagement that people practice, more insightful results emerge. Toward that end, we might look at the church world this way:

- *Unattached.* These are people who had attended neither a conventional church nor an organic faith community (house church, simple church, intentional community) during the past year. Some of them use religious media to provide a "church experience," but they've had no personal interaction with a regularly convened, face-to-face faith community. This segment represents one out of four adults (23 percent) in America. About one-third of the segment is made up of people who have never attended a church at any time in their lives.
- *Intermittents.* These adults are essentially "under-churched"— that is, people who had participated in either a conventional church or an organic faith community within the past year, but not during the past month. Such people constitute about one out of seven adults (15 percent). About two-thirds of this group had attended at least one church event at some time within the past six months.
- *Homebodies.* This group is made up of people who had not attended a conventional church during the past month, but had attended a meeting of a house church (3 percent).
- *Blenders.* Some adults attend both a conventional church and a house church during a given month. Most of these people attend a conventional church as their primary church, but many are experimenting with new forms of faith community in hopes of finding a more fulfilling experience. We

also found some adults who plan to continue attending both forms because each community meets different needs and provides different opportunities. In total, Blenders represent 3 percent of the adult population.

- *Conventionals.* These adults attended a conventional church (a congregational-style, local church) during the past month, but had not attended a house church. Almost three out of five adults (56 percent) fit this description. This participation includes attending any of a wide variety of conventional-church events, such as weekend services, midweek services, special events, or church-based classes.

Looking down the road, we can expect to see the fastest growth in the Homebody and Blender niches; moderate growth in the Intermittent and Unattached segments; and rather significant decline in numbers for the Conventional category.

These five slices of church experience give us a better handle on how the corporate expression of faith fits into people's lives. But getting a full grip is even more complex than implementing the five-part segmentation metric. There is a growing degree of ministry crossover in America, with more than one out of five adults involved in two or more types of churches in a typical month: a conventional church, a house church, a marketplace church, a real-time ministry event on the Internet, or a live ministry event in the community. That produces a variety of crossover segments:

- Among adults who were churched (either conventionally or alternatively), 15 percent had experienced the presence of God or expressed their faith in God through a faith-oriented website within the past month. Half as many (7 percent) said they had such an experience through a real-time event on the Internet.

- One out of eight churched adults (13 percent) said they had experienced the presence of God or expressed their faith in God through a ministry that met in the marketplace (e.g., their workplace, athletic event, etc.).
- Twice as many churched people (28 percent) said they had experienced the presence of God or expressed their faith in God through their involvement with a special ministry event (such as a worship concert or community service activity).
- A majority of churched adults said they had experienced the presence of God or expressed their faith in God through some form of interaction with religious television or radio programs.

Understanding the churched population is tough enough, but seeking to lovingly move the Unattached segment into the ranks of the Homebodies, Blenders, or Conventionals is no simple task. Keep in mind that most of the Unattached are spiritually inclined but have lost interest in the conventional church experience. (They know what they're talking about, too: More than three-quarters used to be consistent church attenders.) Six out of ten Unattached adults (59 percent) consider themselves to be Christians. Even more surprising was the revelation that 17 percent of Unattached adults are born-again Christians—people who have made a personal commitment to Jesus Christ that is very important in their lives and who believe that they will experience heaven after they die because they have confessed their sins and accepted Christ as their Savior. And even though you won't find them in the sanctuary of a local church, they often engage in traditional faith activities during a typical week. For instance, one-fifth

Even more surprising was the revelation that 17 percent of Unattached adults are born-again Christians.

(19 percent) read the Bible and three out of five (62 percent) pray to God.

What distinguishes the Unattached from regular churchgoers? Here are some characteristics that might help you discover how to relate to them more appropriately. They are:

- more likely to feel stressed out
- less likely to be concerned about the moral condition of the nation
- much less likely to believe they are making a positive difference in the world
- less optimistic about the future
- far less likely to believe that the Bible is totally accurate in its principles
- substantially more likely to believe that Satan and the Holy Spirit are symbolic figures rather than real
- more likely to believe that Jesus Christ sinned while He was on earth
- much more likely to believe that the holy literature of the major faiths all teach the same principles, even though they use different stories
- less likely to believe that a person can be under demonic influence
- more likely to describe their sociopolitical views as "mostly liberal" than as "mostly conservative"

In general, our research discovered that Unattached adults tend to be relatively isolated from the mainstream of society, noncommittal in institutional and personal relationships, and typically happy with their independence. Motivating them to make a commitment to a group of people who are focused on something they have shown a limited interest in—spiritual development and the worship of God—is a titanic challenge. The best strategy for getting them to examine and attach to a church is to have someone they know and trust invite them to engage with the faith community in a purposeful way. This often means initiating a first connection other than attending a worship service and trying to ensure that the event will address one of the issues or needs they are struggling with at that moment. It also helps if the person who invites them accompanies them to the church activity. If the guest attends, the next critical component of the process is a personal and sensitive follow-up. The mind-set of the believer must not be one of trying to "convert a sinner," but of being used by God to bless that person in whatever ways emerge.

What's Happening in Faith Education

For decades, Sunday school was the main avenue through which churches taught people about the Christian faith. Today, roughly one out of five adults claims to attend a Sunday school or Christian education class at a church on any given weekend. That proportion has remained surprisingly stable during the past twenty years. And, of course, Sunday school has been the primary connection that the conventional church has with children until they reach adulthood.

A new model of instruction has emerged, recasting the most common form of Christian education or discipleship training.

During the past decade, however, a new model of instruction has emerged, recasting the most common form of Christian education or discipleship training. The emerging trend in Christian education is the small-group ministry. Moving people off campus into informal groups that usually meet in someone's home to study, pray, and interact has been one of the biggest efforts of Protestant churches over the past twenty-five years. In many churches, small groups represent the dominant form of discipleship training. With house churches and other organic formats growing in popularity, conventional churches have not only increased their efforts to shore up their small-group ministries, but many are co-opting the language of the house church world as well. It is becoming less common to hear the off-campus, church-organized groups referred to as cell groups, Bible study groups, or even small groups. More churches are labeling them home groups, house churches, community groups, neighborhood churches, or home fellowships. Regardless of the name, close to one-quarter of adults are currently involved in such an assembly. The percentage of adults engaged in small groups has risen over the past fifteen years by about five percentage points—not a huge increase, but enough to be numerically and culturally significant and to equal if not surpass the number of adults involved in Sunday school.

One of the benefits of small groups appears to be the ability to get men involved.

One of the benefits of small groups appears to be the ability to get men involved. Because men are less likely than women to attend Sunday church services, they are therefore unlikely to be present for on-site Christian education experiences as well. Women are more likely than men to participate in small groups, too, but the gap is smaller, suggesting that many married men are more likely to accompany their wives to a less formal setting for some religious input.

One of the surprises related to small groups is that they do not attract more young adults. Given the penchant of the younger crowd for informal get-togethers in a casual atmosphere and their love of debate and spiritual discussions, many churches had anticipated a greater influx of the under-thirty population into small groups. However, younger adults have been consistently less likely to participate than older adults.

Perhaps the single most unexpected pattern has been the consistently high rate of involvement among black adults. From 2000 to 2010, the African American population has been 70 percent more likely than the national average to attend a small group during a given week.

What's Happening in Giving

One of the continuing controversies in Christian circles is whether or not modern-day Christians are called to tithe. Nobody disputes the idea that the Bible exhorts Christians to be generous and to practice the principles of good stewardship, but many people note that neither Jesus nor His followers harped on the "10 percent rule" in the same way that the Jews accepted the tithe as an indisputable expectation prior to the arrival of Jesus on the scene.

In the Old Testament, tithing emerges as one of the practices that God commanded of Israel. Literally meaning "one-tenth" or "the tenth part," the tithe originated as a tax that the Israelites paid from the produce of the land to support the priestly tribe (the Levites), fund Jewish religious festivals, and help the poor. The ministry of Jesus Christ, however, brought an end to strict adherence to many of the ceremonial codes that were fundamental to the Jewish faith. Tithing was among the casualties. Since the first century, Christians have believed in generous giving, but without an obligation to contribute a specific percentage of their income. There are, however, some sects in the Christian community that teach tithing as a standard expectation, and it is a widespread practice

Nobody disputes the idea that the Bible exhorts Christians to be generous and to practice the principles of good stewardship.

to encourage people attending church services to give the church their "tithes and offerings" when the offering bucket is passed through the congregation.

Frankly, this is another area in which the debate is moot. There is no doubt that, on the whole, American Christians are exceedingly blessed financially. Most adults (around 60 percent) respond to that blessedness by donating some money to a church during the course of a year. The number of people who give back something to a church is not what it should be, but that's not the most glaring statistic. What stands out—and causes the most consternation among church leaders—is the paltry amount of money that most Christians contribute.

Adults who call themselves Christian give away less than 3 percent of their total, pretax income to churches.

On average, adults who call themselves Christian give away less than 3 percent of their total, pretax income to churches and all other nonprofit organizations. Within that total, less than 2 percent of their aggregate income is contributed to churches. For those who give, the median dollars donated per year hovers in the hundred-dollar range. (*Median* means that as many people give *less* than that amount as give more.) Stated differently, half of all adults give less than $100 a year to churches. The mean amount of giving, which takes into account the large sums that are outliers on the curve, is closer to $900 per year. In a nation where the typical churchgoing household makes more than $50,000 per year, averaging less than $1,000 in contributions is embarrassing.

By far the most generous donors are evangelicals. At no time during the past fifteen years have less than 95 percent of evangelicals given money to churches. About four out of five donate a mean of at least $1,000 annually. That's more than triple the national average of donors who give at that level. The research also shows that Protestants give substantially more than Catholics (usually 75 to 100 percent more), though Catholics give smaller amounts more frequently.

The notion of tithing, though, has not made much of a dent among Christian adults.[2] The percentage who tithe has stayed constant since the turn of the decade, falling in the 5 to 7 percent range. A Barna tracking survey reported that the proportion of adults who tithed was 5 percent in 2007; 7 percent in 2006 and 2005; 5 percent in 2004 and 2003; 6 percent in 2002; and 5 percent in 2001.

Among all born-again adults, 9 percent contributed one-tenth or more of their income, which is consistent with the decadal average for born-again adults who tithed. We also found that Protestants are about four times more likely than Catholics to tithe (8 percent vs. 2 percent).

Giving has been affected by the recession, but tithing patterns remained relatively consistent.

In the most recent half decade, giving has been affected by the recession, but tithing patterns remained relatively consistent. Hands down, the most generous segment is evangelicals, and that is seen not only in the aggregate amount of dollars they give to churches, but also through their status as the population segment most likely to tithe. (The percentage of evangelicals who tithe is generally three to four times the national average.) Other groups that have a much higher percentage of tithers when compared to the national average are political conservatives; people who had prayed, read the Bible, *and* attended a church service during a typical week; charismatic or Pentecostal Christians; and registered Republicans— all segments that typically have at least twice as many tithers as the U.S. norm. At the other end of the generosity continuum are several groups that stand out for being the least likely to tithe: people under the age of twenty-five, atheists and agnostics, single adults who have never been married, liberals, and downscale adults. On average, over the past decade, one percent or less of the people in each of those segments tithed in any given year.

Another way that people give is by volunteering their time and skills. Our tracking of volunteerism in the church suggests that the Pareto principle holds true: 80 percent of the work is accomplished by 20 percent of the workers. About three out of ten adults contribute their time and talent to a church during a given week. (Protestants are nearly twice as likely as Catholics to do so.) This is one of the few religious behaviors in which men nearly keep pace with women. Over the last twenty years, the percentage of people surrendering their free time to serve has remained pretty stable.

Some Christians fail to help out because they feel they have nothing special to offer the cause.

If it seems strange that more Christians do not embrace Jesus' mandate that they become servants, we have found that some Christians fail to help out because they feel they have nothing special to offer the cause. Even though the Bible teaches that all followers of Christ are given supernatural abilities by God to serve Him better—abilities known as spiritual gifts—a large share of the Christian public (32 percent) remains either unaware of the existence of these capabilities or aware of the gifts but not cognizant of which ones they possess. Surprisingly, fewer Christians today are aware of the existence of spiritual gifts (68 percent) than was true ten or even fifteen years ago (72 percent and 71 percent, respectively). And even among self-identified Christians who claimed to have heard of spiritual gifts, a majority are unable to identify any gift they believe they have been given.

Among those who took a stab at describing their gifts, the most frequently mentioned were teaching (9 percent), service (8 percent), and faith (7 percent), followed by encouragement

(4 percent), healing (4 percent), knowledge (4 percent), and tongues (3 percent). The gift of leadership was mentioned by just 2 percent.

The differences in the answers provided by evangelicals, non-evangelical born agains, and notional Christians are noteworthy. Evangelicals were the most likely to claim the gifts of teaching (28 percent), service (12 percent), encouragement (10 percent), and administration (7 percent). One of the reasons evangelicals may seem so verbal about their faith and faith-driven con-victions is that so many of them believe

Non-evangelical born-again adults were the most likely to claim the gifts of faith and hospitality.

they are spiritually gifted in the realm of giving verbal guidance (teaching and encouragement). Similarly, evangelicals were far more likely to claim the gifts of administration and service, which reflects the widely cited tendency of the group to be well organized and to be generous in donating their time and energy to causes they deem worthy.

Non-evangelical born-again adults were the most likely to claim the gifts of faith (10 percent) and hospitality (3 percent). Notional Christians were most notable for having the largest percentage who said they had no gift at all (37 percent, compared to 16 percent of evangelicals and 24 percent of non-evangelical born agains).

Over the past fifteen years, the profile of who has which gift has changed a bit. For instance, the percentage who claim to have the gift of encouragement has grown slowly but steadily from 2 percent in 1995 to 6 percent today. During that period, the proportion of born-again adults claiming the gift of evangelism dropped from 4 percent to one percent. Those who are aware of spiritual gifts but cannot identify their own have risen from 8 percent to 13 percent in the past decade.

A specific set of gifts, commonly described as the charismatic gifts, are widely claimed. In total, one out of eight Christian adults said they have one or more of those gifts (healing, interpretation, knowledge, miracles, prophecy, tongues). The people most likely to say they have a charismatic gift are women (twice as likely as men); people without any college education; born-again Christians; and people forty-five or older. Intriguingly, though 13 percent say they have one or more charismatic gifts, the survey revealed that roughly twice that number of Christians describe themselves as charismatic. It may be that those who cannot identify such a gift in their own lives nevertheless acknowledge that such gifts are operative and powerful in the church today, even if God has not (yet) entrusted them with one.

One of the saddest outcomes from our research on spiritual gifts—but sometimes one of the more humorous—relates to the gifts that people claim to have, but which are not among the spiritual gifts God has delivered to advance His Kingdom. (Listings of spiritual gifts appear in Romans 12:6-8; 1 Corinthians 12:7-11, 28-31; Ephesians 4:7-13; and 1 Peter 4:10-11.) Included among the numerous "supernatural abilities" not found in the Bible are the gifts of compromise, clairvoyance, premonition, a sense of humor, singing, health, life, happiness, a job, and a house. Overall, one-fifth of all gifts cited by respondents (21 percent) were attributes not found in the biblical lists of spiritual gifts.

One-fifth of all gifts cited by respondents were attributes not found in the biblical lists of spiritual gifts.

This lack of understanding about how God has prepared us to serve effectively is not a pretty picture. Between those who do not know their gifts (15 percent), those who say they don't have one (28 percent), and those who claim gifts that are not biblical (20 percent), nearly two-thirds of self-identified Christians who claim to have heard about spiritual gifts have not been able to accurately apply to their lives whatever they have heard or what the Bible teaches on the subject.

One cannot help but wonder if the reduction in interpersonal evangelism is at least partially attributable to the fact that only one percent of Christian adults (self-described or born again) claim the gift of evangelism. Though the Bible never suggests that one must possess this gift in order to share the gospel, the tiny proportion of believers who self-identify with the gift reflects the stalled growth of the Christian church in America.

What's Happening in Personal Spiritual Practices

Perhaps the most closely watched personal spiritual practice is Bible reading. Over the last two decades, we have also found that this is one of the most volatile behaviors to track. Back in the early 1990s, more than four out of ten adults read the Bible in a typical week. Bible reading then went into a mild decline, bottoming out at 31 percent in 1995 before beginning a slow, jagged return to the mid-forties by 2004. From 2004 through 2010, about 44 percent of the public claimed to have read the Bible during the week prior to their interview, other than when they were at church or some other religious event.

There are some consistent patterns related to Bible reading. The older a person is, the more likely he or she is to read the Bible regularly. Women are more likely than men. Adults who attend a Protestant church are about twice as likely as Catholics to read the Bible during the week. Blacks are far more likely than other ethnic or racial segments to do so. About nine out of ten evangelicals and two-thirds of all born-again adults read the Bible during the week.

The older a person is, the more likely he or she is to read the Bible regularly.

Prayer is another personal spiritual discipline that gets a lot of attention. Slightly more than four out of five Americans pray during a typical week. In fact, the only population subgroup, among the sixty-plus that we regularly analyze, from which an average of seven out of ten people do not regularly pray are atheists and agnostics. Even the most spiritually disenfranchised groups—including political liberals, adults not registered to vote, and Mosaics—generally register at least seven out of ten who pray during the week. Praying is almost a given among evangelicals, born-again believers, African Americans, and adults who attend non-mainline Protestant churches; in each case, more than 95 percent of the segment pray each week.

The most fervent evangelizers are evangelicals and individuals who are most active in their faith.

One of the hallmarks of evangelical and born-again Christians is their penchant for sharing their faith with others who believe differently. Within that population, a majority try to explain their religious beliefs to others at least once during the course of a year for the purpose of getting the other person to accept Jesus Christ as Savior. Evangelism has waned a bit since the onset of the recession, dropping from six out of ten born agains spreading the gospel between 1991 and 2007 to about five out of ten since then.

The most fervent evangelizers are evangelicals (three-quarters of whom usually share their faith during a typical year) and individuals who are most active in their faith (70 percent or more of those who usually attend church services, read the Bible, and pray during a typical week). The segment of the "saved" community who are least likely to tell others about saving faith through Jesus is mainline Protestants (only about four out of ten share their faith during a typical year). A group that has become more active in evangelism over the past decade is Catholics. Though proselytism is not native to American Catholicism, the many changes that have altered the demographics of the Catholic community are making gospel outreach a more natural, if not yet widespread, practice in that tradition.

Reflections

To the chagrin of some religious leaders, we are in an era of religious and spiritual experimentation in which traditional expectations are widely disregarded. Fortunately, the motivation for people's spiritual exploration is most often a genuine, sometimes desperate, desire to connect more deeply with God. Our surveys indicate that traditions and mores cultivated by core institutions such as churches and families have made the exploration process uncomfortable and inefficient for millions of well-intentioned Americans. Some of the manifestations of this spiritual adventurousness—church hopping, testing new church models, recalibrating the balance between "inreach" and outreach—have stirred healthy, if sometimes heated, controversy. It's all part of the growth process.

> *The motivation for people's spiritual exploration is most often a genuine desire to connect more deeply with God.*

In the midst of such upheaval, trend research identifies some population segments that are experiencing greater success than others at integrating meaningful faith practices into their lives. For instance, women are more active than men in many faith dimensions, such as church attendance, Bible reading, immersion in Christian education, and prayer.

Why?

Similarly, blacks are more likely than whites to engage in virtually every faith behavior we track.

Why?

What can be learned from such trendsetting groups about

making faith practical, appealing, and helpful? Surely there are clues we can pick up and apply to help satisfy the spiritual needs and desires of people who are not as bonded to God as they could be—or want to be, in many cases. If nothing else, the gap in involvement between one group and another should prompt us to continue to explore new formats and relationships that might reveal new ways to enable people to enjoy a more robust relationship with God.

The United States will always be a significant mission field. As long as we have young children within our borders, they will represent the most important focus of our spiritual development efforts. But in addition to our youngsters, there are clearly tens of millions of adults—tens of millions!—whose need for God is urgent, perhaps more urgent than we even realize. We cannot be distracted by secondary objectives. Fretting about church attendance is a secondary objective; enabling people to worship, understand, love, serve, and obey God is our primary aim. Do we worry too much about planting new churches for the sake of filling auditoriums and pointing with satisfaction to growth statistics? Are we too focused on pioneering new models—and their uniqueness or popularity—to worry about their true spiritual impact?

Enabling people to worship, understand, love, serve, and obey God is our primary aim.

In the end, head-count statistics are useful for identifying numerical growth and noteworthy change, and they can point out certain problems, but they are not as helpful in fixing the problems. That's because the only real solutions are personal, one-on-one solutions—that is, one individual demonstrating the care and love of Christ to another individual. We don't shape an entire culture in one fell swoop; we influence one life at a time, and through the cumulative impact of that influence, we begin to alter society.

As you consider the religious behavior patterns outlined in this chapter, don't get caught up in attendance statistics or tithing percentages. Those figures merely reflect a larger, more important issue: where people's hearts reside today. Look at the picture that emerges from the numbers and get a sense of just how healthy the body of Christ is and what could be done to usher those outside the church into it. The game is not won or lost on the basis of attendance figures or classroom seats filled, but on the basis of how the experiences derived in those places and through those events move people's minds and hearts closer to God. Don't confuse the means with the ends; don't mistake activity for significance; don't misconstrue big numbers to imply success; and don't expect perfection when progress is the best we can hope for.

CHAPTER 7

INSTITUTIONAL FAITH

The New Face and Emerging Emphases of Organized Religion

ORGANIZED RELIGION IN America is a huge domain. There are an estimated 340,000 Christian churches in the country (about 320,000 Protestant and 20,000 Catholic), plus another 15,000 to 20,000 other religious centers—churches, mosques, synagogues, temples, meeting rooms—for non-Christian faiths. Together they raise somewhere in the neighborhood of $65 billion every year. That's a pretty serious neighborhood.

Times are certainly changing, but Christianity remains the dominant faith in the United States. Presently, 83 percent of adults consider themselves Christians or affiliated with a Christian faith group. One of the most dramatic shifts in the religious world of late has been the emergence of the "none" category as the second-largest faith group. Atheists, agnostics, and "undecideds" now constitute 11 percent of the national adult population—and an even higher proportion among teenagers. Other groups of noteworthy size include the Church of Jesus Christ of Latter-day Saints (LDS), most commonly known as Mormons (2 percent of the adult population, and sometimes included within the Christian category, depending on one's theological bent); Jews (about 1.5 percent); pantheists (i.e., adherents of Eastern religions such as Buddhism, Hinduism, and Confucianism, also roughly 1.5 percent); and Muslims (not quite one-half of one percent). Other faith groups together make up the remaining one-half of one percent.

The proportion of adults who label themselves as Christians has remained surprisingly steady over the past thirty years.

The size of these groups changes every day. In general, the proportion of adults who label themselves as Christians has remained surprisingly steady over the past thirty years. The group that is growing the fastest in terms of total numbers of new adherents is the "none" segment. The Mormons have remained relatively static in this country, recruiting many new adherents each year but losing an equal number to balance it out. (The LDS church fares much better overseas, where the bulk of its membership now resides, even though it is the largest faith that is native to the United States.) In terms of raw numbers of new adherents, Islam and pantheism are growing, but slowly. Judaism is declining slowly.

Christian churches are divided into the Roman Catholic church and Protestant denominations. There is some disagreement about the number of Protestant denominations, with estimates ranging from about 200 to as many as 6,222, according to one internationally known researcher. It all depends on how one defines and measures them. Our best estimate is about 220 denominations, which range in size from a handful of member churches with just a few hundred people to the Southern Baptist Convention, which has more than forty-two thousand member churches and claims more than sixteen million members. All the Protestant denominations combined attract an estimated 140 million people. For comparison's sake, there are nearly twenty thousand Roman Catholic churches with approximately sixty-seven million members cumulatively.

These numbers are a bit of an apples and oranges comparison, however, because some of the figures refer to membership and others refer to attendance; some of the statistics include children and some don't. One of the first lessons I learned when I dove into the religious research realm is that the same fierce independence that originally caused the Protestant universe to branch into hundreds of distinct groups precludes them from using the same measures, taking measurements at the same time, or reporting their findings in a uniform way. We must always look carefully at religious data so we have a clear idea of what we're analyzing.

It's tough enough for Christian churches to foster loyalty to Jesus Christ, much less to a man-made entity.

Despite the measurement issues, the differences in approach taken by denominations cannot mask an important trend that has been in full force for three decades: Most people no longer *join* a church or denomination. As hard as religious groups have tried to retain the loyalty that comes with membership status, Americans abandoned the idea of loyalty to organizations long ago. It's tough enough for Christian churches to foster loyalty to Jesus Christ, much less to a man-made entity such as a denomination or even a local church. Thus, another warning: For better or worse, "membership" is a rather meaningless statistic in the religious world today.

Looking at affiliation patterns, massive changes have occurred in the past fifty years. In 1960, three-quarters of Americans labeled themselves Protestant, about one-quarter were Catholic, and very few either were associated with another faith group or remained unattached. Today, only about 61 percent claim to be Protestant, about 21 percent associate with Catholicism, 11 percent have no religious affiliation or leaning, and the remaining 7 percent or so are part of some other faith group. Religious affiliation was once unshakable. The Baby Boomers came along and changed that thinking, igniting dozens of new denominations and tens of thousands of new, more contemporary churches. Today's two youngest adult generations (the Busters and Mosaics) are following in their footsteps, questioning the value of any religious affiliation and any long-term relationship with a religious group.

If we measure churches by adult attendance, a number of patterns arise. Six of the oldest Protestant churches—American Baptist Church, USA; United Church of Christ; Episcopal Church; Evangelical Lutheran Church in America; United Methodist Church; and Presbyterian Church in the USA—form what is commonly referred to as the mainline churches. Up until the 1960s, they represented the heartbeat of American Christianity. Today, the mainline has been renamed by some the "sideline" as they continue to stagger from steady losses in membership, attendance, income, and churches per capita.

The greatest energy in the Protestant world today is associated with the evangelical and Pentecostal churches.

The greatest energy in the Protestant world today is associated with the evangelical and Pentecostal churches. The largest brands under that umbrella include the Southern Baptist Convention, Assemblies of God, and a few African American groups, such as the Church of God in Christ (COGIC), National Baptist Convention, and African Methodist Episcopal Church (AME). One of the fastest-growing segments of the Protestant community continues to be nondenominational and independent churches.

Who goes where? When you ask people to identify the denomi-national affiliation of the church they usually attend—in other words, not where they have official member status, or what label they prefer for image or discussion purposes—we find that among adults who consider themselves to be Christian and attend a church, 26 percent attend a Catholic church, 24 percent are part of a main-line congregation, and half (50 percent) connect with a Protestant church not associated with the mainline groups. If we slice the pie differently and include all non-Christian people in the mix, we dis-cover that one out of five adults affiliate with the Catholic Church (21 percent), another one out of five with a mainline church (20 percent), slightly less than one out of five with a non-Christian church or no religious group at all (18 percent), and the other two out of five align with a non-mainline Protestant body (41 percent).

Divided Loyalty

Americans have become church shoppers. It is increasingly com-mon for people to shop and hop—to attend a particular church for a while and then switch allegiance to another church that they believe will better meet their needs. Pew Research Center conducted a study on how many people had left the denomination in which they were raised and reported that almost half of all adults (44 percent) had switched. The Roman Catholic Church was the biggest loser, with almost 10 percent of all adults in the nation having formerly affili-ated with that denomination. Perhaps the magnitude of that loss has seemed less staggering because immigration has enabled the Catholic body to remain robust—in fact, it is one of the relatively few expanding bodies in the United States. The influx of immigrants from Latin American countries has not only increased the size of the American Catholic population, but has also pushed the average age of those who attend those churches below thirty, making it the only church of substantial size to have an age norm that reflects so many young people.[1]

That same study pointed out that Hindus enjoy the highest retention rate of all faith groups in America, keeping 84 percent of their adherents from childhood

Hindus enjoy the highest retention rate of all faith groups in America, keeping 84 percent of their adherents.

through adulthood. Other religious groups with comparatively high retention rates include Jews (76 percent), Orthodox Christians (73 percent), Mormons (70 percent), and Catholics (68 percent). Among the groups with the lowest retention rates are Jehovah's Witnesses (37 percent), several mainline Protestant denominations (including Methodists, Presbyterians, Episcopalians, and Congregationalists) that maintained less than half of their children through adulthood, and nondenominational Protestant churches (only a 44 percent retention rate, partially attributable to mobility).[2]

Why is there such fluidity among religious traditions? Our studies have shown a variety of factors, including household mobility (during the past twenty years, from 10 to 18 percent of households moved during a given year, necessitating movement between churches), marriage (more than one-third of people have married outside their religious tradition and converted to share their spouse's tradition), and changes in personal religious views.

Another important factor is people's confidence in the leaders of the faith tradition in which they were reared. Over the past fifty years, a lot of news has come forth about various faith traditions and denominations, some of it good and some not so good. The image of each group has been partially shaped by such news. The Gallup Organization has tracked people's confidence in various faith groups for more than six decades. Its most recent studies indicate that people's overall confidence in churches and clergy has lately

dropped to historic lows. Currently, only about half of the population gives clergy high marks for their honesty and ethical behavior,
down from two-thirds just twenty-five
years ago. The same pattern is reflected
in views about churches. As new information about a faith group enters the
mainstream, people's allegiance to organizations and leaders changes. Gone
are the days of sticking to a church just
because one's family has always attended there. Loyalty as a cultural
value has seen its best days come and go.[3]

Another important factor is people's confidence in the leaders of the faith tradition in which they were reared.

What's Happening in Church Growth

It is not only denominations that expand and contract; individual
churches do as well. One of the recent infatuations in the church
world has been the emergence of the megachurch, often defined as
congregations that attract two thousand or more people on a typical weekend. Megachurches have been around for many decades,
but non-mainline churches in particular began celebrating the
"big-box" congregations in the 1980s and have never looked back.

There are an estimated fifteen hundred megachurches in the
United States, a whopping increase from the dozen or so that
existed in 1970. The Protestant church universe in particular pays
close attention to attendance figures and watches the efforts of the
largest and fastest-growing churches. Our research discovered that
when Protestant churches attempt to evaluate their success, one of
the primary elements they gauge is attendance. Rather than evaluate spiritual growth, most churches settle for measuring numerical
growth, even though a variety of studies have shown there is little
correlation between those two metrics.

In other nations, some churches have grown to phenomenal

sizes. For instance, in South Korea, the legendary Yoido Full Gospel Church has more than eight hundred thousand members and packs its monstrous worship center for seven services each weekend (translated into sixteen languages and dialects). Christian churches with more than one hundred thousand members exist in places as far-flung as Argentina and Nigeria. Fittingly, it is the United States that seems most obsessed with attendance numbers; that focus follows the national obsession with size and superiority—with being the top dog in one's category. It is surprising, then, that the largest churches in the nation are much

When Protestant churches attempt to evaluate their success, one of the primary elements they gauge is attendance.

smaller than their counterparts overseas. For instance, the biggest American church based on weekly attendance is Lakewood Church in Houston, Texas, pastored by television preacher and best-selling author Joel Osteen. Lakewood claims a weekly average attendance of about forty-five thousand people. The next most populous churches attract twenty to twenty-five thousand per weekend—and there are only a half dozen or so of those—and then about three dozen that draw more than ten thousand each week.

Megachurches can be found in every state, although California and Texas have the greatest concentration of them. More than one-quarter of all megachurches now are multisite congregations, meaning that they meet in more than one location. Often the teaching from the senior pastor of the founding church is played on a big screen at the remote sites, though some churches provide live sermons by a campus pastor at their remote sites. The multisite megachurch approach is, in essence, a new form of denomination; but rather than become a formal denomination, a popular church initiates new campuses to reach different groups of people—or different regions—and considers everyone a member

of the mother church. Many megachurches are nondenominational entities, which facilitates the independence, entrepreneurial
spirit, and innovative thinking that foster this type of expansion.
This growth strategy has become so common that one megachurch
has twenty-nine ministry sites in operation. A growing number of
megachurches are increasing their reach by incorporating sites in
multiple states. Multisite churches will become increasingly common throughout this decade.[4]

How significant are megachurches? Their influence is felt in a
number of ways. First, our data indicate that about one out of eight
adults who attend a church are connected to a megachurch—a
number that is likely to increase. Second, megachurches influence
other churches in terms of their program
decisions. Third, the leaders of our largest
churches are revered as the gurus of "how
to do church," attracting large and loyal
followings of other pastors and congregational leaders who wish to see their own
ministries expand.

> *About one out of eight adults who attend a church are connected to a megachurch.*

What's Happening with Church Norms

All the attention given to megachurches tends to obscure that
99 percent of Protestant churches are *not* in the mega category. In
fact, a majority of Americans attend churches of fewer than two
hundred people. The median attendance at Protestant churches is
ninety adults. The median annual budget for all church activities is
about $165,000 annually—less than the compensation package for
the senior pastors of some megachurches.

Indeed, the view looks very different for the typical Protestant
church in America. Less than one out of five churches overall
increase their attendance in a given year; four out of five Protestant

churches remain stable or see a reduction in adult attendance from year to year. Church analysts inform us that about 3,500 Protestant churches close their doors every year. Their departure is masked in the aggregate figures by a similar number of new churches that are started each year. For the past two decades, the total number of Protestant churches has remained remarkably consistent, despite the substantial openings and closings that occur. Since the start of this millennium, more than thirty-five thousand Protestant congregations have shut down. They have been replaced by a slightly higher number of new churches.[5]

One of the great challenges facing the church in America is the health and vitality of rural congregations.

One of the great challenges facing the church in America is the health and vitality of rural congregations. The typical rural congregation draws less than half the national average of adults. Consequently, less than half of all rural churches are able to afford a full-time pastor, and most rural pastors have no formal training. New seminary graduates are rarely interested in rural pastorates because the salaries are small, benefits are minimal, the congregations are aging and unlikely to expand in numbers, and the prestige is minimal in pastoral circles. The two most frequent outcomes in recent years have been for rural churches to shut their doors once the pastor departs or for congregations to share a pastor with another rural ministry.[6]

But neither megachurches nor rural churches reflect the norm for Protestant congregations, which include the following characteristics:

- An annual budget of $165,670 (in 2009). That's more than double the median budget in 1992 ($81,713), outpacing cost-of-living increases during that time. The growth since 2000 (when the median was $117,000) also reflects a considerable increase in giving, especially since attendance has remained unchanged.

- The bulk of a congregation's budget pays for salaries and maintenance. In 2009, 30 percent of church income was diverted to the pastor's compensation package. Only 3 percent was invested in ministry to teenagers and 2 percent in ministry to children.
- Theologically, most pastors describe their congregations as conservative (82 percent), with only one out of eight (12 percent) labeling their ministry "theologically liberal." Roughly four out of ten pastors also say their churches are "fundamentalist" in doctrine. One out of four churches is Pentecostal or charismatic in orientation.
- Most congregations are rather uniform racially and ethnically. Less than one-tenth of congregations can be thought of as ethnically diverse, and even fewer are truly desegregated. That figure is on the rise, but the trajectory promises a slow build. The research also shows that the churches most resistant to integration are African American, whereas megachurches tend to be more of a melting pot. It remains true, as Martin Luther King pointed out more than forty years ago, that eleven o'clock on Sunday morning is the most segregated hour of the week.
- Protestant churches attempt to integrate technology into their efforts as quickly and seamlessly as possible. Two-thirds of these congregations use an LCD projection system, flashing images on a big screen during programs and services. Six out of ten churches show video clips during their services. Two-thirds have a church website for posting information and allowing people to access ministry resources. The latest advances in technology used by ministries include tweeting during services (using Twitter to digitally and instantly

transmit comments and feedback to people and leaders during a church event), and holographic imagery (3-D projection).

- Charismatic churches are one of the growing forces to be reckoned with in the church world. One out of four Protestant churches in the United States (23 percent) is a charismatic congregation, including four out of ten nondenominational churches. The profile of the typical charismatic congregation is very similar to that of evangelical, fundamentalist, and mainline Protestant churches in terms of attendance. (It is important to note, however, that almost one-quarter of American charismatics—22 percent—are Catholic.) Diverging from the stereotype, Pentecostal churches are more likely than other Protestant churches to use new technologies. Pentecostalism has also truly been embraced by the black community. One out of every six majority-white congregations (16 percent) are Pentecostal, compared to 65 percent of the Protestant churches dominated by African Americans. In terms of resources, Pentecostal churches raise less money per congregation than do other churches; their pastors are paid less (by about five thousand dollars per year); and their pastors are much less likely to have a seminary degree (49 percent do, compared to 70 percent among noncharismatic churches). We also discovered that one substantial aspect of the appeal of Pentecostal churches is the greater freedom of emotional and spiritual expression encouraged in those assemblies.

Clearly, the church world changes over time, though to some the changes may seem glacial in velocity and superficial in nature. Many of these changes reflect shifts in cultural expectations and behavior. For instance, while involvement in churches has become less commonplace, people's sense of personal spiritual interest and engagement has risen. The new forms of faith tend to be decentralized—in terms of geography as well as activity and leadership—while providing congregants with greater control over the process.[7]

What's Happening among Clergy

As leaders go, so go their organizations. That adage certainly holds true among Protestant churches.

The profile of a Protestant senior pastor is one of a middle-aged male with extensive education and a below-average annual income for someone with commensurate training and experience. In brief, here is the profile of Protestant senior pastors and how things have changed in the past two decades.

- 90 percent are men, but the proportion of women in the senior pastor role doubled between 1999 and 2009. The lion's share of the women in the pastorate—58 percent—are affiliated with mainline churches. Female pastors are anything but a mirror reflection of their male counterparts. Women clergy tend to be a bit older, more highly educated (77 percent have a seminary degree vs. 63 percent of male clergy), receive smaller compensation levels ($45,300 for women, $48,600 for men); and lead smaller congregations (average attendance of 81 adults compared to an average of 103 in male-led churches).
- The median age of pastors is now fifty-four. That is an alarming uptick from the average reported in 1992 (forty-four) and 2000 (forty-nine). During that time, the percentage of senior pastors who are under forty has plummeted from 32 percent to only 15 percent. This becomes increasingly significant as a large share of today's pastors—perhaps as many as one-third—prepare to retire before we reach the next decade.
- The median compensation package—which includes the

cost of health care, housing allowance, retirement, and auto allowance—was $49,357 in 2009. That seems substantially higher than the pay they received in 1992 ($32,049) and 2000 ($39,048), but it really has barely stayed even with rises in the cost-of-living index.

· The median compensation is especially low, considering the educational background and professional experience of most pastors. Three-quarters of current pastors attended seminary (which is graduate school), and two-thirds (65 percent) graduated with a seminary degree. Further, the median years of full-time, paid ministry experience under their belts is twenty years. Clearly, one does not enter the ministry to make money!

· Pastors move around rather frequently—sometimes by denominational mandate. The median length of time for a lead pastor in his current church is six years. Though that is an increase from the median in 1992 (when it was just four years), it is comparatively short for such highly trained professionals with significant experience. But a large part of the explanation for this is denominational in nature. Pastors in mainline churches have an average tenure of just four years before moving to another congregation. That is about half the average among Protestant pastors in non-mainline churches. (Perhaps a related factor is that 93 percent of mainline senior pastors consider themselves to be leaders, yet only 12 percent claim to have the spiritual gift of leadership.)

The number of full-time ministry opportunities with churches is very limited: More than three-quarters of all Protestant churches have a single pastor on the payroll. Estimates of the total number of ordained clergy serving in churches range from 500,000 to 700,000 people—less than one-half of one percent of the adult population. Our studies show that one-fourth of Protestant congregations have a paid, full-time worship pastor; one-fifth have a youth pastor (someone who works primarily with teens); one out of ten churches (or fewer) have a full-time pastor for children or junior high students; and one out of ten have a pastor directing Christian education or discipleship activities.

In spite of the relatively limited number of full-time ministry professionals serving through churches, the recession has produced what now amounts to a glut of unemployed, available clergy. With churches cutting back on staff during 2007 through 2010, thousands of seminary-trained pastors were let go, with few openings available. The result is that we went from a dearth to an abundance within just seven years. The initial shortage, by the way, was because almost half of seminary graduates do not enter positions in congregational ministry, choosing parachurch options or other career paths altogether. This is because seminary graduates are often deterred by the length and demands of the ordination process, the comparatively meager pay, excessive congregational demands, and the difficulty of achieving success in church-based ministry in a hardened society.

The recession has produced what now amounts to a glut of unemployed, available clergy.

While some argue that seminaries have held back the church at large by not doing a better job of screening and preparing individuals for ministry, these are tough times for seminaries and Bible colleges, the two primary training grounds for pastors and church staff. Enrollment at Bible colleges has dipped by 60 percent in recent years, and seminaries have also been hurt by declining enrollment (though not as substantially). Student enrollment totals are more important for seminaries than for other schools because their endowment funds are usually smaller (their graduates earn less and donate less), leaving them without a security net for lean financial times. In fact, about four out of every ten independent schools that belong to the Association of Theological Schools (ATS) reported in 2008 that they were "financially stressed," with less than a year's worth of spendable assets on hand. Not surprisingly, this has caused seminaries across the country to reduce programs, lay off staff and instructors, slice salaries and benefits, reorganize, and in some of the more extreme cases, either merge or close.[8]

The upside to these hardships is that churches are relearning how to engage congregants in ministry.

The upside to these hardships is that churches are relearning how to engage congregants in ministry. Returning to the biblical notion of the priesthood of the laity, more churches are finding that they are capable of maintaining their ministry presence and practices without relying on trained professionals to lead. In the long run, this will serve churches and communities well.

What's Happening with Models and Methods

The recession has brought to the fore a number of realizations and changes regarding effective ministry in these changing times. Think about the new ways of ministering you have witnessed in recent years. They probably include the following shifts:

- *From monologue to dialogue.* Younger adults do not hang around long if they are not involved in a conversation about a church's underlying beliefs and practices. While this generally slows down the process, it also incorporates the ideas and energy of a wider pool of people. The dialogical process also minimizes the traditional reliance on platitudes and rhetoric in favor of questions and deeper discussion.
- *From authoritarian to team-based leadership.* Rather than

waiting for the superstar to make pronouncements and give permission to act, the new form of leadership invites all gifted leaders to coordinate their efforts with those of other leaders, focusing on a common vision and crafting ways of collaborating for heightened productivity and impact. The old command and control model is being widely—though still not universally—replaced with a team approach.

- *From observation and appreciation to ideation and participation.* As Boomers age and give way to Busters and Mosaics, the dominant tenor of the church becomes one of soliciting people's input and finding ways for everyone to contribute. Naturally, large shares of typical congregations still applaud ministry rather than perform it, but the ratio is shifting a bit. The old 80/20 rule—80 percent of ministry is done by 20 percent of the congregation—is approaching a 70/30 split.

- *From assumptions to analysis.* For many years, Protestant churches have relied on pastoral assumptions about the spiritual depth, maturity, and engagement of congregants. New technologies have introduced a raft of new self-assessment tools and procedures that are helping leaders get a more accurate reading of those they seek to help. There is still a long way to go, but the movement is tangible. Within the coming year, 30 percent of pastors are likely to take steps to empirically evaluate their church's reputation in the community; 24 percent are likely to assess the demographics and theolographics of their community; and 20 percent are likely to study the spiritual transformation journey in the lives of congregants. This means that a majority of churches are still flying by the seat of their pants, but the momentum building behind the metrics movement will motivate more to participate in the future.[9]

- *From legacy services to pragmatic value.* Churches are often expected to provide a handful of religious services for people, regardless of their connection to the church—baptize, confirm, marry, and bury. But fewer people today are interested in having churches perform those rituals for them. Churches are learning to address other needs that people will accept from a church, such as facilitating personal ministry opportunities (e.g., short-term missions trips, community outreach days), connecting like-minded people, and providing access to facilities and programs (e.g., sports, performing arts) that are otherwise unavailable.

These changing approaches to ministry are in response to the changing values and expectations of Americans. Our ongoing studies regarding people's religious experience and spiritual condition shows that people are demanding a more diverse menu of religious options than ever before. These demands transcend the well-known battles over styles of worship music, extent of involvement in social justice and political issues, dress styles, Bible version preference, and the continuation of Sunday night services and Sunday school classes. The bigger confrontation now being waged is over the very form or model of church life. As time goes on, we are witnessing a growing roster of options from which people can choose. Not all of them will thrive over the next decade, but all of them will be accessible to most people.

Earlier we discussed one of the new options: multisite churches. These come in various forms, such as remote campuses relying on the teaching of a centralized senior leader, delivered by technology, with the corporate vision and decisions determined at the central campus. Another popular format is for the remote campuses to be managed like affiliated churches within a denomination, featuring their own campus pastor (and, perhaps, staff), but fully aligned with and under the auspices of the mother church. Another approach is for the mother church to birth a new ministry in a different location and provide it with full autonomy, but to retain a parent-child relationship.

One of the fastest-growing models is the house church, also commonly called organic church or simple church. Although these gatherings are common in other nations—and they were, after all, the format of the original Christians during the time of the apostles through the rule of Constantine—this model is just beginning to catch on in the United States. Those who advocate for a return to this model go so far as to suggest that the "church as we know it is preventing church as God wants it." The early church, as described in the New Testament, was made up of small groups of people who met in each other's homes, usually convening ten to fifteen people. When a group needed to enlarge, it peacefully divided into multiple groups, maintaining their small size so they could have intimacy and focus. Christians from these small gatherings regularly gathered with believers from other house groups, enjoying citywide faith celebrations that facilitated a greater sense of the body of believers in an area as well as the joy of dynamic worship and growth experiences.[10]

The bigger confrontation now being waged is over the very form or model of church life.

Research among house church adherents has shown that, for these people, participation in an organic setting is not merely about playing church by different rules; it is more about leading a radical lifestyle in which faith is not held separate from the rest of one's daily experience; it is woven into all dimensions of life. Ideally, house church participants incorporate serious prayer, spiritual mentoring, faith-driven serving, and throughout-the-day worship in their everyday regimen. This form of church is based on a different vision for existence, a different type of leader, different spiritual behaviors, and different success metrics than are found in conventional churches.

Depending on how one measures participation in house churches—we have experimented with a half-dozen definitions, producing significantly divergent outcomes—our best estimate is that there are some six to twelve million people in the United States presently involved in true house churches (not cell groups or other in-home gatherings that are more Bible study or sermon-based study group than independent church). More than three-quarters of the pastors of conventional churches recognize the authenticity and legitimacy of house churches—and their structural fit with the changes in postmodern society. With growing numbers of conventional churches attempting to incorporate both the house church concept and language into their ministries, it becomes increasingly difficult to get an accurate reading on the movement. But when defined as "part of a group of believers that meets regularly in a home or place other than a church building, . . . [and] *not* associated in any way with a local, congregational type of church," the results have been consistent and persuasive.[11] These groups meet independently, are self-governed, and consider themselves to be complete churches on their own.

Participation in an organic setting is not merely about playing church by different rules.

Our studies have shown that most house churches (80 percent) meet every week, and the typical gathering lasts for about two hours. But you never know exactly what's going to happen next in most of these meetings: There is generally a determination to follow the guidance of the Holy Spirit (although these groups by and large are not Pentecostal in nature). In contrast to the intentionally predictable format of most conventional churches, the format followed in four of ten house churches (38 percent) varies from meeting to meeting.

Most house church meetings include time for spoken prayer (93 percent), reading from the Bible (90 percent), serving people outside of their group or organizing such times (89 percent), sharing personal needs or experiences (87 percent), eating and hanging out together (85 percent), an open-floor discussion of the teaching or discussion points (83 percent), a prepared-teaching time (76 percent), music or singing (70 percent), an offering from participants that is given to ministries (52 percent), and communion (51 percent). Two out of three house churches (64 percent) have children involved in these activities. The average size of a house church is twenty people, of whom roughly one-third are children.

The research found that primarily two types of people are attracted to house churches. The older participants, largely drawn from the Boomer population, are devout Christians who are seeking a deeper and more intense experience with God and other believers. The other substantial segment is

In contrast to the intentionally predictable format of most conventional churches, the format varies from meeting to meeting.

young adults who are interested in faith and spirituality but have little interest in the traditional forms of church. Their quest is largely one of escaping outdated structures and institutions while staying true to their interest in spiritual development.

House churches are not the only alternative model of church life. Others include cyberchurch fellowships (gatherings via the Internet that use live streaming of events, interactive discussions, podcasts, and social-networking capabilities); intentional communities (groups of believers moving into a targeted neighborhood to live among the people in that area and share the love of Christ with them through their lifestyle); family church (a regular, focused gathering of relatives for spiritual purposes including worship, faith education, and community service); monastic communities (residential communities that live a faith-focused lifestyle apart from society at large); traditional media-driven congregations (churches that address the needs of people via old-school media such as televised worship services and radio broadcast sermons); marketplace ministries (faith communities that meet in the marketplace and invite others in those locations to join the group); and contemplative prayer communities (gatherings of people whose primary focus is worship, growth, and fellowship through shared meditative prayer experiences). There are new forms emerging regularly, but those listed here are the most common.

House churches are not the only alternative model of church life. Others include cyberchurch, family church, and marketplace ministries.

Reflections

The church landscape will continue to evolve into something that would have been unrecognizable a quarter century ago. First, we'll see a continued emergence of the new denominations—the multisite churches. Next, we will have the rise of Hispanic churches and eventually a few breakaway denominations catering to the burgeoning Latino population. Third, keep your eyes on the charismatic and Pentecostal sector of the Protestant marketplace, for it, too, shows signs of maintaining a healthy rate of growth. Finally, add the multiplicity of alternative church forms, led by house churches, marketplace ministries, and cyberchurch fellowships. The end result is a very different universe, where the mainline churches and even some of the evangelical and fundamentalist groups that were solid at the end of the last millennium and the beginning of this one will lose altitude unless they substantially reinvent themselves.

Most people aligned with Christian churches are not attuned to the doctrinal distinctions that spawned the various denominations in the first place. These days, Americans are attracted by personalities, convenience and comfort, organizational reputation and efficiency, and the potential for excitement, lasting relationships, and unique experiences. Given the new pastiche of values that drives us, there will be few tears shed over the rapid demise of the old guard. In its place will be a hearty buzz about the escalation of a new cadre of religious entities.

A very significant challenge for all these new champions of twenty-first-century faith will be to avoid becoming so enamored of traditional measures of success—attendance, income, buildings, longevity, continuity—that they simply become updated versions of the institutions

Mainline churches and even some evangelical and fundamentalist groups will lose altitude unless they substantially reinvent themselves.

and models they were spawned to replace. Maintaining a laser-like focus on their God-given reason for existence—to draw people ever closer to God and His truth—will enable them to experience the joy of facilitating genuine transformation, one precious life at a time.

Perhaps the greatest spiritual legacy of the recession of 2007 to 2010 will be the reemergence of the laity as ministers of the faith. That shift will sharpen domestic ministry productivity and reach and will also release much-needed funding for new ministry ventures and for greater focus on target segments that have generally been overlooked in recent years.

Another pattern that is likely to inspire major positive change is the growing awareness of the importance of better metrics and the willingness of church leaders (both clergy and laity) to get serious about measuring more than attendance. Ironically, it may well be a group of megachurch leaders who spearhead this shift in emphasis; having already cracked the bigness code, they will put their energy into moving people toward spiritual depth. That will be a long-awaited and eagerly welcomed advance in the journey of the body of Christ.

Ultimately, some of the pain we have experienced in recent years will produce the joys of the future. The changes that so many lament today will give rise to a more nimble, alert, discerning, and adventurous church. There are certainly challenges ahead: preparing godly and competent leaders who will protect and pursue God's vision, facilitating the development of a biblical worldview in the lives of children, harnessing media for Kingdom advancement, motivating parents to see their homes as churches rather than residence halls, staying abreast of cultural changes so that the church is taken seriously and serves meaningfully, and developing reliable and significant metrics that keep the body of Christ on track. Shifting from the known to the unknown is always uncomfortable, but intelligent and responsive changes will birth a church better able to minister effectively in the new millennium.

Some of the pain we have experienced in recent years will produce the joys of the future.

CHAPTER 8

OUR PROFILE

Demographics Are Not Destiny

POPULATION ESTIMATES AND projections seem to capture people's imaginations. There is lots of talk about the size and nature of specific populations—the United States as a whole or individual states, cities, or metro areas of interest. But the awful truth about population projections is that they are often inaccurate. In fact, the bigger the population in question, the less likely long-term projections are to be on the money. This is largely because analysts assume that trends presently in place will remain in place. But as you know firsthand, things change and the future is unpredictable. Most of us have trouble accurately describing what we will be doing a week from now, much less one year, ten years, or forty years down the road.

So imagine the challenge of attempting to estimate what 310 million people will be doing, how they will be living, what their desires are, and what they are physically, financially, and emotionally capable of pursuing years from now. Will people decide to have children? How many? In what year? Will families choose to move from their current homes to other locations? How far will they move from their present domiciles? When will they make the move? Those kinds of questions are endless and often seem to exist in a vacuum—but the answers to such questions enable demographers to make the kinds of predictions and projections that lead us to believe that the future will look one way or another.

Imagine the challenge of attempting to estimate what 310 million people will be doing years from now.

Here's a case in point. The United Nations provides projections about the world's future. In 1998, it proclaimed that in 2050 the world's population would likely be 8.9 billion people. That estimate lasted all of two years before the same group revised the estimate to 9.3 billion people. That's like suddenly bolting a second United States plus another Mexico onto the globe—it's an enormous difference. Why the change in projections? Because statisticians at the United Nations noticed unexpected and minute increases in fertility rates in the United States and Europe and recalculated their figures. In fact, demographers are so acutely aware of the fragility of their estimates that they routinely provide three different projections, a low, middle, and high series of figures. (The middle series is what demographers typically use as their estimate for prediction purposes, holding the extremes in abeyance as a hedge against their bet.) The disparity between the high and low numbers can be breathtaking. For instance, a recent UN projection (I'm not picking on them, really) made at the time of this writing indicated that in 2050 the world's total population will be somewhere between 8 billion and 10.5 billion people. That's a spread of 2.5 *billion* people![1]

Does any of this matter, or is it just another hobby for the idle or the statistically obsessed? Bottom line: It matters. Demographic projections are big business because governments and businesses around the world base their current existence and future plans on such expectations. For instance, demographic outlooks provide data on which big-buck decisions are made: the size and education of the future labor force, the number of people who will be retired and living on government assistance, the numbers of people who will rely on government programs (and the tax dollars needed to fund those programs), the medical and health-care needs of an aging population, how many immigrants are allowed in the country, household income levels and the propor- tion available for discretionary spending,

Despite the uncertainties that can lead to misjudg- ments in forecasting, demographics can be invaluable.

and so forth. Joining insights into the numbers and types of people that comprise a specified population enables leaders to make informed decisions.

So, despite the uncertainties that can lead to misjudgments in forecasting, demographics—such as gender, family size, marital status, age, ethnicity, income, and mobility attributes—can be invaluable as we try to understand both the size and nature of a population. Let's take a look at America's population today and where it's probably headed.

What's Happening with Population Growth

The United States is one of the relatively few large nations in the developed world that has been continually expanding its popula- tion base. At a time when western European nations have been experiencing population declines, the United States keeps adding people. The pace of growth has been quite impressive too. It took the country about 130 years to reach one hundred million people; only 52 years to double it; just 39 years to add the next hundred million (in 2006); and we are expected to increase by another hundred million by 2038, only 32 years after reaching the three hundred million plateau.[2]

In the nearer term, the Census Bureau—the world's largest and most heavily funded research firm, which operates as the federal government's official keeper of population statistics and projections—believes we will be home to about 341 million people in 2020. Unless something dramatic and unforeseen happens, the base population will keep growing, to an estimated 373 million in 2030, 405 million in 2040, and 439 million in 2050.[3] If we stay on track with the projection for the coming decade, we will grow at about one percent per year. That may not seem like a blistering pace, but when the base population is more than three hundred million people, each percent adds up pretty quickly.

Our population grows because of the confluence of several factors: live births, health factors, and net immigration.

Without giving it much thought, you might assume that the population increases because people have babies. But it's a bit more complicated than that. Our population grows because of the confluence of several factors. First, the number of live births is the biggest factor, which is affected by both physical factors (e.g., fertility rates, the number of women in their prime childbearing years, the incidence of sexual intercourse) and attitudes (e.g., desire to have children, the number of children desired). Second, there are health factors involved. These include matters such as disease risk, infant mortality rates, and adult mortality rates. Third, net immigration is a major consideration in the United States, more so than in most nations of the world.

Looking at those factors, we discover that America has been doing quite well on the reproductive front. The country has had more than four million births each year since 2000—the first time we've hit the four million mark since 1993. In fact, in 2007 we set a record for births (4.317 million), eclipsing the record set in 1957 during the Baby Boom era. The increase is due to what some demographers cite as a perfect storm of factors: substantial numbers of women delaying childbirth until their forties (which has raised the average age of the first-time mother to twenty-five), plus a growing number of immigrants having babies, high fertility rates due to a growing number of females in their twenties and thirties (which are their most fertile years), and a lower number of abortions. When you put it all together, the United States experiences about 4.3 million live births, net international migration adds about one million people, and we lose around 2.5 million people to death each year. That produces an increase of between 2.5 and 3 million people per year, accounting for a 25- to 30-million person expansion over the run of the decade.[4]

Immigration is an important aspect of our growth—and, in recent years, a point of much moral and political controversy. Our population growth is more than a matter of letting a few new residents cross the border. Between now and 2050, we expect 82 percent of the population growth to be produced by new immigrants and the children they have in the United States. We allow anywhere between

We also become the new home to about five hundred thousand unauthorized foreigners each year.

seven hundred thousand and one million immigrants to legally enter the country each year, not including estimates suggesting we also become the new home to about five hundred thousand unauthorized foreigners each year.

Our nation is fortunate in that we get the cream of the crop of the world's immigrants. Among all immigrants, 55 percent of those who are well-educated come to the United States. That trend is likely to remain in force for the coming decade because such

immigrants are drawn to nations where they have an existing network of family or reliable friends to help them assimilate the new
culture. There are, of course, many uneducated, desperately poor
immigrants, too, and their presence inside our borders has sparked
social tensions. But the United States began as a nation of immigrants. Welcoming people from other nations has been a hallmark
of the country and is now established as a central part of our growth
strategy. The average annual flow of immigrants has consistently
risen during the past century, from an average of roughly a quarter
million per year in the 1950s to an average of more than 325,000 in
the '60s, about 450,000 annually in the '70s, ballooning to 730,000
in the '80s, 900,000 in the '90s, and fluctuating between 700,000
and one million newcomers during the past decade. In fact, the
foreign-born segment of America's population is already close to
13 percent and will continue to grow for the foreseeable future.[5]

What's Happening Regarding Race, Ethnicity, and Aging

It's not hard to see what some analysts have termed "the brown-
ing of America." A trend that began a quarter century ago has
been picking up steam ever since. America is definitely becoming
more ethnically diverse than ever before. During the past decade,
Hispanics overtook African Americans as the second-largest racial/
ethnic segment in the nation. Three more significant trends will
materialize in the coming years:

- By 2015 a majority of the children born in the United States
  each year will be nonwhite.
- By 2023 (or thereabouts) a majority of all children in the
  country will be non-white.
- Around 2048 what we call "minority groups" will overtake the
  size of the white population to become the majority.

Today, about two-thirds of the population is non-Hispanic white, with about 16 percent Hispanic, 13 percent black, 5 percent Asian, and 2 percent Native American. But with greater numbers of Hispanic women in their prime childbearing years and having larger families, the percentage of whites will consistently decline through at least the middle of this century. Hispanic women are giving birth to an average of three children, while non-Hispanic white females are giving birth to fewer than two, and black and Asian women are bearing about 2.1 each. (The rate of replacement—the number of children women must have in order to keep the population base unchanged—is 2.1.)[6]

The percentage of whites will consistently decline through at least the middle of this century.

There are two hundred million non-Hispanic whites in the United States today; forty years from now that total will increase by only three million. During that same time span, the Hispanic population will nearly triple, from 47 million to 133 million. There will be similar massive jumps among blacks (up 61 percent) and Asians (up 173 percent).[7]

Another significant characteristic related to race and ethnicity is age. The median age of non-Hispanic white Americans is currently forty-one. That's older than the median among Asians (36), blacks (31), or Hispanics (28). The difference in the average age between Hispanics and whites is a result of Hispanics being unusually young (three out of ten are under eighteen, compared to two out of ten among whites) and whites dominating the ranks of the over fifty-five crowd (29 percent of whites are fifty-five or older, compared to just 13 percent of Hispanics). In fact, looking at the sixty-five-and-older segment, 16 percent of whites are already there, but just 6 percent of Hispanics are. As the Baby Boomers, most of whom are white, reach their sunset years in the coming decade, that gap will widen.[8]

One consequence of an aging nation is that the gender balance is further disrupted. Because women live longer than men, as a higher proportion of the population reaches older ages, greater numbers of men pass away. There are already four million more women than men in the United States. That gap may well double.

There are already four million more women than men in the United States. That gap may well double.

By the way, life spans continue to be extended thanks to advances in medical care and physical conditioning, reductions in the use of unhealthy substances (e.g., alcohol, tobacco), and better nutrition. The average life span of people born in 2006 is expected to be seventy-five for men and eighty for women. That longevity is further anticipated to be lengthened by about two years for children born ten years from now. Gerontologists have posited that life spans can be extended if we take additional steps to reduce stress, such as transitioning to shorter work weeks (e.g., four ten-hour workdays) and postponing retirement.[9]

What's Happening with Wealth, Work, and Education

While America is an economically blessed nation, most households were hurt by the recession that began in 2007. Household income levels decreased for the first time in years; poverty levels rose; discretionary income dropped; family wealth diminished as people dipped into their savings to make ends meet; record numbers of personal bankruptcies, home foreclosures, and auto repossessions occurred; retirement funds suffered dramatic losses; several million people lost their jobs, while millions of others were underemployed; and the long-established optimism about the future vanished. As I write this (early 2011), the recession is still in full force; it is not a pretty picture, nor one that is rapidly vanishing.

Standard measures of wealth bear out the challenges people are facing. Household income skyrocketed from the 1980s until the start of the downturn, rising from a median of $42,429 in 1980 to $50,557 in 2000, and reaching a high point of $52,163 in 2007. After just one year of the recession, household income had already dropped by 3.6 percent, to $50,303 in 2008, with more reductions in store. Family income (which is always higher than household income because it removes the single-person households and their lower incomes from the mix) experienced a similar pattern of consistent increases through the 1980s and 1990s, slower and less prolific increases from 2000 through 2007, and the beginning of the recession-driven decline in 2007. Family income levels went from $50,366 to $64,755 in 2007—nearly a 30 percent improvement—before the slippage set in, sustaining a 3.3 percent decline to $62,621 in 2008.[10]

Despite that public attitudes toward racism and people of different backgrounds have improved tremendously in the last four decades, income parity has not materialized. In fact, the gaps across the racial and ethnic categories are stupefying. For instance, the median household income among non-Hispanic whites was $55,530 in 2008. That same year, median household incomes were $65,637 for Asians, $37,913 for Hispanics, and $34,218 for blacks.

Public attitudes toward racism and people of different backgrounds have improved tremendously in the last four decades.

Hispanics and blacks had been gaining ground until the recession hit, but they have now surrendered some of the gains made in the last couple of decades. For instance, median black household income was 58 percent of the white median in 1980, 60 percent in 1990, and 68 percent in 2000, but it reverted to 62 percent in 2008. Similarly, the median Hispanic household income was 73 percent of the white median in 1980, 72 percent in 1990, and 76 percent in 2000, but it fell to just 68 percent in 2008.

All of these changes tie into the levels of poverty identified by the government. Though the overall national poverty level has shifted little in the last thirty years (from 13 percent in 1980 to 13.2 percent in 2008), poverty among blacks and Hispanics has plummeted. Among blacks, the poverty rate dropped from 32.5 percent in 1980 to 22.5 percent in 2000, and after dropping even further in the beginning of the 2000s, it rose a bit in response to the recession, reaching 24.5 percent in 2008. Among Hispanics, the rate dropped from 25.7 percent in 1980 to 21.5 percent in 2000 and was still at that level in 2008. Despite these encouraging decreases, the national average has remained relatively stable due to a slight growth in poverty among whites (from 10.2 percent in 1980 to 10.5 percent in 2008), who constitute two-thirds of the population. It is interesting that the poverty rate is much lower among married-couple families (5.5 percent). In fact, one of the proposed antidotes to poverty, especially in the black population (where most families wind up becoming single-parent, mother-led families), is to do whatever it takes to increase the percentage of stable marriages, since poverty is much less of a factor in those households.[11]

One of the proposed antidotes to poverty is to increase the percentage of stable marriages.

The recession notwithstanding, Americans still possess tremendous wealth. Home ownership, which was once the cornerstone of the American dream, has become a normative reality, with two out of three households (66 percent) owning the homes in which they live. After years of reckless spending, Americans are beginning to accumulate some savings, and there is evidence that the hardships introduced by the economic crash have altered many people's spending patterns. The Federal Reserve Board estimated that even though Americans lost more than $12 trillion in wealth due to the economic slide, the aggregate net worth of American households topped $53 trillion in mid-2009. The median net worth of individual families in 2007 was about $120,000—an amount that has surely dipped since that measurement, but which remains a mind-boggling figure to most people around the world. Whether or not we will maintain that wealth—and build on it—depends upon several factors, including our levels of educational achievement and occupational choices.[12]

To better understand wealth and income patterns, then, we must look at educational and occupational trends.

Educational achievement still represents the path to financial stability. In the United States today, among people twenty-five or older, 13 percent have not completed high school; 31 percent ended their education after attaining their high school diploma; 17 percent took some college classes but did not earn a degree; 9 percent have a two-year associate's degree; 19 percent have a bachelor's degree; and 10 percent have both a bachelor's degree and an advanced degree. This profile is far better than what characterized our country forty years ago. At that time only 52 percent of people graduated from high school (compared to 87 percent now) and slightly less than 11 percent finished a college degree (versus 29 percent these days). Of course, the portrait varies by demographic attributes. While a majority of Asians (53 percent) complete a college degree, the same can be said for only 20 percent of blacks and 13 percent of Hispanics. (Thirty percent of non-Hispanic whites have a college diploma.) Some of the most dramatic changes in educational achievement relate to women, of whom just 8 percent received a four-year college degree in 1970, but among whom 29 percent do today.[13]

> *Educational achievement still represents the path to financial stability in the United States today.*

The relationship between education and income is clear: The more advanced your education, the greater the likelihood of raising your annual earnings. The research shows that people in the thirty-five to fifty-four age bracket who do not have a college diploma earn roughly $25,100 per year; those who completed a high school education make about $36,300; people with some college experience take in $42,900; those who earned an associate's degree average $43,900; those with a bachelor's degree earn $65,600; a master's degree generates $78,600; a doctorate is worth $102,500 annually; and people with a professional degree rake in $131,000. It is unfortunate that today's young adults often graduate from college with a pile of school debt on their hands. Over the long haul, though, having the educational credentials to open the doors to better-paying jobs tends to be a good investment.[14]

Having the educational credentials to open the doors to better-paying jobs tends to be a good investment.

Parents have shown a growing willingness to participate in the educational preparation of their children when they are very young. More than four out of five parents of preschoolers now read to their children at least three times a week; three out of four work with their children on knowing letters, numbers, and words; and slightly more than half tell their children stories at least three times a week. All of those statistics show an increase over the past fifteen years. Recent studies have shown that one of the most important determinants of students' classroom performance is their home environment and the degree of academic encouragement and support they receive from their families.[15]

In spite of these positive trends, a growing body of research indicates that our young people are not making the grade. Standardized educational achievement tests, which have become a controversial component in their own right in the past decade, regularly show that our students do not reach the "proficient" mark that reflects "solid academic performance." The Department of

Education reports that just 39 percent of fourth-grade students and 31 percent of eighth-grade students are proficient in math. Similar numbers of students reach the proficient level in reading: 32 percent among fourth graders and 29 percent among eighth graders.[16]

As the world stage has changed in recent years, one of the undeniable truths is that Americans must increasingly be able to compete in a global economy, or at least be able to understand and respond wisely to emerging international realities. There are all kinds of studies that demonstrate American students are falling behind many of their global counterparts. Among the best-known sources of such statistics are those compiled by the thirty OECD nations (the most developed countries).[17] During the past decade, American students have consistently generated mean scores that are below the OECD average on the standardized math, science, and reading literacy tests, and our students have ranked in the middle of the pack in those fields. The most recent comparisons indicated that American students ranked twenty-fourth of twenty-nine reporting nations in mathematics and seventeenth in sci-

Standardized educational achievement tests regularly show that our students do not reach the "proficient" mark.

ence. Other outcomes of those international comparisons revealed that the United States spends way above average on primary and secondary education, the cost of a college experience is a barrier for many, and the college dropout rate of American students is well above average. One result of these patterns is a static literacy level among adults: Testing since 1992 shows there has been no significant gain in adult literacy in the United States in nearly two decades—at a time when other nations are seeking to (and sometimes successfully managing to) pass the United States in the economic fast lane.[18]

Among the striking factors from global comparative research

are the improvements realized by nations that many Americans are barely aware of. Substantial gains have been made in educational investment, quality, and achievement in countries such as Finland, Turkey, Hungary, and the Czech Republic, not to mention economic rising stars like South Korea. In other words, the global competition our students (and labor force) face is not just from the usual suspects (China, India, Brazil, Japan, Germany) but from a growing contingent of determined nations that are steadily eroding the differences in educational achievement, paving the way for a more competitive economic future.

A growing contingent of determined nations are steadily paving the way for a more competitive economic future.

As the United States gets back on its feet in the wake of the devastating effects of the recession, our economy will rely on a better educated and more focused labor force to sustain the recovery and build a strong economic foundation for the future. Our economy is expected to add up to fifteen million new jobs during this decade, with a growing share of these jobs requiring at least some college education. Almost all of the new jobs—96 percent—are anticipated to be within the service sector. The most prolific gains will be in the areas of professional and business services (27 percent of the new jobs), health care and social assistance (26 percent), and construction (8 percent). The types of professional and business services positions that will fuel job growth include consultants in management, science, and technology; computer system designers; and those who specialize in employment services. The health-care positions most likely to blossom will be physician's assistants, those who provide in-home health care, people who assist the elderly and disabled, and nurses. The biggest employment losses are expected to be realized in goods producing and manufacturing, as millions of those jobs are lost to overseas companies that can exploit lower costs for employee wages and benefits.[19]

What's Happening with Household Mobility

With all that happens in our lives—education, marriage, having children, working—it's not surprising that a lot of movement occurs. When the nation emerged, few people moved more than a stone's throw from their family of origin, working the fields with extended family members. But as technology has changed our means of economic support and mobility, our tendency to move has changed as well. In the 1980s, almost one out of five people (17 percent) changed their place of residence in a typical year.

As technology has changed our means of economic support and mobility, our tendency to move has changed as well.

Since then, that number has been sliced by more than 50 percent, to slightly less than 12 percent in 2008. When most people move, they don't go very far: Two-thirds stay within the same county, and an additional one-fifth move within the same state. One reason for the decline in household mobility has been the recession: With no jobs to motivate relocation, more people have stuck with their existing jobs or stayed in their current residences; and with no promise of raises or even continued income, fewer people have attempted to upgrade the quality of their housing by moving to bigger, newer, or nicer homes. The most common reasons for relocating tend to be housing related (responsible for about 40 percent of all moves), family related (about 30 percent), and work related (about 20 percent).[20]

The recession certainly changed our relocation patterns. Places that had been migration magnets, such as Las Vegas and Orlando, actually experienced an outflow of residents during the early stages of the downturn. Places in the Midwest and Northeast that had witnessed a steady stream of departures became the paragons of stability as people with jobs, houses, and family in the area stayed put during the uncertain times. In fact, the group most likely to move was renters: They were five times more likely than homeowners to shift locations during the first couple of years of the recession.

What are the go-to locations today? In 2009 and 2010, the states that were the biggest population losers were Michigan and Nevada. In terms of metropolitan areas, Washington, DC, and Boston are among the recent winners, while Atlanta and Phoenix had net gains that were much smaller than they had experienced in previous years. California and Florida are curious cases because they have been experiencing substantial domestic out-migration that is largely canceled out by international immigration. But all of these patterns change according to market conditions and the political winds, so don't put too much stock in data that are affected by major reversible events (such as a recession). Ongoing tragedies such as the 2010 BP oil leak in the Gulf of Mexico will have a more enduring impact on relocation.[21]

Places that had been migration magnets actually experienced an outflow of residents during the early stages of the downturn.

Reflections

The demographic patterns and changes described here provide a variety of opportunities in the midst of transition.

First, we have a chance to serve people as they make the transition from familiar lifestyles to new, and often untried, approaches to life. In particular, we might prepare for the onslaught of Boomers reaching retirement age. It is quite likely that an unprecedented proportion of Boomers will refuse to stop working once they reach the age of sixty-five. That's partially a reflection of financial need (many had their retirement funds decimated by the recession), partially a refusal to give up positions of authority

(a substantial share of Boomers who hold positions of authority
in business and churches are reluctant to allow young people to
take the reins or make critical decisions), and partially a reflection
of their nervousness about what to do when they have to move
outside their comfort zones. Perhaps you have a family member,
a colleague from work, a friend from church, or a neighbor who
is approaching the "golden years." Take some time to observe this
person's transition needs and see if there is a way you can help him
or her make the shift to the next phase of life.

Boomers will once again become a controversial generation during these next two decades as they redefine the "mature lifestyle."
They are healthier at their age than their parents or grandparents
were, but they will still need help in transitioning to the next
phases of their lives. What can be done to help aging Boomers
deal with the sense of loss they experience as their health precludes
them from doing some activities they
used to do, or as their friends and family members pass away more frequently,
or as leaving their places of employment
robs them of their identity and sense of
meaning, or as their lack of positions
of authority leaves them feeling useless?

*We have a chance
to serve people as they
make the transition from
familiar lifestyles to new
approaches to life.*

Once again, a bit of creative thinking and a desire to have a positive impact on other people's lives might lead to some personally
fulfilling activity.

Another critical transition point relates to the ethnic and racial
transformation that is redefining America. How are you accom-
modating the needs of people who are different from you? For
those who wish to make a positive difference in the world, there
are some forty million Americans living in poverty and another
forty million who are on the edge. Is there some way you can serve
them: tutoring their children, inviting them over for a meal once a

week, carpooling with them, etc.? Naturally, all of these suggestions require some sacrifice and inconvenience, but even these little acts of love could be life changers for people who are less advantaged.

As you examine your own life in light of the demographic patterns defining America, remember that despite what some sociologists say, demographics are not destiny. Behavioral patterns such as those described in these pages are based on averages. But averages mask that few individuals actually possess characteristics and experiences that perfectly conform to all the norms. A good way to read and use demographic information is to understand what *usually* happens and use that insight to prepare yourself to buck the trends for your own benefit. The "average" Hispanic will not graduate from college, but if you're Hispanic, that pattern is not a reality that you should accept as a limitation on your own potential. The "average" person with a high school diploma earns less than $40,000 a year, but that

Even little acts of love could be life changers for people who are less advantaged.

need not be seen as a ceiling you cannot exceed. For every attribute that is studied, there are outliers—people who are so far outside the primary range that they may not even show up on the chart. There is no reason why you cannot be a positive outlier if you do what you can to achieve your dreams. After all, it is when people refuse to accept the averages as limitations that those averages change.

CHAPTER 9

TOGETHER WE CAN
REDIRECT THESE TRENDS

ONE OF OUR CULTURE's mantras is, "It is what it is." I'd like to rec-
ommend a return to a forgotten expression that used to character-
ize our mind-set: "Life is what you make it."

The America we have today is the America we've allowed to happen. We don't have to like what we see, but we do have to deal with
it. If you don't like the portrait of the current and future America
that I've drawn—and for the sake of the nation and the Kingdom
of God, I hope you don't—then let's change it. That's the whole
point of studying trends: If you know where you stand and what's
coming, you can redirect it. In this case, we can and we should.

It has been said that there are three types of people when it
comes to the future: those who will watch what happens, those
who will make it happen, and those who will wonder what happened. Which of those three types will you be? The choice is yours:
All three archetypes are possible.

Let me suggest that if you consider yourself a Christian—a true *follower* of Christ, not just someone who knows *about* Christ— then you are called to follow His example and create the future. That may sound overwhelming, but remember, with Christ all things are possible. With His power and wisdom at your disposal, you can do great things that will bless millions of people. But becoming an agent of transformation— someone who is blessed to be a blessing— does not just happen. You have to be informed, purposeful, and committed.

If you consider yourself a Christian, then you are called to follow His example and create the future.

I hope the information in this book has sufficiently informed you about current conditions and future possibilities to raise your levels of understanding and confidence. Armed with that knowledge and called by God to influence the world one life at a time, now is your moment—your chance to make a lasting, positive difference in the world by anticipating the future and shaping it in ways that demonstrate your love for God and His people and your commitment to His life principles. You cannot afford to wait for the future to come to you. There is nothing worse than being a victim of a world you could have influenced but chose not to.

As you analyze the slice of reality into which God has placed you, begin with a plan of action based on what you foresee in the days ahead and how you want to mold that future. Any good plan starts with *informed readiness*. You must first become the person that God gave you life to become. To facilitate that, take your cues from God, not the world. You can do that only if you have a dynamic and vibrant relationship with Him. God, not the world, defines your purpose—to love Him with all your heart, soul, mind, and strength and to love others as you love yourself. A vital connection with God cannot happen in an hour a week in a religious environment; it must be a 24-7 engagement in which you are surrendered to Him. It is a relationship you cannot control and should not want to control; why not let your all-powerful, omniscient, loving Father guide your ways? What better alternative could there possibly be?

What kind of habits have you developed for your life? Just as cultural trends are simply the accumulation of maturing habits, your life is a series of habits that become predictable patterns (i.e., trends). Have you performed the same kind of no-holds-barred examination of your life and its patterns that you're willing to perform on our culture? An intense survey of the only universe you control—*you*—is critically important so you can have a realistic sense of where you stand and where you want to go. Only then can you devise a strategy for getting from here to there. It is not until you get serious about implementing that plan and becoming God's disciple that you can effectively partner with Him to change the world.

Take your cues from God, not the world. You can do that only if you have a dynamic and vibrant relationship with Him.

As you honestly examine your life to see where you stand, you need some metrics to help you measure the things that matter. Here are a few suggestions, taken straight from the Bible:

- Examine your worship of God: He yearns for and revels in your worship of Him.
- Determine how fully you love Him. This is not a question about emotion or feelings; it is about depth of commitment and absolute loyalty.
- How well are you representing God by serving other people? Just as Jesus Christ visited earth to demonstrate the life of a servant, so are we called to be alert to opportunities to take care of the needs of others, acting as the mouth, hands, and feet of God Himself.

- Do you consistently obey His commands? To do so, of course, you must know them.
- Surrender your will in favor of adopting His. Do you know what His will is and what it looks like in practice in the twenty-first century?

If you do these things—worship God alone, love Him completely, take care of other people, obey His commands—you will have not only revolutionized your own life, but your influence on the world will have begun in earnest. Yes, God can change the world through you, but you have to prove that you will allow God to transform you first. And you have to accept that meaningful change can be produced only when you cooperate with God. You cannot give what you don't have. You cannot be who you're not. The world will not follow you if you look and behave just like the world. What is impossible for you is possible for God. Only if you align yourself with the right Leader, and devote yourself to carrying out His vision and plans, will you be able to go places you never dreamed were possible. It's all about Him. It starts with your decision to let it be about Him and to seal that choice with your unyielding commitment to being the person He created you to be.

Genuine transformation is about loving God and people with everything you have.

Having recently completed six years of research on the question of how God transforms us, I can tell you that genuine transformation is about loving God and people with everything you have. To reach that state, you must be permanently changed. First, you have to be broken by God—broken over your sins against Him, over your focus on self, and over your reliance on society for your cues and marching orders. And it gets tougher once you are shattered by what you've done and who you've become. At that point, you have to surrender the fullness of your life to God and submit yourself to His will. That's a searing process: being humbled by your bad choices, getting over yourself, recognizing the holiness of your creator Father, accepting His forgiveness and love, and returning that love by throwing out your own plans and expectations and completely adopting His. Only then can you truly love God and others. Without this kind of inner transformation, you'll choose to love yourself more than Him. When push comes to shove and difficult choices have to be made, you'll opt for those things that advance you rather than God.

Brokenness, surrender, submission, and deep love—those are the "big four" that most of us ignore most of our lives to our own detriment and that of the people we've been placed on earth to love and serve.[1]

> *You'll find some common threads through the way God works in the lives of surrendered servants.*

It is important to embrace that transformation, because without it our metrics will be self-centered. Sure, we might have measures that examine our impact on other people, but we are essentially pursuing what *we* think needs to be done, and what *we* would like to accomplish, rather than allowing God to make those determinations for us and then to work through us in unexpected ways.

You'll find some common threads through the way God works in the lives of surrendered servants. First, you'll relax: You cannot accomplish what God calls you to do; only He can do it through you. Second, you'll be part of the true church—that is, a collection of people who have chosen to abandon their own hopes and dreams in favor of God's. The power of a community united behind God's vision for the world, and operating in the authority of His Holy Spirit, will simply blow you away. Third, your impact will transcend whatever words or marketing efforts you deploy to bring attention to what God is doing through you. This is the ultimate form of Christian evangelism: God transforming lives through the commitment of those whose lives He has already transformed. Fourth, you will no longer struggle to worship Him, and you will experience joy unlike anything you've imagined. This doesn't mean you will not encounter hardships, persecution, times of sacrifice, or moments of doubt—God has already promised that you will. But that's part of the journey too, and it makes the outcomes even sweeter.

It's not simple, and it's not an overnight process, but it begins with a promise to really go for it.

Let me now return to our earlier consideration of the one-life-at-a-time approach. To help make that strategy tangible, imagine this: Suppose you get serious about addressing what these trends are doing to America and to the church and choose to commit to irrevocably altering the trajectory of your own life's trends in order to be genuinely transformed by God. It's not simple, and it's not an overnight process, but it begins with a promise to yourself and God that you will really go for it.

Let's imagine that a hundred thousand people will read this challenge, allow the Holy Spirit to inspire and convict them, and therefore commit to reconfiguring their life's trends so their objectives and efforts line up with God's will. That would be remarkable, wouldn't it?

But continue to roll out this scenario. You and your transforming peers would not commit yourselves to God in a cultural vacuum. So imagine if each person's spiritual renaissance affected just a few people—say one family member, two close friends, two work associates, and two fellow church members—who were so inspired by what they saw God doing in the lives of the transformed that they, too, chose to reframe their life's trajectory and allowed God to transform them. That would raise the community of the newly transformed to about three-quarters of a million people. That's not bad. Yes, it would take some time for this to happen, but let's say that it occurs within a three-year period, which seems reasonable.

But then you have to believe that such a reinvigorating process could not be contained; it would repeat itself. If that were to happen, then each of the newly transformed individuals would in turn affect the lives of just a few people who are drawn to the metamorphosis they see. This time, our three-quarters of a million blossom into a community totaling upwards of five million people on the journey. Play that out one more time, and we'd have reached perhaps thirty-five million people in the course of a decade. Thirty-five million people! That is far greater than the existing sum of all Christians in the United States who are currently broken, surrendered, submitted lovers of God who are allowing Him to transform the world through them. About four to five times greater![2]

Would it matter, or would that simply become another niche to track? I'd wager that it would matter—big time. People of passion draw attention, and they experience sustained influence. Envision the changes that would follow. The raging policy debates over moral behavior would become moot in the face of a growing and unwavering segment of people who are living examples of truth and integrity. The need for unique, world-class leaders to stand up and take charge of a massive effort would be alleviated by the obvious leadership provided directly by God through His Holy Spirit. The frantic efforts of churches to attract more people would become irrelevant because Americans would be exposed to people who *are* the church of Jesus Christ, in the flesh, without buildings and programs.

People of passion draw attention, and they experience sustained influence. Envision the changes that would follow.

Do you know what's so outrageous about this wild fantasy? It was God's original plan: Send His Son to visit the earth. Model the principles and resultant behaviors. Intensely invest in a handful of followers. Let them spread the message and the way. Watch it grow and change the world. The big differences between the plan outlined above and Jesus' experience are that He is not here in the flesh to jump-start the process, and I'm proposing that we start with a hundred thousand people instead of twelve. Neither of those conditions should be a deal breaker, though. Jesus is present with us spiritually, and the process is the same regardless of the numbers. This is doable.

Jesus is present with us spiritually, and the process is the same regardless of the numbers.

My closing question for you is this: Is *Futurecast* simply a book with information you find interesting, or is it a book that you will allow God to use to reveal the trends in your life and to challenge you to change the trajectory of those trends, first in your life, then perhaps in the lives of others, one life at a time? When you boil it down, those are really your only options. And in the end, that's a choice only you can make.

Choose wisely.

Defining Our Terms

Generations

It seems that every magazine or book on the market uses different definitions for the various generations—Builders, Boomers, Busters, Mosaics, and Digitals; or Gen X, Gen Y, Millennials, Echo Boomers, Silent, Greatest, GI, etc. The reason for the lack of consistency is that there is no such thing as a generation—it is a sociological construct that lacks a definitive anchor and description.

Nearly thirty years ago, The Barna Group adopted one of the popular definitions of generations: They represent eighteen- to twenty-year periods. We have stuck with that definition for the sake of consistency. So when you read about the generations throughout this book (or in other research from me or from The Barna Group), here are the groups we are referring to:

- Builders—born from 1927 through 1945
- Boomers—born from 1946 through 1964
- Busters—born from 1965 through 1983
- Mosaics—born from 1984 through 2002
- Digitals—born from 2003 through 2021

Faith Segments

Over the years, The Barna Group has done extensive research in relation to people's religious faith. There are many ways of categorizing people within that realm. In a recent book—*The Seven Faith Tribes*—I analyzed more than thirty thousand people in order to profile their lives in relation to their faith beliefs and behaviors. The result was a discussion about the seven faith tribes of America—Captive Christians, Casual Christians, Jews, Mormons, Pantheists, Muslims, and Skeptics.[1] You will see reference to some of those tribes in this book.

But you will also see mention of other ways of categorizing people. Among those alternative groupings are "born-again Christians" and "evangelical Christians." In those cases, people assigned to those categories are there *not* on the basis of survey respondents embracing those labels; we typically do not use those terms in our research. Born-again Christians are people we categorize as such on the basis of their statement that they have made a personal commitment to Jesus Christ that is important in their lives in the present and who also contend they will go to heaven after they die only because they have confessed their sins and accepted Jesus Christ as their Savior.

Evangelicals are actually a subset of born-again adults—about one-sixth of the born-again public. They, too, are categorized as such without necessarily calling themselves evangelical. They not only meet the born-again criteria but also seven other theological perspectives. (Those include saying their faith is very important in their lives today; believing they have a personal responsibility to share their religious beliefs about Christ with non-Christians; believing that Satan exists; believing that eternal salvation is possible only through grace, not works; believing that Jesus Christ lived a sinless life on earth; asserting that the Bible is accurate in all that it teaches; and describing God as the all-knowing, all-powerful, perfect deity who created the universe and still rules it today.)[2] Being classified as either a born-again Christian or an evangelical is independent of the person's church attendance or the denominational affiliation of the church he or she most frequently attends.

How do self-reported evangelicals differ from those adults whom we categorize as evangelical on criteria other than being born again? Among the self-reported evangelicals, 13 percent do not believe that their religious faith is very important in their lives today; 27 percent do not strongly affirm that the Bible is totally accurate in all of the principles it teaches; 49 percent do not believe they have a responsibility to share their religious beliefs with other people; 67 percent do not reject the notion that Satan is merely symbolic; 58 percent do not firmly reject the idea that a person can earn eternal salvation; 39 percent do not reject the idea that Jesus sinned while He was on earth; and 13 percent have a nonbiblical view of the nature of God.

APPENDIX B

About the Research

Research Sourcing

Throughout this book you will read facts, figures, and statements that do not have a note attached. Those are bits of information that come from the national surveys conducted by The Barna Group during 2008 through 2010. Our surveys are generally conducted by telephone, with a special effort made to include people who no longer have landlines in their homes but now rely solely on mobile telephones. Sometimes we will incorporate online surveys into the final sample as well in an effort to reach people who do not respond to telephone surveys—typically young adults. All surveys among the adult public involved a minimum of one thousand people randomly selected from across the forty-eight continental states (my apologies to residents of Hawaii and Alaska).

Listed below are the details of each Barna Group study utilized.

Studies among Adults

All of the following studies were conducted among national random samples of adults. Upon completion of each survey, minimal statistical weights were applied to the data to allow the results to more closely correspond to known national demographic averages for several variables. In all surveys since 2008, the sample universe included people drawn from cell-phone households. All studies relied on callbacks to households not reached after the first attempt; a maximum of six callbacks were made to each non-responsive household, with contact attempts made at differing times of the day and days of the week. The average length of each survey was between fifteen and twenty minutes.

Field Date	Sample Size	Maximum Sampling Error
August 2010	1,000	+ 3.2 percentage points
February 2010	1,005	+ 3.2 percentage points
February 2010	1,001	+ 3.2 percentage points
September 2009	1,002	+ 3.2 percentage points
July 2009	1,000	+ 3.2 percentage points
November 2008	1,203	+ 2.9 percentage points
October 2008	1,005	+ 3.2 percentage points
August 2008	1,003	+ 3.2 percentage points
May 2008	1,003	+ 3.2 percentage points
January 2008	1,006	+ 3.2 percentage points
December 2007	1,005	+ 3.2 percentage points
August 2007	1,000	+ 3.2 percentage points
January 2007	1,003	+ 3.2 percentage points
October 2006	1,003	+ 3.2 percentage points
August 2006	1,005	+ 3.2 percentage points
May 2006	1,003	+ 3.2 percentage points
January 2006	1,003	+ 3.2 percentage points

Studies among Protestant Clergy

All of the following studies were conducted by telephone among national random samples of senior pastors, using quotas based upon each denomination's estimated incidence among all Protestant churches. Each church was contacted multiple times in an effort to reach the senior pastor and complete the interview. The average length of each interview was between seventeen and twenty-two minutes.

Field Date	Sample Size	Maximum Sampling Error
December 2009	611	+ 4.1 percentage points
August 2009	603	+ 4.1 percentage points
October 2008	605	+ 4.1 percentage points
December 2007	605	+ 4.1 percentage points
November 2007	615	+ 4.1 percentage points

Studies among Teenagers

All of the following studies were conducted among national random samples of teenagers (ages thirteen to eighteen). The sample universe was households, so each household contacted was screened for the presence of teenagers and then interviews were conducted with teenagers located in the sampled homes. Upon the completion of each survey, minimal statistical weights were applied to the data to allow the results to more closely correspond to age and gender distribution of teens. Quotas were used related to location, again based on Census Bureau figures for teenagers. Surveys conducted since 2008 have built in special efforts to include people reached via cell phone. All of these teen studies utilized callbacks to qualified households in which the resident teen was not reached on the first attempt. The average length of each survey was between sixteen and twenty minutes.

Field Date	Sample Size	Maximum Sampling Error
November 2009	602	+ 4.1 percentage points
July 2006	618	+ 4.1 percentage points

For more information about the research conducted by The Barna Group, visit www.barna.org. Additional perspectives from George Barna can be seen at www.georgebarna.com.

Acknowledgments

I'M THANKFUL FOR the help provided by many people in relation to this book.

Nancy Barna played a huge role in the process. Sure, she's my wife, so she's stuck with me. (Okay, not according to chapter 3, but you get the idea.) She not only fed me and took care of the house, the kids, and the animals while I worked absurd hours on this book, but she even gave up several days of her precious time to help organize some of the archived information I needed. Nancy, thank you. I love you and appreciate you and have benefited immeasurably from your ability to step in and fill the gaps. You have always proven to be a super partner. I hope the influence of this book is worth your investment in it.

Esther Fedorkevich is my agent, friend, and fellow revolutionary. Esther, your willingness to be a sounding board has been invaluable. Your ideas offered at critical moments in this process have been crucial. As usual, you have deftly handled this project and played a significant role in its seeing the light of day. You are always a blessing to me. May God reward your wisdom, diligence, and loyalty and bless your family for sacrificing you during our adventures in publishing.

David Kinnaman is now the majority owner of The Barna Group; I am pleased that David is taking the company forward. He graciously provided me with unrestricted access to all of the studies we did while I was still the owner of the company, as well as a few that have been undertaken since then. Without that gift, this book would be very different and, at best, incomplete. Thank you, David. You are a good friend, a terrific researcher, and a genuine follower of Jesus. I pray that God will prosper you and the company in all the years to come.

My business partners in The Strategenius Group—Connie DeBord, Robert Hawkins, and Joel Tucciarone—gave me what I needed during an intense couple of weeks during the writing of this book: encouragement and space. Thank you, my friends, and may the Lord continue to use us in serving others as compassionately as you have served me.

A boatload of people prayed for me during the writing of this book. You know who you are. What you hold in your hands is the fruit of our prayers. I hope you are pleased with this resource. Thank you for your support.

Bibliography

Anderson, Chris. *The Long Tail*. New York: Hyperion, 2006.

Barna, George. *Maximum Faith: Live Like Jesus*. New York: SGG Publishing, 2011.

———. *Revolution*. Carol Stream, IL: Tyndale House Publishers, 2005.

———. *The Seven Faith Tribes*. Carol Stream, IL: Tyndale House Publishers, 2009.

———. *Transforming Children into Spiritual Champions*. Ventura, CA: Regal Books, 2004.

Brooks, Arthur. *Gross National Happiness*. New York: Basic Books, 2008.

———. *Who Really Cares*. New York: Basic Books, 2006.

Burd-Sharps, Sarah, Kristen Lewis, and Eduardo Borges Martins. *The Measure of America*. New York: Columbia University Press, 2008.

Canton, James. *The Extreme Future*. New York: Dutton, 2006.

Christensen, Clayton, Scott Anthony, and Erik Roth. *Seeing What's Next*. Boston: Harvard Business School Press, 2004.

Dreher, Rod. *Crunchy Cons*. New York: Crown Forum, 2006.

Durant, Will and Ariel. *The Lessons of History*. New York: Simon & Schuster, 1968.

Easterbrook, Gregg. *The Progress Paradox*. New York: Random House, 2003.

Friedman, George. *The Next 100 Years*. New York: Doubleday, 2008.

Hutchison, Thomas, Amy Macy, and Paul Allen. *Record Label Marketing*. Burlington, MA: Focus Press, 2010.

Kohut, Andrew, and Bruce Stokes. *America Against the World*. New York: Times Books, 2006.

Lake, Celinda, and Kellyanne Conway. *What Women Really Want*. New York: Free Press, 2005.

Luntz, Frank. *What Americans Really Want . . . Really*. New York: Hyperion, 2009.

Penn, Mark. *Microtrends*. New York: Twelve, 2007.

U.S. Census Bureau. *Statistical Abstract of the United States: 2010*. Lanham, MD: Bernan Press, 2010.

Underhill, Paco. *The Call of the Mall*. New York: Simon & Schuster, 2004.

Watson, Richard. *Future Files*. London: Nicholas Brealey Publishing, 2008.

Winograd, Morley, and Michael Hais. *Millennial Makeover*. New Brunswick, NJ: Rutgers University Press, 2008.

Zakaria, Fareed. *The Post-American World*. New York: W.W. Norton, 2008.

Zogby, John. *The Way We'll Be*. New York: Random House, 2008.

Notes

Chapter 1: How We Live and How We Want to Live:
Our Lifestyles and Aspirations

1. U.S. Census Bureau, *Statistical Abstract of the United States: 2010*, table 674, http://www.census.gov/compendia/statab/2010/tables/10s0674.pdf; Pew Research Center, "Median Household Income: 1970-2007," http://pewsocialtrends .org/pubs/?chartid=527; "Median U.S. Household Income by State," *U.S. News & World Report*, October 5, 2010, http://politics.usnews.com/opinion/articles/2010 /10/05/median-us-household-income-by-state.html.
2. http://www.pew.org, data released April 9, 2008; "How Americans Spend Now," *Time*, April 27, 2009, 23–30.
3. Dave Manuel, "Savings Rates in the United States Have Collapsed Since Mid '80s," March 1, 2010, http://www.davemanuel.com/2010/0301/a-history-of-personal -savings-rates-in-the-united-states; "Personal Income and Outlays: September 2010," U.S. Department of Commerce, Bureau of Economic Analysis, November 1, 2010, 6.
4. Associated Press, "Slowly, Americans Regain Wealth Lost to Recession," *Baltimore Sun*, March 12, 2010; Rich Miller and Alison Sider, "Surging U.S. Savings Rate Reduces Dependence on China," Bloomberg News Service, June 26, 2009, http://www.bloomberg.com/apps/news?pid=newsarchive&sid=aome1_t5Z5y8; Jeffrey M. Jones, "Americans Shift Expectations about Retirement Funding," Gallup.com, April 29, 2010, http://www.gallup.com/poll/127592/Americans-Shift -Expectations-Retirement-Funding.aspx.
5. Dennis Jacobe, "Nearly Half of Small-Business Owners May Never Retire," Gallup Organization, October 1, 2010, http://www.gallup.com/poll/143351/nearly-half -small-business-owners-may-retire.aspx.
6. Robert J. Samuelson, "How the Mighty Have Fallen," *Newsweek*, July 11, 2009, http://www.newsweek.com/2009/07/10/how-the-mighty-have-fallen.html; Catherine

Rampell, "Shift to Saving May Be Downturn's Lasting Impact," *New York Times*, May 9, 2009, http://www.nytimes.com/2009/05/10/business/economy/10saving .html; Gallup.com, data released April 29, 2010; "25 People to Blame for the Financial Crisis," *Time*, February 23, 2009.

7. "Flow of Funds Summary Statistics, Fourth Quarter 2009," Federal Reserve Board, March 11, 2010; Brian K. Bucks, Arthur B. Kennickell, Traci L. Mach, and Kevin B. Moore, "Changes in U.S. Family Finances from 2004 to 2007: Evidence from the Survey of Consumer Finances," February 2009, http://www.federalreserve.gov/pubs /bulletin/2009/pdf/scf09.pdf.

8. Robert Samuelson, "How the Mighty Have Fallen," *Newsweek*, July 11, 2009, http://www.newsweek.com/2009/07/10/how-the-mighty-have-fallen.html.

9. U.S. Census Bureau, *Statistical Abstract of the United States: 2010*, tables 658, 662, http://www.census.gov/compendia/statab/2010/tables/10s0658.pdf, http://www .census.gov/compendia/statab/2010/tables/10s0662.pdf; TNS study reported in an e-letter from Quirk's Marketing Research, December 22, 2009.

10. Timothy W. Martin, "Hard Times Turn Coupon Clipping Into the Newest Extreme Sport," *Wall Street Journal*, March 8, 2010, http://online.wsj.com/article/SB1000142 405274870361590457505341322990166o.html.

11. "U.S. Consumer Participation in Loyalty Programs Jumps Nearly 20% Amidst Recession, Says Latest Colloquy Research," Colloquy press release, July 1, 2009, http://www.colloquy.com/files/pro70109.pdf.

12. Data from *Farmer's Friendly Review* newsletter, winter/spring 2010, 1.

13. Sharon Jayson, "Point Values Add Up to Far More Stress These Days," *USA Today*, May 5, 2008, D4.

14. Robert Frank, "The Perfect Salary for Happiness: $75,000," *Wall Street Journal*, September 7, 2010; http://blogs.wsj.com/wealth/2010/09/07/the-perfect -salary-for-happiness-75000-a-year.

15. Samantha Braverman, "Would Americans Rather Be Younger, Thinner, Richer, or Smarter?" Harris Interactive, August 26, 2010, http://www.harrisinteractive .com/NewsRoom/HarrisPolls/tabid/447/mid/1508/articleId/555/ctl/Read Custom%20Default/Default.aspx.

16. Nationwide survey by AAA, reported by Reuters on September 25, 2009.

17. George Barna, "Media Exposure, Addiction," GeorgeBarna.com, January 25, 2010, http://www.georgebarna.com/2010/01/media-exposure-addiction.

18. *Rasmussen Reports*, August 21, 2009; OmniPoll, The Barna Group, from studies conducted in 2008 and 2009; U.S. Census Bureau, *Statistical Abstract of the United States: 2010*, tables 1225, 1226, 1232, http://www.census.gov/compendia /statab/2010/tables/10s1225.pdf, http://www.census.gov/compendia/statab/2010 /tables/10s1226.pdf, http://www.census.gov/compendia/statab/2010/tables/10s1232 .pdf; Pew Research Center, data released July 29, 2009.

19. U.S. Census Bureau, *Statistical Abstract of the United States: 2010*, table 1203, http:// www.census.gov/compendia/statab/2010/tables/10s1203.pdf.

20. Ibid., table 1212, http://www.census.gov/compendia/statab/2010/tables /10s1212.pdf.

21. E-mail received from Forrester Research, July 21, 2008.

22. This study was conducted by OnePoll, based on interviews with 2,000 women, reported at www.salon.com on April 9, 2010.

23. Based on research conclusions contained in an e-mail from Forrester Research, February 11, 2010.

24. Research Note, www.pewresearch.org, posted November 4, 2009.

25. USC Annenberg School Center for the Digital Future, "2009 Digital Future Report," April 28, 2009, http://www.digitalcenter.org/pdf/2009_Digital_Future_Project _Release_Highlights.pdf.

26. Jenna Wortham, "Face-to-Face Socializing Starts with a Mobile Post," *New York Times*, October 19, 2009, http://dealbook.nytimes.com/2009/10/19/face-to-face -socializing-starts-with-a-mobile-post.

27. "The Power of Teens Who Use Social Media," *Opposing Views*, May 25, 2010, http://www.opposingviews.com/i/the-power-of-teens-who-use-social-media; "Teen Social Media Influencers Wield Power Online and Offline," June 6, 2010, http://trends.myyearbook.com.

28. Jeffrey Zaslow, "Friendship for Guys (No Tears!)," *Wall Street Journal*, April 7, 2010, http://online.wsj.com/article/SB10001424052702304620304575166090090482912 .html.

29. U.S. Census Bureau, *Statistical Abstract of the United States: 2010*, tables 94, 95, http://www.census.gov/compendia/statab/2010/tables/10s0094.pdf, http://www .census.gov/compendia/statab/2010/tables/10s0095.pdf.

30. Melissa A. Bisson and Timothy R. Levine, "Negotiating a Friends with Benefits Relationship," *Archives of Sexual Behavior*, September 13, 2007, 66–73, http://www.springerlink.com/content/t22037j0215j4367; U.S. Census Bureau, *Statistical Abstract of the United States: 2010*, table 1299, http://www.census.gov /compendia/statab/2010/tables/10s1299.pdf.

31. Larry Gordon, "Mixed-gender Dorm Rooms Are Gaining Acceptance," *Los Angeles Times*, March 15, 2010, http://articles.latimes.com/2010/mar/15/local/la-me -dorm-gender15-2010mar15.

Chapter 2: Family Life: Foundations, Continuity, Disruptions, and Possibilities

1. Benedict Carey and Tara Parker-Pope, "Marriage Stands Up for Itself," *New York Times*, June 26, 2009, http://www.nytimes.com/2009/06/28/fashion/28marriage .html; U.S. Census Bureau, *Current Population Reports*, "Household and Family Characteristics: March 1991," P20-458; U.S. Census Bureau, *Statistical Abstract of the United States: 2010*, table 56, http://www.census.gov/compendia/statab/2010 /tables/10s0056.pdf.

2. Michael McManus, "The Issue for Conservatives Is Marriage," *Virtue Online*, May 4, 2009, http://www.virtueonline.org/portal/modules/news/article.php?storyid=10367.

3. "In Love? It's Not Enough to Keep a Marriage, Study Finds," Reuters, July 14, 2009, based on data drawn from the study "What's Love Got to Do with It?" Australian National University, 2009.

4. Leslie Bennetts, "The Truth about American Marriage," *Parade*, September 21, 2008,

http://www.parade.com/hot-topics/2008/09/truth-about-american-marriage. Survey results: http://www.parade.com/hot-topics/2008/09/truth-about-american -marriage-poll-results.

5. Ibid. See also Bob Berkowitz and Susan Yager-Berkowitz, *He's Just Not Up for It Anymore* (New York: HarperCollins, 2008).

6. Leslie Bennetts, "The Truth about American Marriage," *Parade*, September 21, 2008; survey data from research by Zogby International, November 2009; Benedict Carey and Tara Parker-Pope, "Marriage Stands Up for Itself," *New York Times*, June 26, 2009, http://www.nytimes.com/2009/06/28/fashion/28marriage.html.

7. Leslie Bennetts, "The Truth about American Marriage," *Parade*, September 21, 2008; survey data from research by Zogby International, November 2009; Benedict Carey and Tara Parker-Pope, "Marriage Stands Up for Itself," *New York Times*, June 26, 2009; Bob Berkowitz and Susan Yager-Berkowitz, *He's Just Not Up for It Anymore* (New York: HarperCollins, 2008).

8. Jeffrey S. Passel, Wendy Wang, and Paul Taylor, "Marrying Out: One-in-Seven New U.S. Marriages Is Interracial or Interethnic," Pew Research Center, http:// pewsocialtrends.org/files/2010/10/755-marrying-out.pdf.

9. Carl Weisman, *So Why Have You Never Been Married?* (Far Hills, NJ: New Horizon, 2008), 16.

10. U.S. Census Bureau, *Statistical Abstract of the United States: 2010*, table 94, http://www.census.gov/compendia/statab/2010/tables/10s0094.pdf.

11. "State by State: The Legal Battle Over Gay Marriage," National Public Radio, http://www.npr.org/templates/story/story.php?storyId=112448663; Sheri and Bob Stritof, "Same Sex Marriage License Laws: United States," http://marriage.about .com/cs/marriagelicenses/a/samesexcomp.htm; "Same-sex Marriage in the United States," Wikipedia, http://en.wikipedia.org/wiki/Same-sex_marriage_in_the _United_States.

12. Brian Powell, Catherine Bolzendahl, Claudia Geist, and Lala Carr Steelman, *Counted Out: Same-Sex Relations and Americans' Definitions of Family* (New York: Russell Sage Foundation, 2010). See also Pat Wingert and Barbara Kantrowitz, "What Makes a Family?" *Newsweek*, September 30, 2010; http://www.newsweek.com/2010/10/04 /what-makes-a-family-more-americans-say-gays-count.html.

13. Charles Colson, *BreakPoint* commentary, May 22, 2009; "The Future of Marriage and Non-Traditional Relationships," http://polyinthemedia.blogspot.com/2010/03 /future-of-marriage-and-non-traditional.html; "Polyamory Is the Fastest Growing Style of Relationship," http://polyinthemedia.blogspot.com/2010/05/polyamory-is -fastest-growing-style-of.html.

14. U.S. Census Bureau, *Statistical Abstract of the United States: 2010*, tables 78, 94, http://www.census.gov/compendia/statab/2010/tables/10s0078.pdf, http://www .census.gov/compendia/statab/2010/tables/10s0094.pdf.

15. Michael McManus, "A New Agenda for Conservatives," *Virtue Online*, November 4, 2009, http://www.virtueonline.org/portal/modules/news/article.php?storyid=11510; U.S. Census Bureau, *Statistical Abstract of the United States: 2010*, table 1300, http:// www.census.gov/compendia/statab/2010/tables/10s1300.pdf.

16. The terms *evangelical Christian* and *born-again Christian* are not based on self-classification in The Barna Group surveys. Born-again Christians are defined as

people who say they "have made a personal commitment to Jesus Christ that is still important in their lives today," and who also indicate they believe that when they die they will go to heaven because they have confessed their sins and have accepted Jesus Christ as their savior. Respondents are not asked to describe themselves as "born again." Evangelicals meet the born-again criteria as well as seven other conditions. Those include saying their faith is very important in their lives today; believing they have a personal responsibility to share their religious beliefs about Christ with non-Christians; believing that Satan exists; believing that eternal salvation is possible only through God's grace, not good deeds; believing that Jesus Christ lived a sinless life on earth; asserting that the Bible is accurate in all of the principles it teaches; and describing God as the all-knowing, all-powerful, perfect deity who created the universe and still rules it today. Respondents were not asked to describe themselves as evangelical. Being classified "born again" or "evangelical" is not dependent on church attendance or the denominational affiliation of the church attended.

17. Jeff Jones and Lydia Saad, "Values and Beliefs: 2010," The Gallup Organization, May 6, 2010, http://www.gallup.com.

18. U.S. Census Bureau, *Statistical Abstract of the United States: 2010*, tables 34, 56, http://www.census.gov/compendia/statab/2010/tables/10s0034.pdf, http://www.census.gov/compendia/statab/2010/tables/10s0056.pdf.

19. Census Bureau News, July 28, 2008; private correspondence with Michael McManus, June 6, 2008, based on research conducted for and contained in his book *Living Together* (New York: Simon & Schuster, 2008).

20. Private correspondence with Michael McManus, June 6, 2008, and July 18, 2008, based on research conducted for and contained in his book *Living Together* (New York: Simon & Schuster, 2008); Lydia Saad, "By Age 24, Marriage Wins Out," The Gallup Organization, August 11, 2008, http://www.gallup.com/poll/109402/age-24-marriage-wins.aspx; U.S. Census Bureau, *Statistical Abstract of the United States: 2010*, tables 63, 94, http://www.census.gov/compendia/statab/2010/tables/10s0063.pdf, http://www.census.gov/compendia/statab/2010/tables/10s0094.pdf.

21. Sharon Jayson, "Report: Cohabiting Has Little Effect on Marriage Success," *USA Today*, March 2, 2010, http://www.usatoday.com/news/health/2010-03-02-cohabiting02_N.htm; Sharon Jayson, "Couples Study Debunks 'Trial Marriage' Notion of Cohabiting," *USA Today*, July 8, 2009, http://www.usatoday.com/news/nation/2009-07-08-living-together_N.htm.

22. Sharon Jayson, "Couples Study Debunks 'Trial Marriage' Notion of Cohabiting," *USA Today*, July 8, 2009.

23. See note 20.

24. U.S. Census Bureau, *Statistical Abstract of the United States: 2010*, tables 59, 67, 682, http://www.census.gov/compendia/statab/2010/tables/10s0059.pdf, http://www.census.gov/compendia/statab/2010/tables/10s0067.pdf, http://www.census.gov/compendia/statab/2010/tables/10s0682.pdf.

25. Benjamin Scafidi, "The Taxpayer Cost of Divorce and Unwed Childbearing," Institute for American Values, April 15, 2008, 5; Charles Colson, *BreakPoint* commentary, January 14, 2010.

26. Pamela Paul, "The Un-Divorced," *New York Times*, July 30, 2010; http://www.nytimes.com/2010/08/01/fashion/01Undivorced.html.

27. U.S. Census Bureau, *Statistical Abstract of the United States: 2010*, tables 78, 99, http://www.census.gov/compendia/statab/2010/tables/10s0078.pdf, http://www.census.gov/compendia/statab/2010/tables/10s0099.pdf; "Births, Marriages, Divorces, and Deaths: Provisional Data for August 2009," Centers for Disease Control, *National Vital Statistics Report*, vol. 58, no. 18, http://www.cdc.gov/nchs/data/nvsr/nvsr58/nvsr58_18.htm.

28. "Births, Marriages, Divorces, and Deaths: Provisional Data for August 2009," Centers for Disease Control, *National Vital Statistics Report*, vol. 58, no. 18, http://www.cdc.gov/nchs/data/nvsr/nvsr58/nvsr58_18.htm; Robert Rector, "Understanding Illegitimacy," *National Review Online*, April 12, 2010, http://www.nationalreview.com/articles/229515/understanding-illegitimacy-robert-rector.

29. Robert Rector, "Understanding Illegitimacy," *National Review Online*, April 12, 2010; "The New Face of Motherhood," *Pastors Weekly Briefing*, vol. 18, no. 20, May 14, 2010, http://www.parsonage.org/images/pwbe/issues/PWB-100514.html; data drawn from a *CBS News/New York Times* survey, April 2009.

30. See note 29.

31. "Having Kids Makes You Happy," *Newsweek*, July 7, 2008, 62, http://www.newsweek.com/2008/06/28/having-kids-makes-you-happy.html; "The New Face of Motherhood," *Pastors Weekly Briefing*, vol. 18, no. 20, May 14, 2010, http://www.parsonage.org/images/pwbe/issues/PWB-100514. html; data drawn from a *CBS News/New York Times* survey, April 2009.

32. Pew Research Center, research notes posted May 6, 2010, http://www.pew.org; Centers for Disease Control reports on assisted reproductive technology: http://www.cdc.gov/art/ART2006/section5.htm#f49, and http://www.cdc.gov/art/ART2007/section5.htm; "The Adopted Child," National Adoption Information Clearinghouse, http://www.aacap.org/galleries/FactsForFamilies/15_the_adopted_child.pdf.

33. Robert J. Samuelson, "America Falling into Parent Trap," *Orange County Register*, August 6, 2010, http://www.ocregister.com/articles/children-261070-child-family.html?wap=0.

34. Sharon Jayson, "Parents, Kids Today More in Harmony than Prior Generations," *USA Today*, August 12, 2009, http://www.usatoday.com/news/nation/2009-08-12-generation-gap-pew_N.htm.

35. Sharon Jayson, "New Daditude: Today's Fathers Are Hands-on, Pressure Off," *USA Today*, June 20, 2009, http://www.usatoday.com/news/nation/2009-06-16-dad-fathers-parenting_N.htm; Sharon Jayson, "Family Life, Roles Changing as Couples Seek Balance," *USA Today*, April 19, 2009, http://www.usatoday.com/news/health/2009-04-18-families-conf_N.htm; "71 percent Still Say Being a Father Most Important Role for a Man," *Rasmussen Reports*, June 20, 2010, http://www.rasmussenreports.com/public_content/lifestyle/holidays/june_2010/71_still_say_being_a_father_most_important_role_for_a_man.

36. "America's Children: Key National Indicators of Well-Being, 2009," http://www.childstats.gov/americaschildren09; "The Myth of the Over-Scheduled Child," *Connect with Kids* newsletter, October 22, 2008, http://www.connectwithkids.com/tipsheet/2008/408_oct22/thisweek/081022_child.shtml.

37. Sharon Jayson, "It's Cooler than Ever to Be a Tween, but Is Childhood Lost?" *USA Today*, February 4, 2009, http://www.usatoday.com/news/health/2009-02-03-tweens

-behavior_N.htm; Sharon Jayson, "How Stressed Are Kids? More than We Think," *USA Today*, November 3, 2009, http://www.usatoday.com/news/health/2009-11-04 -APAkidstress04_ST_N.htm.

38. Sharon Jayson "There's a Reason You're Happiest on Weekends," *USA Today*, January 12, 2010, http://www.usatoday.com/news/health/2010-01-12-weekends12_ ST_N.htm; Sharon Jayson, "How Stressed Are Kids? More than We Think," *USA Today*, November 3, 2009, http://www.usatoday.com/news/health/2009-11-04 -APAkidstress04_ST_N.htm.

39. Robin Marantz Henig, "What Is It About 20-Somethings?" *New York Times*, August 18, 2010, http://www.nytimes.com/2010/08/22/magazine/22Adulthood-t .html?_r=3&src=me&ref=homepage.

40. Blair Minton, "Tremendous Potential for Affordable Assisted Living," Center for Excellence in Assisted Living, May 2010, http://www.theceal.org/column. php?ID=34; "Aging Services: The Facts," *Leading Age*, http://www.aahsa.org/facts; "Thirteen Million Baby Boomers Care for Ailing Parents, 25% Live with Parents," *Senior Journal*, October 19, 2005, http://seniorjournal.com/NEWS/Boomers/5-10 -19BoomersCare4Parents.htm.

41. For more information on the research, see George Barna, *Transforming Children into Spiritual Champions* (Ventura, CA: Regal, 2003), and George Barna, *Revolutionary Parenting* (Carol Stream, IL: Tyndale House Publishers, 2007).

42. For more about the possibilities generated by investing in young people's lives, the obstacles to the parent/church partnership, and strategies for overcoming those barriers, see George Barna, *Transforming Children into Spiritual Champions* (Ventura, CA: Regal, 2003).

43. This does not mean that people do not change at all in their adult years. On average, the changes evident in adult lives are minimal. Occasionally, however, God introduces some major event, relationship, or idea into people's lives and their worldview radically changes. That is not normal, but it does happen. The Holy Spirit can change any person, at any time, for any reason, in any way, without warning.

Chapter 3: Attitudes and Values: The Mind Stuff That Defines Us

1. Justin Pope, "Admissions Boards Face Grade Inflation," Associated Press, November 18, 2006; Gordon C. Winston, "The Decline in Undergraduate Teaching," http://www.williams.edu/wpehe/DPs/DP-24.pdf; M. Donald Thomas and William L. Bainbridge, "Grade Inflation: The Current Fraud," *Effective School Research*, January 1997, http://schoolmatch.com/articles/esrjan97.htm; Raina Kelley, "Generation Me," *Newsweek*, April 18, 2009, http://www.newsweek.com/2009 /04/17/generation-me.html.

2. Jason F., "Forbes Misses the Point of the 4-Day Work Week," *Signal vs. Noise*, August 20, 2008, http://37signals.com/svn/posts/1209-forbes-misses-the-point -of-the-4-day-work-week; Bryan Walsh, "The Four-Day Work Week Is Winning Fans," *Time*, September 7, 2009, http://www.time.com/time/magazine/article /0,9171,1919162,00.html.

3. Arthur Brooks, *Gross National Happiness* (New York: Basic Books, 2008); Marshall and Kelly Goldsmith, "How Happiness Happens," *Businessweek*, December 11, 2009, 92, http://www.businessweek.com/magazine/content/09_51/b4160092992355.htm; Rana Foroohar, "The Recession Generation," *Newsweek*, January 9, 2010, http://www.newsweek.com/2010/01/08/the-recession-generation.html.

4. Rana Foroohar, "The Recession Generation," *Newsweek*, January 9, 2010, http://www.newsweek.com/2010/01/08/the-recession-generation.html.

5. *Rasmussen Reports*, October 8, 2009; November 6, 2009; May 10, 2010; http://www.rasmussenreports.com.

6. Lydia Saad, "Americans' Confidence in Military Up, Banks Down," June 24, 2009, http://www.gallup.com/poll/121214/Americans-Confidence-Military-Banks-Down .aspx; "Virtually No Change in Annual Harris Poll Confidence Index from Last Year," March 9, 2010, http://www.businesswire.com/news/home/20100309005415 /en/Virtually-Change-Annual-Harris-Poll-Confidence-Index.

7. *Rasmussen Reports*, March 4, 2010, www.rasmussenreports.com.

8. "AARP Survey: 70 Percent of Americans Believe the Country Has Not Lived up to Kennedy's Inaugural Request," PR Newswire, January 19, 2009, http://newsblaze .com/story/2009011906130300001.pnw/topstory.html.

9. Raina Kelley, "Generation Me," *Newsweek*, April 18, 2009, http://www.newsweek .com/2009/04/17/generation-me.html; Sharon Jayson, "Year in Review: Narcissism, Stress in Psych News Spotlight," *USA Today*, December 30, 2009, http://www.usatoday.com/news/health/2009-12-31-yearendbehavior31_ST_N.htm.

10. "69 Percent Say Americans Are Becoming More Rude, Less Civilized," *Rasmussen Reports*, August 17, 2010, http://www.rasmussenreports.com/public_content /lifestyle/general_lifestyle/august_2010/69_say_americans_are_becoming_more _rude_less_civilized.

11. Ibid.

12. Edward Wyatt, "More than Ever, You Can Say That on Television," *New York Times*, November 13, 2009, http://www.nytimes.com/2009/11/14/business/media/14vulgar .html.

13. Chantal M. Lovell, "3 UR Professors Study Increase in Disrespect in Classroom," *Redlands Daily Facts*, May 24, 2010, http://www.redlandsdailyfacts.com/ci_15151889 ?source=rss_emailed; "Swearing Habit," *Connect with Kids* newsletter, April 21, 2010, http://www.connectwithkids.com/tipsheet/2010/486_apr21/thisweek/100421 _swearing.shtml; K. J. Mullins, "Bullies, Drugs, and Disrespect Top Concerns for Schools," *Digital Journal*, April 29, 2010, http://www.digitaljournal.com /article/291366.

14. *Rasmussen Reports*, October 9, 2009, www.rasmussenreports.com; "Character Study Reveals Predictors of Lying and Cheating," Josephson Institute report, October 29, 2009, http://josephsoninstitute.org/surveys/index.html.

15. "Character Study Reveals Predictors of Lying and Cheating," Josephson Institute report, October 29, 2009, http://josephsoninstitute.org/surveys/index.html; "The Ethics of American Youth: 2008," Josephson Institute report, http://charactercounts .org/programs/reportcard/2008/index.html.

16. Nicholas Kulish, "Author, 17, Says It's 'Mixing,' Not Plagiarism," *New York Times*,

February 11, 2010, http://www.nytimes.com/2010/02/12/world/europe/12germany.html.

17. Alan Siegel, "The Stimulus America Needs: Trust," *Christian Science Monitor*, January 27, 2009, http://www.csmonitor.com/Commentary/Opinion/2009/0127/p09s01-coop.html; data from Pew Research Center, April 15, 2008, http://www.pewresearch.org; data from *Rasmussen Reports*, October 27, 2009, http://www.rasmussenreports.com.
18. Lymari Morales, "Distrust in U.S. Media Edges Up to Record High," The Gallup Organization, September 29, 2010, http://www.gallup.com/poll/143267/distrust-media-edges-record-high.aspx.
19. *Rasmussen Reports*, "66 percent of Voters Are Angry at the Media," June 15, 2010, http://www.rasmussenreports.com/public_content/politics/general_politics/june_2010/66_of_voters_are_angry_at_the_media.
20. Christine Lagorio, "A New Age of Celebrity Worship," *CBS News*, March 3, 2006, http://www.cbsnews.com/stories/2006/03/03/health/webmd/main1366162.shtml.
21. Charles Jennings, "The Power of X: Experiential Learning in Today's World," October 7, 2009, http://charles-jennings.blogspot.com/2009/10/power-of-x-experiential-learning-in.html.
22. Jeffrey M. Jones, "Americans' Outlook for U.S. Morality Remains Bleak," Gallup Organization, May 17, 2010, http://www.gallup.com/poll/128042/americans-outlook-morality-remains-bleak.aspx.
23. Jeff Jones and Lydia Saad, "Gallup Poll Social Series: Values and Beliefs," Gallup Organization, May 26, 2010, http://www.gallup.com/poll/File/133337/Moral_Acceptability_May_26_2010.pdf.

Chapter 4: Media, Technology, and Entertainment: The Tools and Conduits That Define Our Lives

1. Among the eight forms of media we tested in our national survey of 1,004 adults, there was not one form that even half of the respondents said had significant influence on them. Only one-third (34 percent) said the most influential of those eight media—books—had significant influence on their thinking and behavior, while the purportedly least-influential media (movies and the Internet) were said by just 7 percent to have significant influence on them.
2. Several years ago we conducted research on influence and discovered that seven combined entities—music, books, Internet content, movies, televised content, laws, and our families—have most of the influence on what we think and do. Other media—such as radio and video games—also contribute a discernible degree of influence on how we live. For more information on that research, see George Barna, *Revolution* (Carol Stream, IL: Tyndale House Publishers, 2005).
3. U.S. Census Bureau, *Statistical Abstract of the United States: 2010*, table 1094, http://www.census.gov/compendia/statab/2010/tables/10s1094.pdf. This research was conducted by Veronis Suhler Stevenson. The methodology used appears to significantly underestimate the amount of time devoted to Internet usage, pegging it at about four hours per week. The Barna Group studies, similar to those of several

other research groups, estimate Internet use to be about fifteen to twenty hours per week among those who use the Net.

4. International Federation of the Phonographic Industry, January 3, 2008.

5. Pew Research Center, "49%—The Beatles: Here, There, Everywhere," http://pewresearch.org/databank/dailynumber/?NumberID=844.

6. Nielsen SoundScan, "2009 U.S. Music Purchases up 2.1% over 2008; Music Sales Exceed 1.5 Billion for Second Consecutive Year," *BusinessWire*, January 6, 2010, http://www.businesswire.com/news/home/20100106007077/en/2009-U.S.-Music -Purchases-2.1-2008-Music.

7. *BBC News*, "Legal Downloads Swamped by Piracy," January 16, 2009, http://news .bbc.co.uk/2/hi/technology/7832396.stm.

8. Thomas Hutchison et. al., *Record Label Marketing*, 42–45; Ed Christman, "US Album Sales Fall 12.8% in 2010, Digital Tracks Eke Out 1% Gain," *Billboard*, January 5, 2010, http://www.billboard.com/news/u-s-album-sales-fall-12-8 -in-2010-digital-1004137859.story#/news/u-s-album-sales-fall-12-8-in-2010 -digital-1004137859.story.

9. Arik Hesseldahl, "The iPod is Dead. Long Live the iPod," *Businessweek*, July 26, 2009, http://www.businessweek.com/technology/content/jul2009 /tc20090726_261031.htm.

10. See note 8.

11. "Best-selling Albums in the United States Since SoundScan Tracking Began," Wikipedia article accessed January 30, 2011, http://en.wikipedia.org/wiki /Best-selling_albums_in_the_United_States_since_Nielsen_SoundScan_tracking _began#2000.5B18.5D.5B21.5D.

12. Ed Christman, "'Thriller' Sales Soar Close to Eagles' 'Hits,'" Reuters, July 19, 2009, http://www.reuters.com/article/idUSTRE56I2B820090719.

13. Sean Michaels, "Most Music Didn't Sell a Single Copy in 2008," *Guardian*, December 23, 2008, http://www.guardian.co.uk/music/2008/dec/23/music-sell-sales.

14. Grammy.com, "Global Concert Business Healthy in 2009," December 11, 2009, http://www.grammy.com/blogs/global-concert-business-healthy-in-2009; Ray Waddell, "U2 Manager Delighted to Bring Stage Show Full Circle," Reuters, September 23, 2009, http://www.reuters.com/article/idUSTRE58M17Q20090923; *Rolling Stone*, October 15, 2009, 42; Edna Gundersen, "U2 Turns 360 Stadium Tour into Attendance-shattering Sellouts," *USA Today*, October 5, 2009, http://www.usatoday.com/life/music/news/2009-10-04-u2-stadium-tour_N.htm; Mark Joseph, "Molly Jenson and the House Concert Phenomenon," *The Huffington Post*, August 5, 2009, http://www.huffingtonpost.com/mark-joseph/molly-jenson -and-the-hous_b_251469.html; John McAlley, "Too Big for Texas," National Public Radio, October 13, 2009, http://www.npr.org/blogs/monkeysee/2009/10/too_big _for_texas_u2s_clay_vs.html.

15. Tom Lowry, "Vevo Aims to Help Music Companies Cash In on Video," Businessweek, December 6, 2009, http://www.businessweek.com/technology /content/dec2009/tc2009126_307441.htm.

16. Paul Bonanos, "'All You Can Eat' Music Services Still Don't Have Everything You Want to Hear," GigaOM.com, March 17, 2010, http://gigaom.com/2010/03/17 /all-you-can-eat-music-services-still-dont-have-everything-you-want-to-hear.

17. Charles M. Blow, "Swan Songs?" *New York Times*, July 31, 2009, http://www
.nytimes.com/2009/08/01/opinion/01blow.html?scp=1&sq=swan+song+8%2F1
%2F2009&st=nyt; Matt Rosoff, "10 Music-tech Trends That Will Shape the Next
Decade," *CNET*, December 28, 2009, http://news.cnet.com/8301-13526_3
-10422428-27.html.

18. Arbitron, Inc., "Use of Social Media Explodes," April 8, 2010, http://arbitron
.mediaroom.com/index.php?s=43&item=682.

19. Tom Webster, "The Infinite Dial: Digital Platforms and the Future of Radio,"
Edison Research, April 8, 2010; Marisa Taylor, "A 'Traditional' Radio for the Internet
Age," *Wall Street Journal*, March 20, 2010, http://online.wsj.com/article/SB100014
24052748703580904575132032760207868.html; Om Malik, "Pandora: Streaming
Everywhere on Everything," *Businessweek*, January 12, 2010, http://www
.businessweek.com/technology/content/jan2010/tc20100112_584610.htm.

20. Andy Fixmer and Ronald Grover, "For MySpace, a Fresh Coat of Paint,"
Businessweek, October 27, 2010, http://www.businessweek.com/magazine
/content/10_45/b4202042143361.htm.

21. That fewer adults use the Internet at a place of employment can be misleading. Just
over half of all people in the labor force use the Internet at work, but because only
66 percent of adults are in the labor force, the aggregate usage-at-work figure appears
lower than it is. See U.S. Census Bureau, *Statistical Abstract of the United States: 2010*,
table 1120, http://www.census.gov/compendia/statab/2010/tables/10s1120.pdf.

22. U.S. Census Bureau, "Computer and Internet Use in the United States: 2007,"
http://www.census.gov/population/www/socdemo/computer/2007.html.

23. Arbitron, Inc., "Use of Social Media Explodes," April 8, 2010, http://arbitron
.mediaroom.com/index.php?s=43&item=682.

24. eTForecasts, "Internet User Forecasts by Country," http://www.etforecasts.com
/products/ES_intusersv2.htm; e-mail correspondence from Forrester Research, sent
February 29, 2008.

25. John Horrigan, "Use of Cloud Computing Applications and Services," Pew Research
Center, September 12, 2008, http://www.pewinternet.org/Reports/2008/Use-of
-Cloud-Computing-Applications-and-Services/Data-Memo.aspx; Ted Hoy, "The
Next Revolution: Cloud Computing and Web 3.0," *Chief Marketer*, November 9,
2009, http://chiefmarketer.com/technology/1109-cloud-computing/index.html.

26. Benny Evangelista, "TV Viewers Falling for the Evil Plot," *San Francisco Chronicle*,
July 29, 2009, http://www.sfgate.com/cgi-bin/blogs/techchron/detail?entry
_id=44457; Pew Research Center, "Internet and American Life Project: April
2009—Economy," April 19, 2009, http://pewinternet.org/Shared-Content/Data
-Sets/2009/April-2009-Economy.aspx; e-mail from Forrester Research, sent
July 24, 2009.

27. Pew Research Center, "Internet and American Life Project: April 2009—Economy,"
April 19, 2009, http://pewinternet.org/Shared-Content/Data-Sets/2009/April-2009
-Economy.aspx; e-mail from Forrester Research, sent July 24, 2009; Lance Whitney,
"More TVs Hopping onto the Internet," *CNET*, February 24, 2010, http://news
.cnet.com/8301-17938_105-10458846-1.html.

28. Kristin McGrath, "Status Update: Facebook Logs 500 Million Members," *USA*

Today, July 21, 2010, http://www.usatoday.com/tech/news/2010-07-21-facebook
-hits-500-million-users_N.htm.

29. Jeremiah Owyang, "A Collection of Social Network Stats for 2009," *Web Strategy*,
January 11, 2009, http://www.web-strategist.com/blog/2009/01/11/a-collection
-of-soical-network-stats-for-2009; Jean-Louis Gassée, "The 2010 Tech Watch List,"
Monday Note, January 3, 2010, http://www.mondaynote.com/2010/01/03/the
-2010-tech-watch-list/#more-2343.

30. U.S. Census Bureau, *Statistical Abstract of the United States: 2010*, table 1243,
http://www.census.gov/compendia/statab/2010/tables/10s1243.pdf; Deborah Yao,
"Forecaster Boosts U.S. Ad Revenue Outlook for 2010," Associated Press, January 9,
2010, http://abcnews.go.com/Business/wireStory?id=9603254; Ian McKee, "TV Ad
Revenue Declines 22% in 2009 in USA," The Power of Influence, December 30,
2009, http://thepowerofinfluence.typepad.com/the_power_of_influence/2009/12
/the-television-industry-in-the-us-is-expected-to-see-lower-than-expected-revenues
-of-156-billion-in-2009-that-will-make-fo.html.

31. Matt Richtel and Brian Stelter, "In the Living Room, Hooked on Pay TV," *New
York Times*, August 22, 2010, http://www.nytimes.com/2010/08/23/business
/media/23couch.html; Roger Cheng, "Cutting the Cable Cord Gets Easier," *Wall
Street Journal*, October 13, 2010, http://online.wsj.com/article/SB100014240527487
03440004575548083813748368.html.

32. Sue Zeidler, "Global Box Office Hit Record in 2008," Reuters, March 31, 2009,
http://uk.reuters.com/article/idUKN3144101520090331?pageNumber=1.

33. AP release, June 22, 2009; Ronald Grover, Adam Satariano, and Ari Levy, "Netflix
vs. the Hollywood Studios," *Businessweek*, December 29, 2009, http://www
.businessweek.com/magazine/content/10_02/b4162054151330.htm.

34. Jessica Mintz, "Redbox's Machines Take On Netflix's Red Envelopes," Associated
Press, June 22, 2009, http://www.usatoday.com/tech/news/2009-06-22-redbox_N
.htm; Lauren A. E. Schuker and Ethan Smith, "Hollywood Eyes Shortcut to TV,"
Wall Street Journal, May 22, 2010, http://online.wsj.com/article/SB10001424052748
704167704575258761968531140.html.

35. *Variety*, September 7–13, 2008, 6.

36. *Rasmussen Reports*, February 6, 2010.

37. U.S. Census Bureau, *Statistical Abstract of the United States: 2010*, table 1100,
http://www.census.gov/compendia/statab/2010/tables/10s1100.pdf; Steven Piersanti,
"The Ten Awful Truths About Book Publishing," Berrett-Koehler Publishers, June 15,
2009, http://www.bkpextranet.com/AuthorMaterials/10AwfulTruths.htm.

38. *Entertainment Weekly*, September 18, 2008, 28; *Rasmussen Reports*, November 17,
2008; data supplied by the American Association of Publishers in August 2010.

39. Julie Bosman, "In Study, Children Cite Appeal of Digital Reading," *New York Times*,
September 29, 2010, http://www.nytimes.com/2010/09/29/books/29kids.html.

40. "Google eBooks," http://googlesystem.blogspot.com/2010/12/google-ebooks.html;
Sam Diaz, "Google Challenges E-readers by Taking E-books Directly to Browser,"
ZDNet, October 15, 2009, http://www.zdnet.com/blog/btl/google-challenges-e
-readers-by-taking-e-books-directly-to-browser/26051; James Crawford, "On the
Future of Books," Inside Google Books (blog), October 14, 2010, http://booksearch
.blogspot.com/2010/10/on-future-of-books.html.

41. Pew Project for Excellence in Journalism, "The State of the News Media 2010," March 2010, http://www.stateofthemedia.org/2010.
42. Pew Project for Excellence in Journalism, "The State of the Media 2008," March 2008, http://www.stateofthemedia.org/2008/Journalist%20report%202008.pdf.
43. Rasmussen Reports, "67% Say News Media Have Too Much Influence over Government Decisions," January 14, 2010, http://www.rasmussenreports.com /public_content/politics/general_politics/january_2010/67_say_news_media_have _too_much_influence_over_government_decisions.
44. Pew Project for Excellence in Journalism, "The State of the News Media 2010," March 2010, http://www.stateofthemedia.org/2010.
45. E-mail sent from Forrester Research, January 25, 2008; Pew Research Center, "Adults and Video games," Pew Internet & American Life Project, December 7, 2008, http://www.pewinternet.org/Reports/2008/Adults-and-Video-Games/1-Data-Memo .aspx.
46. Jamin Brophy-Warren and David Lidsky, "Power Play," *Fast Company*, May 2010, 42.
47. Common Sense Media, "Is Texting Taking Over Your Teen?" http://www.common sensemedia.org/texting-taking-over-your-teen; Common Sense Media, "Responsible Text Messaging Tips," http://www.commonsensemedia.org/responsible-text -messaging-tips; Tim Parry, "Twitter Better for Nonsense than Business Sense," *Chief Marketer*, August 24, 2009, http://multichannelmerchant.com/social-media /twitter/0824-twitter-business-pointless-babble/index.html.
48. U.S. Census Bureau, *Statistical Abstract of the United States: 2010*, table 1111, http://www.census.gov/compendia/statab/2010/tables/10s1111.pdf; data from the Centers for Disease Control and Prevention, reported by the *New York Times*, May 13, 2010.

Chapter 5: Americans' Religious Beliefs: The New Train of Thought

1. I have written extensively about different ways of categorizing people in relation to their faith. A couple of different perspectives are contained in *The Seven Faith Tribes* (Carol Stream, IL: Tyndale House Publishers, 2009) and *Revolution* (Tyndale, 2005).
2. This profile is based on people's self-report of alignment with a Protestant or Catholic church or of calling themselves Christian but not aligning with Protestantism or Catholicism. Similarly, the number who say they are associated with another faith group (Mormon, Muslim, Jew, etc.) is based on self-reporting.
3. In Barna Group surveys, an "evangelical" is someone who meets nine criteria based on answers to survey questions. They are people who say their faith is very important in their lives today; believe they have a personal responsibility to share their religious beliefs about Christ with non-Christians; believe that Satan exists; believe that eternal salvation is possible only through grace, not works; believe that Jesus Christ lived a sinless life on earth; assert that the Bible is accurate in all that it teaches; and describe God as the all-knowing, all-powerful, perfect deity who created the universe and still rules it today. In addition, they meet the "born-again" criteria by saying they have made a personal commitment to Jesus Christ that is still important

in their lives today and that they believe that when they die they will go to heaven because they have confessed their sins and have accepted Jesus Christ as their savior. Being classified as an evangelical is *not* dependent upon church attendance, the denominational affiliation of the church attended, or calling oneself an evangelical.

4. People who are non-evangelical born-again Christians meet the born-again survey criteria but do not meet the other evangelical criteria (see prior footnote for descriptions). Respondents are *not* classified as "born again" on the basis of choosing that description for themselves.

5. Notional Christians are defined as people who consider themselves to be Christian but do not meet the born-again criteria used in the survey (see note 3 in this chapter for description).

6. St. Matthews Churches, "Bible Facts," http://www.saintmatthewschurches.com /BibleFacts.aspx, accessed June 10, 2010; Daniel Radosh, "The Good Book Business," *The New Yorker*, December 18, 2006, http://www.newyorker.com/archive/2006/12 /18/061218fa_fact1; David Cameron, "Internet Bible Sales on the Rise for New Reasons," ArticlesBase, October 31, 2008, http://www.articlesbase.com/religion -articles/internet-bible-sales-on-the-rise-for-new-reasons-623017.html.

7. See note 6.

8. For a more complete discussion about the early church and how the current state of the local church has evolved, see Frank Viola and George Barna, *Pagan Christianity?* (Carol Stream, IL: Tyndale House Publishers, 2008).

Chapter 6: America's Religious Behavior: Practicing What We Think We've Preached

1. Over the past twenty years we have toyed with different ways of measuring attendance to see what the variations are. In the different experiments we have conducted, the results have never diminished the attendance total by more than five percentage points. On the other hand, none of the alternative methods we have used has ever produced an increase in church attendance.

2. Barna Group data pertaining to tithing includes all money given away by individuals, not just money donated to churches.

Chapter 7: Institutional Faith: The New Face and Emerging Emphases of Organized Religion

1. Pew Forum on Religious and Public Life, "U.S. Religious Landscape Survey: Summary of Key Findings," February 2008, http://religions.pewforum.org/reports.

2. Pew Forum on Religious and Public Life, *U.S. Religious Landscape Survey*, February 2008, 30–31.

3. Jeffrey M. Jones, "U.S. Clergy, Bankers See New Lows in Honesty/Ethics Ratings," Gallup, December 9, 2009, http://www.gallup.com/poll/124628/Clergy-Bankers -New-Lows-Honesty-Ethics-Ratings.aspx; Lydia Saad, "Americans' Confidence in

Military Up, Banks Down," Gallup, June 24, 2009, http://www.gallup.com/poll
/121214/Americans-Confidence-Military-Banks-Down.aspx.

4. *Outreach* magazine, special issue on "The Outreach 100," September 2009, http://
www.outreachmagazine.com/resources/outreach100/2009-outreach100/3158-2009
-Outreach-100-Tracks-Top-Churches.html.

5. Based partially on studies described in an article in *UA News*, a publication of the
University of Arizona, June 6, 2008, describing analyses performed by a team of
University of Arizona sociologists using data from the National Congregations Study.

6. David Van Biema, "Rural Churches Grapple with a Pastor Exodus," *Time*, January
29, 2009, http://www.time.com/time/magazine/article/0,9171,1874843,00.html.

7. Other helpful sources of information about congregational conditions are the
National Congregations Study (http://www.soc.duke.edu/natcong) and Hartford
Institute for Religion Research's "Fast Facts" page (http://hirr.hartsem.edu/research
/fastfacts/fast_facts.html#numcong).

8. G. Jeffrey MacDonald, "Seminaries Face Financial Woes," *USA Today*, March 17,
2009, http://www.usatoday.com/news/religion/2009-03-17-seminaries_N.htm.

9. *Theographics*˜ is a term we coined in the 1990s to summarize the diverse measures
that researchers and analysts use to create a profile of people's religious beliefs and
behaviors. It refers to the statistical data that describe the religious and spiritual
components of a population.

10. Wolfgang Simson, *The House Church Book* (Carol Stream, IL: Tyndale House
Publishers, 2009).

11. For further information about house church research, see George Barna, "How
Many People Really Attend a House Church? Barna Study Finds It Depends on the
Definition," *Barna Group*, August 31, 2009, http://www.barna.org/organic-church
-articles/291-how-many-people-really-attend-a-house-church-barna-study-finds-it
-depends-on-the-definition; George Barna, "House Churches Are More Satisfying
to Attenders Than Are Conventional Churches," Barna Group, January 8, 2007,
http://www.barna.org/organic-church-articles/112-house-churches-are-more
-satisfying-to-attenders-than-are-conventional-churches.

Chapter 8: Our Profile: Demographics Are Not Destiny

1. Martin Walker, "The World's New Numbers," *The Wilson Quarterly*, Spring 2009,
24–31.

2. U.S. Census Bureau, "U.S. Population Increases," http://2010.census.gov
/mediacenter/awareness/us-population-increases.php.

3. U.S. Census Bureau, *Statistical Abstract of the United States: 2010*, tables 1–3,
http://www.census.gov/compendia/statab/2010/tables/10s0001.pdf, http://www
.census.gov/compendia/statab/2010/tables/10s0002.pdf, http://www.census.gov
/compendia/statab/2010/tables/10s0003.pdf.

4. Ibid., tables 5, 80, http://www.census.gov/compendia/statab/2010/tables/10s0005
.pdf, http://www.census.gov/compendia/statab/2010/tables/10s0080.pdf.

5. U.S. Census Bureau, "Census Bureau News," September 21, 2009; Laura B. Shrestha,
The Changing Demographic Profile of the United States, Domestic Social Policy

Division, Congressional Research Service, Library of Congress, May 5, 2006, http://www.fas.org/sgp/crs/misc/RL32701.pdf; Stefan Theil, "The Incredible Shrinking Continent," *Newsweek*, March 1, 2010, 38–39; Martin Walker, "The World's New Numbers," *The Wilson Quarterly*, Spring 2009, 24–31.

6. U.S. Census Bureau, *Statistical Abstract of the United States: 2010*, tables 2, 10, 79–81, http://www.census.gov/compendia/statab/2010/tables/10s0002.pdf, http://www.census.gov/compendia/statab/2010/tables/10s0010.pdf, http://www.census.gov/compendia/statab/2010/tables/10s0079.pdf, http://www.census.gov/compendia/statab/2010/tables/10s0080.pdf, http://www.census.gov/compendia/statab/2010/tables/10s0081.pdf.

7. Ed Pilkington, "U.S. Set for Dramatic Change as White America Becomes Minority by 2042," *The Guardian*, August 15, 2008, http://www.guardian.co.uk/world/2008/aug/15/population.race.

8. U.S. Census Bureau, *Statistical Abstract of the United States: 2010*, tables 10, 11, http://www.census.gov/compendia/statab/2010/tables/10s0010.pdf, http://www.census.gov/compendia/statab/2010/tables/10s0011.pdf.

9. Deborah Kotz, "Majority of Babies Will Live to 100," *U.S. News & World Report*, October 2, 2009, http://health.usnews.com/health-news/family-health/articles/2009/10/02/majority-of-babies-will-live-to-100-how-will-they-do-it.html; U.S. Census Bureau, *Statistical Abstract of the United States: 2010*, table 102, http://www.census.gov/compendia/statab/2010/tables/10s0102.pdf.

10. U.S. Census Bureau, *Statistical Abstract of the United States: 2010*, tables 674, 680, http://www.census.gov/compendia/statab/2010/tables/10s0674.pdf, http://www.census.gov/compendia/statab/2010/tables/10s0680.pdf; Carmen DeNavas-Walt, Bernadette D. Proctor, and Jessica C. Smith, U.S. Census Bureau, Current Population Reports, P60-236, *Income, Poverty, and Health Insurance Coverage in the United States: 2008*, U.S. Government Printing Office, Washington, DC, 2009. Unofficial estimates from the Census Bureau, based on their monthly American Community Survey data, suggest that median household income may have dropped another 3 percent in 2009.

11. U.S. Census Bureau, *Statistical Abstract of the United States: 2010*, table 695, http://www.census.gov/compendia/statab/2010/tables/10s0695.pdf; U.S. Census Bureau News Release, "Income, Poverty, and Health Insurance Coverage in the United States: 2008," September 1, 2009.

12. Emily Kaiser, "U.S. Household Wealth Up for First Time Since 2007," Reuters, September 17, 2009, http://www.reuters.com/article/idUSTRE58G55F20090917; U.S. Census Bureau, *Statistical Abstract of the United States: 2010*, table 705, http://www.census.gov/compendia/statab/2010/tables/10s0705.pdf; ESRI, "2009/2014 Demographic Trends," http://www.esri.com/library/fliers/pdfs/2009-2014-demographic-trends.pdf.

13. U.S. Census Bureau, *Statistical Abstract of the United States: 2010*, tables 224–226, http://www.census.gov/compendia/statab/2010/tables/10s0224.pdf, http://www.census.gov/compendia/statab/2010/tables/10s0225.pdf, http://www.census.gov/compendia/statab/2010/tables/10s0226.pdf.

14. Ibid., tables 226, 227, http://www.census.gov/compendia/statab/2010

/tables/10s0226.pdf, http://www.census.gov/compendia/statab/2010/tables /10s0227.pdf.

15. Ibid., table 229, http://www.census.gov/compendia/statab/2010/tables/10s0229.pdf.

16. Ibid., table 260, http://www.census.gov/compendia/statab/2010/tables/10s0260.pdf.

17. OECD stands for Organization for Economic Cooperation and Development. It includes England, the European nations, Australia, Canada, Mexico, South Korea, the Scandinavian nations, and others. These nations share educational and economic statistics and compare how each nation is doing on comparable measures.

18. National Center for Educational Statistics, "Fast Facts: International," U.S. Department of Education, http://nces.ed.gov/fastfacts/#, accessed June 13, 2010; OECD, *Education at a Glance: 2008, Key Results*, September 9, 2008, http://www .oecd.org/dataoecd/10/10/41274071.pdf; National Center for Educational Statistics, "Fast Facts: Assessments," U.S. Department of Education, http://nces.ed.gov /fastfacts/display.asp?id=69, accessed January 4, 2011.

19. Bureau of Labor Statistics, "Economic Projections: 2008-2018 News Release," December 10, 2009, http://www.bls.gov/news.release/archives/ecopro_12102009 .htm.

20. U.S. Census Bureau, "Census Bureau News," April 22, 2009; U.S. Census Bureau, *Statistical Abstract of the United States: 2010*, tables 30, 31, 33, http://www.census .gov/compendia/statab/2010/tables/10s0030.pdf, http://www.census.gov/compendia /statab/2010/tables/10s0031.pdf, http://www.census.gov/compendia/statab/2010 /tables/10s0033.pdf.

21. U.S. Census Bureau, "Census Bureau News," December 23, 2009; Michael Barone, "Migration Gives South and West Big Gains," *US News & World Report*, January 16, 2009, http://www.usnews.com/blogs/barone/2009/01/16/migration-gives-south -and-west-big-gains-census-bureau-statistics-show.html; Rebecca Wilder, "Recession Slammed Domestic Migration," *News N Economics*, December 24, 2009, http://www .newsneconomics.com/2009/12/recession-slammed-domestic-migration.html; Conor Dougherty, "Sun Belt Loses Its Shine," *Wall Street Journal*, March 24, 2010, http:// online.wsj.com/article/SB10001424052748704211704575140132450524648.html.

Chapter 9: Together We Can Redirect These Trends

1. This discussion of the spiritual transformation process is based on a long-term research project and subsequent case studies, detailed in my book *Maximum Faith: Live Like Jesus* (New York: SGG Publishing, 2011).

2. For the statistical explanation of how many Americans have been broken of sin and self by God, surrendered their life to Him, submitted to His will, and pursued God and people with profound love and service, see *Maximum Faith: Live Like Jesus*, referenced above.

Appendix A: Defining Our Terms

1. For complete information on each of these tribes, and what the presence of such divergent faith groups sharing our culture means for the future, see *The Seven Faith Tribes* (Carol Stream, IL: Tyndale House Publishers, 2009).

2. This approach is based on core elements of the definition of an evangelical contained within the statement of faith of the National Association of Evangelicals. We have been measuring evangelicals in the same manner since 1991.

About BarnaBooks

BARNABOOKS IS an imprint of Tyndale House Publishers, one of the largest Christian publishing companies in the United States. The BarnaBooks imprint was launched in 2005 with George Barna's book *Revolution*. The mission of BarnaBooks is to provide new voices with a platform to challenge and stimulate the Christian sector. Incorporating original data from surveys conducted by The Barna Group is one of the line's distinctives.

Resources that become part of this line fit within any of eight core aspects of ministry that we believe are most critical to the future of the church in America. Those areas are:

- Worldview development
- New models for communities of faith
- Media content and influence
- Ministry to children
- Facilitating effective leadership
- Strengthening families
- Understanding and influencing cultural trends
- Enabling positive, biblical life transformation

For more information about BarnaBooks, visit www.tyndale.com /barnabooks.

About George Barna

GEORGE BARNA HAS filled executive roles in politics, marketing, advertising, media development, research, and ministry. He founded the Barna Research Group in 1984 (now The Barna Group) and helped it become a leading marketing research firm focused on the intersection of faith and culture. His research has focused on a wide variety of topics, including faith dynamics, leadership, cultural trends, family development, spiritual transformation, and church health.

Since selling a majority share of The Barna Group, he has continued to play a guiding role in the company. He is also the founder of Metaformation, a company dedicated to helping people optimize their life journey, and a senior partner in The Strategenius Group, which provides strategic marketing and business development services.

Barna has written more than forty books, primarily addressing leadership, social trends, church dynamics, and spiritual development. They include best sellers such as *Revolution, Pagan Christianity?* (with Frank Viola), *Transforming Children into Spiritual Champions, The Frog in the Kettle,* and *The Power of Vision.* His most recent titles have included *Maximum Faith: Live*

Like Jesus, The Cause Within You (with Matthew Barnett), and *Master Leaders*. Several of his books have received national awards, and his works have been translated into more than a dozen foreign languages. He serves as the general editor of the BarnaBooks line published through Tyndale House Publishers. He has had more than one hundred articles published in periodicals and regularly writes analyses for *The Barna Update*, a biweekly research report accessed online (www.barna.org), and a blog on his personal website (www.georgebarna.com). His work is frequently cited as an authoritative source by the media. He has been hailed as "the most quoted person in the Christian church today" and has been named by various media as one of the nation's most influential Christian leaders.

After graduating summa cum laude from Boston College, Barna earned two master's degrees from Rutgers University. At Rutgers, he was awarded the Eagleton Fellowship. He also has a doctorate from Dallas Baptist University. George lives with his wife and three daughters in Southern California. He is a huge fan of the Lakers, Yankees, great blues and shredder guitar playing, suspense novels, pizza, and the beach.

FOR MORE INFORMATION ON TRENDS VISIT www.georgebarna.com OR www.barna.org

Barna Books encourage and resource committed believers seeking lives of vibrant faith—and call the church to a new understanding of what it means to be the Church.

For more information, visit www.tyndale.com/barnabooks.

BARNA

CP0309